T0110433

STANLEY WELLS

Shakespeare and Co.

Stanley Wells is the author of *Shakespeare: For All Time,* chairman of the Shakespeare Birthplace Trust, Emeritus Professor of Shakespeare Studies at the University of Birmingham, general editor of the Penguin and Oxford editions of Shakespeare's works, and co-editor of *The Oxford Companion to Shakespeare.* He lives in England.

Shakespeare and Co.

Christopher Marlowe
Thomas Dekker
Ben Jonson
Thomas Middleton
John Fletcher
and Other Players in His Story

STANLEY WELLS

VINTAGE BOOKS
A Division of Random House, Inc.
New York

The Library of Congress has cataloged the Pantheon edition as follows:
Wells, Stanley W., [date]
Shakespeare and co.: Christopher Marlowe, Thomas Dekker,
Ben Jonson, Thomas Middleton, John Fletcher,
and the other players in his story / Stanley Wells.
p. cm.
Includes bibliographical references and index.
1. Shakespeare, William, 1564–1616—Contemporaries.
2. Shakespeare, William, 1564–1616—Friends and associates.
3. Shakespeare, William, 1564–1616—Relations with actors.
4. Theater—England—London—History—16th century.
5. Theater—England—London—History—17th century.
6. London (England)—Social life and customs—16th century.
7. London (England)—Social life and customs—17th century.
I. Title. II. Title: Shakespeare and company.
PR2911.W45   2007
822.3'3—dc22
2006038010

Vintage ISBN: 978-0-307-28053-4

Author photograph © Shakespeare Birthplace Trust

www.vintagebooks.com

For
CLEMENCY
at last

Contents

List of Illustrations

Preface

This book attempts to place Shakespeare in relation to the actors and other writers, mainly playwrights, of his time in an accessible and where possible entertaining manner. In doing so it responds to and develops recent currents of critical and scholarly thought which see Shakespeare not as a lone eminence but as a fully paid-up member of the theatrical community of his time, a working playwright with professional obligations to the theatre personnel without whose collaboration his art would have been ineffectual, and one who, like most other playwrights of the age, actively collaborated with other writers, not necessarily always as a senior partner. This view found editorial expression in the Oxford edition of the *Complete Works* (General Editors Stanley Wells and Gary Taylor, 1986, second edition 2005) and its accompanying *Textual Companion* (by Stanley Wells, Gary Taylor, John Jowett and William Montgomery, Oxford, Clarendon Press, 1987). It has also been the subject of a number of studies, notably Brian Vickers's polemical and contentious but valuable *Shakespeare, Co-author* (Oxford, Oxford University Press, 2002), some of which are cited in the notes to this book.

I have not attempted to give chapter and verse for all the biographical facts mentioned in the text, but have benefited greatly from entries in the *Oxford Dictionary of National Biography* (Oxford, Oxford University Press, 2004), especially the following:

Edward Alleyn, by S. P. Cerasano.
Robert Armin, by Martin Butler.
Francis Beaumont, by P. J. Finkelpearl.
Richard Burbage, by Mary Edmond.

Thomas Dekker, by John Twyning.
John Fletcher, by Gordon McMullan.
Ben Jonson, by Ian Donaldson.
Will Kemp, by Martin Butler.
John Lyly, by G. K. Hunter.
Christopher Marlowe, by Charles Nicholl.
John Marston, by James Knowles.
Francis Meres, by David Kathman.
Thomas Middleton, by Gary Taylor.
Thomas Nashe, by Charles Nicholl.
Richard Tarlton, by Peter Thomson.
John Webster, by David Gunby.

The availability on-line of this invaluable work of reference has been of enormous assistance.

Records of theatrical performance in the Shakespearian period are patchy and sparse; many plays did not reach print, and those that did were often published years, sometimes many years, after they were written and first acted. To give only one example, around half of Shakespeare's plays did not appear in print until 1623, seven years after he died, and by then some of them were at least thirty years old. As a result, it is often impossible to date plays of the period with any precision. I have tried to follow the best received opinion, and to indicate where uncertainty about chronology is of material significance.

Quotations from writers of the period are given in modern spelling except where there is a special reason to reproduce features of the original printing or manuscript. Quotations from Shakespeare are normally from the Compact Edition of the Oxford *Complete Works*, second edition, which adds *Edward III* and prints the whole of *Sir Thomas More*. Stage directions in this edition are cited as an additional number after act, scene and line, for example '4.4.127.1', or with a zero in place of line number if at the head of a scene. A list of non-Shakespearian plays quoted is given below, with a note of the editions used. For ease of access as well as for the excellent quality of the editing I have frequently used the Oxford English Drama (Oxford World's Classics) series. Other series, especially the Revels plays published by Manchester University Press, and the New Mermaids published by A. and C. Black, can also be recommended. When responsibly edited modernized editions were not available I have modernized the quotations myself.

It is difficult to convey a sense of relative monetary values. Advice to multiply early modern sums by a specific number can only result in crude equivalents. During this period the poor were often extremely poor, and the rich enormously wealthy. It may be worth remembering that in 1600 an average labourer's wage would have been about eight pence a week, and a craftsman might have received a shilling (twelve pence). I have not attempted to give metric equivalents.

I am grateful to Martin Toseland, formerly of Penguin Books, for initial encouragement, to Laura Barber, also formerly of Penguin Books, for invaluably rigorous and creative criticism of the first five chapters, to Helen Conford for assistance in the final stages of the work, to Elizabeth Stratford for meticulous copy-editing, and to Judith Wardman for her index. Dr Martin Wiggins kindly read Chapter 3, and Dr John Jowett Chapter 6, to their benefit. Dr Paul Edmondson has been a constant source of help and encouragement at every stage of my work.

EDITIONS OF NON-SHAKESPEARIAN PLAYS

The Alchemist, by Ben Jonson, in *Ben Jonson: The Alchemist and Other Plays*, ed. Gordon Campbell (Oxford, Oxford University Press, 1995).

Alexander and Campaspe, by John Lyly, ed. David Bevington and G. K. Hunter (Manchester, Manchester University Press, 1999).

Alphonsus, King of Aragon, by Robert Greene, ed. W. W. Greg, Malone Society Reprints (Oxford, Oxford University Press, 1926).

Antonio and Mellida, by John Marston, in *John Marston: The Malcontent and Other Plays*, ed. Keith Sturgess (Oxford, Oxford University Press, 1997).

The Arraignment of Paris, by George Peele, ed. Harold H. Child, Malone Society Reprints (Oxford, Oxford University Press, 1910).

The Atheist's Tragedy, by Cyril Tourneur, in *Four Revenge Tragedies*, ed. Katherine Eisaman Maus (Oxford, Oxford University Press, 1995).

Bartholomew Fair, by Ben Jonson, in *Ben Jonson: The Alchemist and Other Plays*, ed. Gordon Campbell (Oxford, Oxford University Press, 1995).

The Case is Altered, by Ben Jonson, in *Ben Jonson*, ed. C. H. Herford and Percy and Evelyn Simpson, 11 vols. (Oxford, Clarendon Press, 1925–52), vol. iii.

The Devil is an Ass, by Ben Jonson, in *Ben Jonson: The Devil is an Ass and Other Plays*, ed. M. J. Kidnie (Oxford, Oxford University Press, 2000).

Dido, Queen of Carthage, by Christopher Marlowe and Thomas Nashe, in *Christopher Marlowe: The Complete Plays*, ed. Frank Romany and Robert Lindsey (London, Penguin Books, 2003).

Doctor Faustus, by Christopher Marlowe, in *Christopher Marlowe: Doctor Faustus and Other Plays*, ed. David Bevington and Eric Rasmussen (Oxford, Oxford University Press, 1995).

The Duchess of Malfi, by John Webster, in *John Webster: The Duchess of Malfi and Other Plays*, ed. René Weis (Oxford, Oxford University Press, 1996).

Eastward Ho, by George Chapman, Ben Jonson and John Marston, in *Ben Jonson*, ed. C. H. Herford and Percy and Evelyn Simpson, 11 vols. (Oxford, Clarendon Press, 1925–52), vol. iv.

Edward II, by Christopher Marlowe, in *Christopher Marlowe: Doctor Faustus and Other Plays*, ed. David Bevington and Eric Rasmussen (Oxford, Oxford University Press, 1995).

Every Man in His Humour, by Ben Jonson, ed. J. W. Lever (Lincoln, Nebr., University of Nebraska Press, 1971).

Every Man Out of His Humour, by Ben Jonson, in *Ben Jonson*, ed. C. H. Herford and Percy and Evelyn Simpson, 11 vols. (Oxford, Clarendon Press, 1925–52), vol. iii.

The Faithful Shepherdess, by John Fletcher, in *The Dramatic Works in the Beaumont and Fletcher Canon*, General Editor Fredson Bowers, 10 vols. (Cambridge, Cambridge University Press, 1966–96), vol. ii.

Friar Bacon and Friar Bungay, by Robert Greene, ed. Daniel Seltzer (London, Edward Arnold, 1965).

A Game at Chess, by Thomas Middleton, ed. T. Howard-Hill (Manchester, Manchester University Press, 1993).

Hymenaei, by Ben Jonson, in *Ben Jonson*, ed. C. H. Herford and Percy and Evelyn Simpson, 11 vols. (Oxford, Clarendon Press, 1925–52), vol. vii.

If this be not a Good Play, the Devil is in it, by Thomas Dekker, in *The Dramatic Works of Thomas Dekker*, ed. Fredson Bowers, 4 vols. (Cambridge, Cambridge University Press, 1953–61), vol. iii.

The Jew of Malta, by Christopher Marlowe, in *Christopher Marlowe: Doctor Faustus and Other Plays*, ed. David Bevington and Eric Rasmussen (Oxford, Oxford University Press, 1995).

The Knight of the Burning Pestle, by Francis Beaumont, ed. Sheldon P. Zitner (Manchester, Manchester University Press, 1984).

A Looking Glass for London and England, by Robert Greene and Thomas Lodge, ed. W. W. Greg, Malone Society Reprints (Oxford, Oxford University Press, 1932).

A Mad World, My Masters, by Thomas Middleton, in *Thomas Middleton: A Mad World, My Masters and Other Plays*, ed. Michael Taylor (Oxford, Oxford University Press, 1995).

The Maid's Tragedy, by Francis Beaumont and John Fletcher, in *Four Jacobean Sex Tragedies*, ed. Martin Wiggins (Oxford, Oxford University Press, 1998).

The Malcontent, by John Marston, in *John Marston: The Malcontent and Other Plays*, ed. Keith Sturgess (Oxford, Oxford University Press, 1997).

The Phoenix, by Thomas Middleton, in *The Works of Thomas Middleton*, ed. A. H. Bullen, 8 vols. (London, John C. Nimmo, 1885–6).

The Return from Parnassus, Parts One and Two, in *The Three Parnassus Plays*, ed. J. B. Leishman (London, Ivor Nicholson and Watson, 1949).

The Revenger's Tragedy, in *Four Revenge Tragedies*, ed. Katherine Eisaman Maus (Oxford, Oxford University Press, 1995).

The Roaring Girl, by Thomas Dekker and Thomas Middleton, ed. Paul Mulholland (Manchester, Manchester University Press, 1987).

Satiromastix, by Thomas Dekker, in *The Dramatic Works of Thomas Dekker*, ed. Fredson Bowers, 4 vols. (Cambridge, Cambridge University Press, 1953–61), vol. i.

Sejanus, His Fall, by Ben Jonson, in *Ben Jonson: The Devil is an Ass and Other Plays*, ed. M. J. Kidnie (Oxford, Oxford University Press, 2000).

The Shoemaker's Holiday, by Thomas Dekker, ed. R. L. Smallwood and Stanley Wells (Manchester, Manchester University Press, 1979).

Singing Simpkin, by Will Kemp, in Charles Read Baskervill, *The Elizabethan Jig* (Chicago, University of Chicago Press, 1929, repr. New York, Dover Books, 1965), pp. 444–9.

Sir Thomas More, by Anthony Munday and others (in the Oxford Shakespeare, second edition, 2005).

The Spanish Tragedy, by Thomas Kyd, in *Four Revenge Tragedies*, ed. Katherine Eisaman Maus (Oxford, Oxford University Press, 1995).

Summer's Last Will and Testament, by Thomas Nashe, in *Thomas Nashe: Selected Works*, ed. Stanley Wells (London, Edward Arnold, 1964).

Tamburlaine, by Christopher Marlowe, in *Christopher Marlowe: Doctor Faustus and Other Plays*, ed. David Bevington and Eric Rasmussen (Oxford, Oxford University Press, 1995).

The Tamer Tamed, or the Woman's Prize, in *The Dramatic Works in the Beaumont and Fletcher Canon*, General Editor Fredson Bowers, 10 vols. (Cambridge, Cambridge University Press, 1966–96), vol. iv.

The Travels of the Three English Brothers, by William Rowley, John Day and George Wilkins, in *Three Renaissance Travel Plays*, ed. Anthony Parr (Manchester, Manchester University Press, 1995).

Volpone, by Ben Jonson, in *Ben Jonson: The Alchemist and Other Plays*, ed. Gordon Campbell (Oxford, Oxford University Press, 1995).

The White Devil, by John Webster, in *John Webster: The Duchess of Malfi and Other Plays*, ed. René Weis (Oxford, Oxford University Press, 1996).

The Witch, by Thomas Middleton: *A Critical Edition of Thomas Middleton's 'The Witch'*, ed. Edward J. Esche (New York, Garland, 1993).

The Woman Hater, by Francis Beaumont, in *The Dramatic Works in the Beaumont and Fletcher Canon*, General Editor Fredson Bowers, 10 vols. (Cambridge, Cambridge University Press, 1966–96), vol. i.

A Yorkshire Tragedy, by Thomas Middleton, from the Oxford edition of Middleton's *Complete Works* (forthcoming).

I

The Theatrical Scene

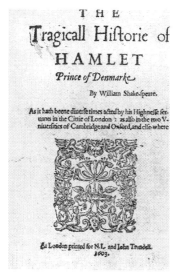

1. The title page of the first, unauthorized, edition of Hamlet *boasts of its performance by the King's Men in London, and in the university cities of Oxford and Cambridge.*

Early one morning in 1600 or 1601, boys ran around London sticking up bills announcing that if you went to the Globe playhouse on the south bank of the River Thames that afternoon you could see a new play called *Hamlet*. They pasted the bills on the doors of taverns and houses, and on pissing-posts provided for the convenience of those who walked the streets. The lads pulled down out-of-date bills announcing earlier performances and chucked them away. Hastily printed, these pieces of paper were of the moment. They brought profit to printers such as William Jaggard, later to be one of the publishers of the collected edition of Shakespeare's plays known as the First Folio, which appeared in 1623. From 1602 Jaggard held a monopoly on the production of playbills. Not a single one survives, but at least we have a transcript of one that was displayed by travelling players in Norwich in 1624; it read: 'Here within this place at one of the clock shall be acted an excellent new comedy called *The Spanish Contract* by the Princess' servants; *vivat rex*.'[1]

The new bills named the play to be performed, with a few words of description and commendation such as 'the right excellent conceited tragedy of *Hamlet, Prince of Denmark*'. They told you that it was to be acted by the Lord Chamberlain's company at the Globe. They did not necessarily say who wrote it: the company's reputation was high, whatever it played. It frequently performed before the Queen and her courtiers, as publishers were proud of boasting on the title pages of the relatively small number of plays that got into print.

By the time Shakespeare wrote *Hamlet* his name, as well as that of the company for which he exclusively wrote, was becoming an attraction both to readers and to theatregoers. Born in 1564, and therefore 37 years old in 1601, he was best known to readers as the author of two popular narrative poems, the immensely successful, rather saucy *Venus and Adonis* (1593) and its tragic successor, *The Rape of Lucrece* (1594). He had already written or co-written more than twenty plays. Indeed by this date he had completed both his cycles of English history plays, most of his romantic comedies, and his tragedies from *Titus Andronicus* through *Romeo and Juliet* to *Julius Caesar*. A founding member as both actor and shareholder of the Lord Chamberlain's Men, established in 1594, he was now a prosperous and admired member of his profession. Though he lived in modest lodgings when he was in London, he owned a fine house and garden in his home town of Stratford-upon-Avon, where his wife and his two daughters, Susanna and Judith, remained – his only son, Hamnet, had died in 1597. There he was a prominent householder and landowner: in 1602, not long after writing *Hamlet*, he paid £320 for land in Old Stratford, as well as buying a cottage close to his home, presumably for one of his servants. And only three years later he made an even bigger investment of £440 in a lease of the Stratford tithes. These were large sums. Theatre was a profitable business. And it brought fame as well as money. Several of his plays had appeared in print, at first anonymously, as was common enough, but increasingly since 1598 with his name on their title pages, which in appearance and wording resembled playbills. So those who wrote the advertisement for the first performance of *Hamlet* may well have included its author's name among its attractions.

The most theatrically and dramatically ambitious as well as the longest play yet written for the English stage, *Hamlet* represented a high-water mark in Shakespeare's rapidly developing career. It was and remains the most continuously entertaining tragedy ever written, brilliantly theatrical yet also intellectually and emotionally challenging, a demonstration of technical prowess and linguistic skill beyond that possessed by any of Shakespeare's contemporaries. It was rapidly recognized as a masterpiece that appealed equally to intellectuals and to the theatregoing populace at large. Soon after it took the town by storm the Cambridge scholar and controversialist Gabriel Harvey (1552/3–1631) – an intellectual snob if ever there was one – scribbled in his copy of Chaucer's poems a note to the effect that 'The younger sort take much delight in Shakespeare's *Venus and Adonis*, but his *Lucrece*, and his tragedy of *Hamlet, Prince of Denmark*, have it in them to please the wiser sort'.[2]

But numerous allusions in plays written for the popular theatre soon after the tragedy appeared show that it pleased the younger as well as the wiser sort, the groundlings as well as the cognoscenti. After this, Shakespeare could not avoid becoming a classic. He was to die in 1616 at the age of 52; in a poetic tribute published in the First Folio, seven years later, his colleague Ben Jonson was to write that he was 'not of an age, but for all time'. This was prophetic. At least since the later part of the eighteenth century, Shakespeare has been accorded semi-divine status and his reputation has spread world-wide. The period in which he wrote is constantly referred to as 'the age of Shakespeare'. His plays have eclipsed those of his contemporaries in theatrical popularity and in critical esteem. His status has become iconic.

For all Jonson's hyperbole, however, Shakespeare *was* 'of an age', and it was an age rich in theatrical and dramatic talent and achievement. He worked within the same intellectual and theatrical environment as his contemporaries, was subject to the same commercial and social pressures, and interacted with fellow dramatists and actors throughout his career.

At the time of his birth, in 1564, professional drama was in its infancy. There were no public playhouses. Plays, mostly lasting no more than an hour each, were acted by amateurs and by small professional groups attached to households of the aristocracy. They performed in the halls of great houses, in guildhalls and inns, even sometimes in churches. The first London playhouse, the Red Lion, went up in 1567, when Shakespeare was 3 years old, and it survived for only a few months. He was 12 when, in 1576, the construction of the Theatre in Shoreditch, well north of the City of London walls, heralded the golden age of English drama. Acting companies rapidly grew in size, plays became more ambitious in scope, and the first great generation of English poetic dramatists emerged.

As a writer, Shakespeare seems to have been a late starter. It is impossible to date the beginning of his career with any precision, but he married at the age of 18, in 1582, his last children – twins – were born in Stratford in 1585, and he is first heard of as a writer in 1592, when he was 28. By then he had probably written several plays. In the earliest of them, including *The Two Gentlemen of Verona*, the three parts of *Henry VI*, *The Taming of the Shrew* and *Titus Andronicus*, he was responding to the work of immediate predecessors and early contemporaries such as John Lyly, George Peele, Thomas Kyd, Robert Greene and above all Christopher Marlowe. This was the Elizabethan generation of dramatists. All except Lyly had died before Shakespeare wrote *Hamlet*.

As his career developed, he faced challenges from the emerging talents of playwrights who included George Chapman, Thomas Dekker, Ben Jonson, Thomas Heywood, John Marston, John Fletcher, Thomas Middleton and Francis Beaumont – the Jacobean generation. Towards the time of his death in 1616 other names appeared on the scene, most notably John Webster; the playwriting careers of Philip Massinger and John Ford still lay ahead. With Middleton and Fletcher (as well as with George Wilkins, who died in 1618) he collaborated; all of the men in the second and third groups named outlived him (except Beaumont, who predeceased him by only six weeks) and learnt from him. Shakespeare's work helped to shape theirs, and their work in turn influenced his.

Shakespeare worked exceptionally closely too with his fellow actors

– exceptionally, because no other dramatist of the period had so long and close a relationship with a single acting company. And that company, which started off as the Lord Chamberlain's Men and earned the ultimate accolade of being named the King's Men when King James succeeded Queen Elizabeth in 1603, was recognized both in England and on the Continent as the finest in the land, with leading actors who would have been stars whenever they were born.

This book aims to place Shakespeare within his theatrical context, to chart his relationships with his fellow actors and dramatists, and to sketch the shifting reputations and lasting achievements of his fellow playwrights. First, let us try to imagine ourselves into the theatrical world inhabited by Shakespeare and his colleagues. What would have been the experience of London citizens who picked up those playbills advertising the first performance of *Hamlet*?

Queen Elizabeth was on the throne. She and her courtiers loved to see plays, but the government was keenly aware of the need to control the activities of players and playwrights in the interests of law and order. Some of their regulations had far-reaching consequences for the content of plays and for the overall conduct of the profession. As early as 1559 a proclamation forbade the performance of plays treating of 'matters of religion or of the governance of the estate of the Commonwealth', since these are topics that should be discussed only by 'men of authority, learning and wisdom', not 'to be handled before any audience but of grave and discreet persons'.[3] This prohibition had a profound effect on the content of plays, inhibiting direct dramatic treatment of religious and political subjects. Dramatists often attempted to evade it, and it was difficult to enforce, but a patent awarded to Edmund Tilney for the office of Master of the Revels in 1581 required all plays to be performed before him or his deputies before being offered to the public; he was to hold this office until he died in 1610. (The patent is summarized in Documents, pp. 233–4 below.)

Other regulations affected the social status of players. An Act of Parliament of 29 June 1572 concerned with 'The Punishment of Vagabonds' and 'the relief of the poor and impotent' attempted to define 'rogues, vagabonds, and sturdy beggars' who will be punished for their 'lewd manner of life'. They include 'all fencers, bearwards, common players in interludes, and minstrels not belonging to any baron of this realm' who are not licensed by at least two Justices of the Peace. The qualification is important: not all actors are rogues and vagabonds. The Queen herself in 1583 awarded her patronage to a group of actors, the Queen's Men, cherry-picked from other companies to tour the country.[4] Initially they also played in London, but they concentrated on touring from 1594. From that year the long-established Lord Admiral's Men played mainly at the Rose playhouse in Southwark, south of the river, the only playhouse of the period of which substantial remains survive. The year 1594 also saw the establishment of the Lord Chamberlain's Men, with Shakespeare as one of their first shareholders. They played initially at the Theatre, before building the Globe close to the Rose in 1599. The Queen's Men's repertory included four surviving plays, *The Famous Victories of Henry the Fifth*, *The Troublesome Reign of King John*, *The True Tragedy of Richard the Third* and *King Leir*, all of unknown authorship, on topics that Shakespeare was to take up later, and it is quite possible that he belonged to this company before moving to the Lord Chamberlain's Men. After Elizabeth died, in 1603, only members of the royal family awarded their patronage to playing companies. As the King's Men, Shakespeare and his colleagues would have worn the royal livery, at least on formal occasions such as the Coronation procession in 1604, for which the company's leaders were each awarded four and a half yards of scarlet cloth.

There were no playhouses in the provinces, and even in London the City authorities frowned on dramatic performances. The Puritans among them regarded playhouses, in which boys impersonated women on the stage, and where serious matters might be lightly treated and comedy was often lewd, as hotbeds of sin. And they feared, reasonably enough, that large assemblies of people would attract rogues and whores and would spread infection in time of plague. As a result, they usually permitted public theatres to be built only outside the boundaries of the City. The Globe had stood since 1599 not far from the southern river bank, in the parish of Southwark. Close by were the Rose, built in 1587, the Swan, of 1595, and other places of public entertainment such as inns, bull- and bear-baiting rings – some of which doubled as playhouses – and brothels. Easily visible from the City, the Globe, along with the tower of the church of St Mary Overy's, now Southwark cathedral, reared over its neighbours. A three-tiered, thatched structure, it was topped by a little hut. Here the raising of a flag indicated that a performance was in the offing, and as the time for its start approached closer a trumpeter blew once, then again, and then for the third and last time. (Audiences must have been reminded of this when they heard the trumpet calls of Edgar's three challenges within the play of *King Lear*, 5.3.[5]) It was early afternoon: as the theatres were open to the air, they could operate only in daylight hours.

Thus informed and summoned, men, women and young persons – even children – streamed into the theatre from all quarters. Although then, as now, theatre audience numbers fluctuated, they could be large. When it was packed tight, as at the sensational performances of Middleton's *A Game at Chess* in 1624, the second Globe, built in 1614 on the foundations of the first, is reported to have held well over three thousand spectators at once. Many playgoers came across the river over London Bridge, some walking, some riding on horseback, a few travelling with servants in their carriages. Others arrived by water, ferried across the busy river in one of the small wherry boats that plied their trade there. Best remembered of the water men is John Taylor, a colourful character who wrote and published reams of doggerel verse recounting his exploits and venting his complaints against, among others, theatre owners and proprietors of hackney carriages which threatened his trade. As he ferried theatregoers across the river he may well have regaled them with samples of his versified wit such as:

> The woman, spaniel, the walnut tree.
> The more you beat them the better they be.

Or he might have challenged them to match his (not quite perfect) palindrome 'Lewd did I live, & evil I did dwel', of which he writes: 'This line is the same backward, as it is forward, and I will give any man five shillings apiece for as many as they can make in English.'[6] There was one year, 1608, in which playgoers could have walked over the frozen river, perhaps hoping to see early performances of *Coriolanus* or, indeed, a revival of *Hamlet*. Francisco's words in that play's opening scene, ' 'Tis bitter cold, / And I am sick at heart', would have struck a special chord if the players were indeed bold enough to brave the elements. But more probably they gave in to the weather and joined the crowds skating, drinking and eating from improvised kitchens on the ice.[7] At other times Taylor's clients would have walked the few steps from the landing stage to the playhouse to pay a penny each to the doorkeeper.

Theatregoers included foreigners and other visitors to the city as well as Londoners. The English theatre was literally something to write home about, as we see in an account of a visit to the Globe for a performance of *Julius Caesar* in 1599 (the year it was first acted) by a Swiss physician, Thomas Platter, only a month or two after the playhouse opened its doors.[8] He seems to have been surprised to learn that 'every day around two o'clock in the afternoon two and sometimes even three plays are performed at different places, in order to make people merry'. He goes on to describe the theatre buildings. Of the seating arrangements he writes:

The places are built in such a way that they act on a raised scaffold, and everyone can well see everything. However, there are separate galleries and places, where one sits more pleasantly and better, therefore also pays more. For he who remains standing below pays only one English penny, but if he wants to sit he is let in at another door, where he gives a further penny; but if he desires to sit on cushions in the pleasantest place, where he not only sees everything well but can also be seen, then he pays at a further door another English penny.[9]

Platter notes that while some spectators stood, others paid more to sit. Notoriously, Hamlet refers to those who stood in the yard as groundlings:

O, it offends me to the soul to hear a robustious, periwig-pated fellow tear a passion to tatters, to very rags, to split the ears of the groundlings, who for the most part are capable of nothing but inexplicable dumb shows and noise. (*Hamlet*, 3.2.8–13)

The word 'groundlings' may have amused those who flocked to early performances of the play, but equally it may have offended them. We know the word as a theatre term entirely from its use here in *Hamlet*, but it would either have been unfamiliar to or have had quite different connotations for the play's first audiences. The first datable use of it in print is in 1601, very close to the time at which Shakespeare wrote *Hamlet*, in Philemon Holland's eloquent translation of Pliny's *Natural History*. It originally meant a small fish that lived in mud at the bottom of the water.[10] Hamlet's term is a metaphor, chosen presumably because the groundlings gaped up at the actors on the platform above them like fish from the bottom of a stream. Did they take offence at it? Or did they interpret his remarks as part of the satirical characterization of a lofty aristocrat? Or was there a genial rapport between stage and yard which enabled them to enjoy his comments as good-natured banter? Did those in the galleries pat themselves on the back in a complacent sense of superiority? Or is it even possible that Shakespeare dodged confrontation by omitting or altering this passage in performance? In the first printed text of the play, the so-called 'bad', or 'short', quarto of 1603, which may be closer to early performances than the much longer 'good' quarto of 1604, and than the different text in the First Folio, the less explicit word 'ignorant' appears instead of 'groundlings'.[11]

At the turn of the century theatre was a growth industry, as exemplified by the building of two large new playhouses: the Globe in 1599 and the Fortune in 1600. People flocked to see plays for various reasons. Some hoped for straightforward entertainment. Some looked for edification, for instruction in English and Roman history, in mythology and in stories of ancient and modern heroes. Some sought to enter a world of the fantasy and imagination, or romanticized reflections of their own lives. Some went to be provoked to think about contemporary social and political issues, even though legal restraints meant that these usually had to be indirectly treated. Until the late 1590s romantic and historical subject matter prevailed, with plays set in distant lands and in the more or less remote past – as Shakespeare's were to be for the whole of his career. But from 1597 onwards the emergence of what became the Jacobean generation of dramatists, including Jonson, Dekker and Middleton, saw a broadening of subject matter, with plays set (sometimes covertly) in contemporary London and satirical of the society that produced them. And as we shall see there were plays that fuelled or provoked subversion or dissent.

How did audiences behave? It is hard to know: many commentators wrote from positions of prejudice. Certainly playgoers came from varied ranks of society, and some theatres attracted more fashionable audiences than others. In an epigram published around 1611 the poet Sir John Davies emphasized social inclusiveness:

> we see at all the playhouse doors
> When ended is the play, the dance, and song,
> A thousand townsmen, gentlemen and whores,
> Porters and servingmen together throng . . .[12]

Puritan opponents of theatre and other polemicists liked to suggest that the yard, at least, teemed with prostitutes and pickpockets, and that playgoing was an inevitable prelude to whoring. In 1580, when public theatres had existed in England only for a few years, Anthony Munday, himself a playwright, wrote of 'the chapel of Satan – I mean the Theatre', where visitors would find 'no want of young ruffians, nor lack of harlots utterly past all shame, who press to the fore-front of the scaffolds to the end to show their impudency and to be as an object to all men's eyes'.[13] Munday takes such obvious delight in his invective that it is difficult to see him as an objective witness. Similarly the tub-thumping Puritan Philip Stubbes wrote bitterly in 1583 that 'these goodly pageants being ended, every mate sorts to his mate, everyone brings another homeward of their way very friendly, and in their secret conclaves covertly they play the sodomites or worse'.[14] (The word 'sodomite' could mean any kind of sexual transgressor.) But the credibility of one, at least, of the theatrical diatribes dwindles when we realize that Stephen Gosson, himself a playwright, in his hypocritically penitential *School of Abuse* of 1579, was paraphrasing Ovid's fifteen-hundred-year-old *Art of Love* while ostensibly writing about the audiences of his own time.[15]

Undoubtedly audiences could include miscreants. Opportunistic pickpockets operated in the yard: their technique was vividly described by the playwright, poet and prose writer Robert Greene:

The nip [thief] standeth leaning like some mannerly gentleman against the door as men go in, and there finding talk with some of his companions, spyeth what every man hath in his purse, and where, in what place, and in which sleeve or pocket he puts his bung [purse], and according to that so he worketh either where the thrust is great within, or else as they come out at the doors.[16]

Thieves could be summarily punished. In 1600 the actor Will Kemp, who until recently had been a member of the company that was to give the first performances of *Hamlet*, wrote of 'a noted cutpurse, such a one as we tie to a post on our stage for all people to wonder at, when at a play they are taken pilfering'.[17] And in the anonymous play *Nobody and Somebody* of around 1606, it is said that 'Somebody once picked a pocket in this playhouse yard, was hoisted on the stage and shamed about it'.[18] These thieves were lucky not to be turned over to the law: anyone convicted of stealing more than twelve pence could be hanged.

There can be no doubt too that prostitutes solicited in the theatres (as they notoriously went on doing into the eighteenth, nineteenth and even twentieth centuries), but strong efforts were made to control their activities. Platter notes that 'Good order is also kept in the city in the matter of prostitution' and that a woman's clients were punished 'with imprisonment and fine', while the woman herself was taken to Bridewell – the 'house of correction' for vagabonds and whores, lying between Fleet Street and the Thames – 'where the executioner scourges her naked before the populace'. Nevertheless, Platter states, 'great swarms of these women haunt the town in the taverns and playhouses'.[19]

Worse still, theatres were at times the scene of serious rioting, sometimes provoked by the nature of the entertainments on offer. The most spectacular event of this kind occurred in 1616. Christopher Beeston, actor and theatre manager, had built a new indoor theatre, the Cockpit, on Drury Lane.[20] On Shrove Tuesday, traditionally a holiday for apprentices and others, three or four thousand apprentices rioted, one group of them making for the theatre. They surrounded it,

broke in, wounded divers of the players, broke open their trunks, and what apparel, books, or other things they found they burnt and cut in pieces; and not content herewith, got on the top of the house and untiled it, and had not the Justices of Peace and Sheriff levied an aid and hindered their purpose, they would have laid that house likewise [i.e. like four houses in Wapping which their fellows had destroyed] even with the ground. In this skirmish one prentice was slain, being shot through the head with a pistol, and many other of their fellows were sore hurt, and such of them as are taken his Majesty hath commanded shall be executed for example' sake.[21]

Bad behaviour among the audience would have affected the way plays were received, and some writers blamed the unfavourable reception even of plays that are now regarded as classics on the stupidity of playgoers. John Webster wrote in the preface to *The White Devil* (1612) that his play had been

presented in so open and black a theatre that it wanted (that which is the only grace and setting out of a tragedy) a full and understanding auditory; and that since that time I have noted, most of the people that come to that playhouse resemble those ignorant asses (who visiting stationers' shops, their use is not to inquire for good books, but new books).

This gives at least a hint that the play might have done better at a different theatre and at a different time of year – it was played, probably in mid-winter, at the Red Bull, Clerkenwell, where audiences were accustomed to more populist fare. Ben Jonson, too, complained of unresponsive audiences; of his learned tragedy *Sejanus, His Fall*, he wrote that it 'suffered no less violence from our people here than the subject of it' – who was dismembered and torn limb from limb – 'did from the rage of the people of Rome'. Jonson's comedy *Epicene; or The Silent Woman* was no better received when acted by a boys' company in 1609, but there the audience seem to have voted with their feet; the comedy is said to have been nicknamed 'The Silent Audience'.

Just as opponents of the theatre exaggerated playgoers' immorality, so too those who reported rowdy behaviour may have been over-inclined to present the exception as the rule. Shortly after *Hamlet* was first performed, the Privy Council itself had to admit that many playgoers were far more respectable than it had supposed. Requiring in 1602 that idle and disorderly persons frequenting public places should be press-ganged for the army, members of the Council were surprised to learn that in the playhouses the Council's officers, who searched them even before the brothels and taverns, found among the playgoers not only 'gentlemen and servingmen but lawyers, clerks, country men that had law causes, ay the Queen's men, knights, and as it was credibly reported one Earl'.[22]

They would not, however, have found members of the English royal family. Queen Elizabeth, and later King James, never attended public playing spaces; rather, the theatre went to them. One of the semi-official ways of circumventing the opposition of the puritanical city fathers was to claim that performances in public playhouses were essentially rehearsals for those given, especially during the Christmas season, at court. The players were well rewarded in both cash and prestige for these events. Nevertheless, high-ranking aristocrats and princely foreign visitors who would have been invited to attend court performances went to the public theatres too. They included great ladies, ambassadors of foreign countries, and foreign noblemen such as Prince Frederick of Württemberg, who saw *Othello* at the Globe in 1610.[23] The Earls of Rutland and Southampton (the latter, Shakespeare's patron, was the dedicatee of his narrative poems) were reported to spend all their time 'merely [i.e. purely] in going to plays every day' during the summer of 1599. They had time on their hands, as they had returned early from supporting the Earl of Essex in his ill-fated campaign against the Irish rebels.[24] Many writers went to the theatre. Playwrights attended performances of plays by their colleagues and rivals, John Donne was known as a 'great frequenter of plays', and John Milton, whose first publication was his sonnet addressed to Shakespeare, saw plays at the Fortune when he was only 12 years old (and others elsewhere a couple of years later).[25] It is intriguing, too, to speculate that the audience for the first performance of *As You Like It*, probably in 1600, may have included Thomas Lodge, the learned physician, formerly a writer of plays, poems and prose fiction, on whose romance *Rosalynde* Shakespeare had – with or without the author's agreement – closely based his play.

Admittedly, neither high rank nor intellectual capacity is a guarantee of attentive behaviour. In at least one playgoer inattentiveness took the form of studious withdrawal rather than extrovert brawling. It was said of the swottish Father Augustine Baker that as a law student in the late 1590s he would go to see plays but 'never went without a pocket book of the law, which he did read when the play or any sort of it pleased him not'. (Baker's other way of relaxing was to read Latin comedies and the learned writings of Erasmus.)[26] But audiences could be deeply absorbed in the plays they most enjoyed: so, in the 1640 version of preliminary verses to the First Folio, the poet and translator Leonard Digges says he has seen

> when Caesar would appear,
> And on the stage at half-sword parley were
> Brutus and Cassius; O, how the audience
> Were ravished, with what wonder they went hence . . .

Digges (who admittedly is concerned to boost Shakespeare's reputation) goes on to say that audiences were less responsive to Ben Jonson's heavier-going classical tragedies *Sejanus* and *Catiline*:

> When some new day they would not brook a line
> Of tedious though well-laboured Catiline:
> Sejanus too was irksome, they prized more
> Honest Iago, or the jealous Moor.[27]

The most eloquent tribute to the raptness with which even the least well educated members of an audience could respond comes in the Prologue to Thomas Dekker's *If this be not a Good Play, the Devil is in it* (1611), where he writes of poets who

> Can call the banished auditor home and tie
> His ear with golden chains to his melody;
> Can draw with adamantine pen even creatures
> Forged out of th'hammer on tiptoe to reach up
> And from rare silence clap their brawny hands
> T'applaud what their charmed soul scarce understands.

> (lines 31–6)

Here Dekker praises the power of dramatic verse to draw even the most unlikely listeners out of themselves, working a spell that enforces attention and compels an understanding which transcends the powers of reason. 'Much', as the Duke says in Shakespeare's early play *The Two Gentlemen of Verona*, 'is the force of heaven-bred poesy' (3.2.71).

But the best evidence that, in spite of occasional exceptions, audiences of the period were worthy of the plays they were given is surely provided by the plays themselves. Popular successes of the time, such as *The Spanish Tragedy*, *Dr Faustus*, *Hamlet*, *Othello* and *Volpone*, make heavier demands on the intellects, the emotions, the imaginations and the sheer stamina of playgoers than almost any works written in the centuries since then for the popular theatre. In the 1580s and earlier 1590s especially, references to classical mythology and literature abound, often (even in immensely popular works such as Shakespeare's *Titus Andronicus* and Thomas Kyd's *The Spanish Tragedy*) accompanied by passages in Latin. Occasionally (as in the French scenes in Shakespeare's *Henry V*, or the Spanish spoken by Surly in Jonson's *The Alchemist*) dialogue is written in foreign tongues. In Marston's *Antonio and Mellida*, which is liberally besprinkled with quotations in Latin from Seneca, the hero and heroine, like Romeo and Juliet, share an extended sonnet between them – but this one is in Italian (4.1.181–98). (Admittedly this provokes a page to exclaim: 'I think confusion of Babel is fallen upon these lovers that they change their language.') Many plays presuppose in their audiences a level of education equivalent to that which their authors received in the grammar schools and universities of the realm. Audiences who made popular successes out of these plays must surely have been as deserving of respect, as responsive and responsible in their behaviour, as any of later ages.

When imagining audiences it is necessary to make a distinction between those at the custom-built public, 'arena' theatres, such as the Rose, the Globe and the Fortune, and the so-called private, indoor theatres, such as the tiny playhouse situated within the precincts of St Paul's cathedral, and the larger Blackfriars, both of which were adapted from pre-existing buildings. The term 'private' is misleading. Though these playhouses were more exclusive than the arenas, that was simply because they charged more for admission. Whereas the arena playhouses were open to the air, the private theatres were roofed. They were much smaller than the arenas, and – no doubt partly for that reason – were initially run for companies composed exclusively of boys, deriving originally from choir schools such as those of the Chapel Royal and St Paul's cathedral.

Private theatres operated only sporadically during the period, but some playwrights, including John Lyly in the early years, and John Marston and Ben Jonson later, wrote largely or – as Lyly did – exclusively for them. They had two periods of glory. The first began in 1576 when rooms in the old Dominican monastery of the Black-friars were converted into an indoor theatre which was used by boy players for eight years. It was in that year that James Burbage, whose son Richard was to become the leading actor of Shakespeare's company, the Lord Chamberlain's Men, built the Theatre. Events relating to this building led to the second great flowering of the boys' companies. The Lord Chamberlain's Men's ground lease was due to expire in 1597, and in 1596 James Burbage reconverted the Blackfriars with the aim of providing an indoor home for the Lord Chamberlain's Men. It was only possible to contemplate using a building in this exclusive area as a theatre because it was not technically part of the City and so did not fall under the jurisdiction of the Lord Mayor, who with his colleagues would have been bound to object. Even so, local residents (who included the Lord Chamberlain himself, deeply involved with the players though he was) successfully petitioned the Privy Council against its use for plays. The fear was that it would 'grow to be a very great annoyance and trouble, not only to all the noblemen and gentlemen thereabout inhabiting but also a general inconvenience to all the inhabitants of the same precinct', both because it would attract a lot of undesirables to the area – a special and very real danger in time of plague – and also, the residents complained, because 'the same playhouse is so near the church that the noise of the drums and trumpets will greatly disturb and hinder both the ministers and parishioners in time of divine service and sermons'.[28] As a result of this, on the expiry of their lease the Lord Chamberlain's Men moved the timbers of the Theatre over the river to construct the Globe, and leased the Blackfriars to a boys' company – who used for their music softer-toned woodwind rather than the brass instruments of the adult companies – which performed there from 1600. Not until 1608, when it was taken over by what was now the King's Men, was the private theatre available for an adult company, and plague delayed its opening until late in 1609. It was especially valuable during the winter, when use of the Globe and of the other open-air theatres would have been difficult.

The Lord Chamberlain's Men's acquisition of the Blackfriars brought about a shift in playwriting techniques. Whereas in the public theatres plays were acted without a break, in the private theatres they were customarily divided into five acts, for the practical reason that candles used for illumination had to be trimmed at frequent intervals. To keep the audience entertained, music was performed during the act breaks as well as before (and during) the performance. The theatre's musicians had a high reputation. The structure of these theatres also made possible more spectacular visual effects than in the open-air public arenas. The dramaturgy of Shakespeare's final plays exemplifies the shift, though it is not entirely radical as plays still needed to be performable in public as well as private spaces. Spectacular effects such as the masque in *The Tempest* and the descent from the heavens of Jupiter in *Cymbeline* might have been easier at the Blackfriars than at the Globe; yet *Pericles*, which also features a deity who appears from above, was written before the Blackfriars became available. No play is more appropriate for performance at the Blackfriars than *All is True* (later known as *Henry VIII*), by Shakespeare and his younger colleague John Fletcher, since the auditorium there is where the actual trial of a central character, Katherine of Aragon – a trial which is dramatized in the play – had taken place; yet we know from contemporary reports that the play was first given at the Globe, in 1613, and there is no record of its having been played at the Blackfriars (which does not prove that it was not). The Globe burned down during one of its earliest performances.

Admission to private theatres cost more than to the arenas: a basic sixpence for admission to the galleries, more for a seat in the pit, and still more for a stool on the stage itself, where fashion-conscious young men enjoyed being seen as well as seeing.[29] Playgoers at private theatres thought of themselves as a cut above those who frequented the arena stages. So in 1600, John Marston, in a play called *Jack Drum's Entertainment*, performed in the private theatre of St Paul's, had a character say that he liked 'the audience that frequenteth there / With much applause. A man shall not be choked / With the stench of garlic, nor be pasted / To the barmy jacket of a beer-brewer'[30] – the implication being that groundlings at theatres such as the Globe would smell unsavoury, an accusation repeated in Thomas Middleton's satirical pamphlet *Father Hubburd's Tales* (1604) when he writes of 'a dull audience of stinkards sitting in the penny galleries of a theatre and yawning upon the players'.[31]

Thomas Platter, visiting the Globe in 1599, notes that 'during the play food and drink is carried around among the people, so that one can also refresh oneself for one's money'.[32] This last phrase suggests, improbably, that perhaps the refreshments were included in the price of admission. But Platter's remark reminds us that, at least until around 1609, performances in the public theatres were given without a break. Although we are accustomed to reading the plays in editions into which act and scene divisions are introduced, we should remember that, until the opening of the Blackfriars, playwrights of the period – though they may have been influenced by the five-act structure of classical drama, as Shakespeare certainly was in, for instance, *Henry V*, with its Chorus before and after each act – nevertheless generally conceived of their plays as continuous units. Every edition of a Shakespeare play printed during his lifetime, and most of those by his contemporaries, is undivided; clearly the writers expected these plays to be acted without interruption. So if people wanted to eat and drink, they had to do so while the play was being performed. This custom led to one happy consequence, at least, when the Globe burnt down in 1613; the only injury, we learn from a letter written by Sir Henry Wotton (reproduced in full on pp. 210–11), was to a man whose breeches caught fire: he was able to quench the conflagration with bottled ale snatched, perhaps, from one of the fleeing vendors.

Platter is interesting on costuming. 'The play-actors are dressed most exquisitely and elegantly, because of the custom in England that when men of rank or knights die they give and bequeath almost their finest apparel to their servants, who, since it does not befit them, do not wear such garments, but afterwards let the play-actors buy them for a few pence.' The idea that it did not 'befit' servants to wear fine garments relates to a series of sumptuary laws enacted during the later part of the sixteenth century which attempted, with limited success, to impose a class system of dress. It was decreed by proclamation in 1574 that none might wear 'Any silk of the colour of purple, cloth of gold tissued, nor fur of sables, but only the King, Queen, King's mother, children, brethren, and sisters, uncles and aunts; and except dukes, marquises, and earls, who may wear the same in doublets, jerkins, linings of cloaks, gowns, and hose; and those of the Garter, purple in mantles only'.[33] These laws, which were hard to enforce, were repealed in 1604, but relics of the system linger on even today in the on-duty costumes of, for instance, schoolchildren, the medical profession, members of the armed forces, traffic wardens, and peers of the realm.

Platter's note, even though he may have based it on the kind of gossip to which tourists are susceptible, reinforces the fact that the actors would, where appropriate, be handsomely dressed, and also – like much other evidence – suggests that they would largely have worn contemporary costume, whatever the period in which the play was set.

A cache of papers left by the theatre owner and financier Philip Henslowe, known loosely as his diary and relating principally to the affairs of the Rose playhouse between 1590 and 1604, reveals much about all aspects of theatrical life, including the actors' costumes. Henslowe often records the expenditure of far more than 'a few pence' on costumes for particular performances, and on material for the company's seamstresses and tailors to make up. On 9 May 1598, for instance, he lent £7 'to buy a doublet and a pair of hose laid thick with gold laces', and on 21 August £10 for 'a suit and a gown' for the play of *Vayvode*; later that month he laid out £2. 16s. 6d. 'to pay the lace man's bill' along with 28s. 6d. for the tailor's bill (the lace man received frequent payments); in November he lent £7 'to buy women's gown [sic] and other things for [appropriately] *The Fountain of New Fashions*', and in the following January 'taffeta for two women's gowns for *The Two Angry Women of Abingdon*' cost him £9. Sometimes he operated a hire purchase system: a player named Richard Jones paid him five shillings a week (except for one week when he couldn't manage it) over a period of twelve weeks for 'a man's gown of peach colour in grain' (that is, indelible, fast-dyed) in the latter part of 1594. These were large sums at a time when a teacher or clergyman might think himself lucky to be paid £20 a year. Clearly the company laid great importance on appearing in fresh and, when appropriate, fine, array.

Theatre companies worked on a co-operative system. The major companies needed around fifteen to twenty regular performers.

Although some of Shakespeare's plays have more than fifty speaking parts, most of them can be acted by a group of fifteen or so, with many of the actors taking two or more roles. There would be a number of stakeholders, fluctuating perhaps from eight to a dozen, known as the sharers who would normally also be active as actors and possibly writers. At least one of them would take on the responsibilities of company manager, looking after financial matters. The company would need professional boy actors, often apprenticed to leading actors, to play women's roles; three or four are enough for most plays of the period, but some roles – such as Rosalind in Shakespeare's *As You Like It*, the Duchess of Malfi in Webster's tragedy, and Beatrice-Joanna in Middleton and Rowley's *The Changeling* – are immensely demanding. In addition, the company would take on hired men, paid by the week, according to the varying requirements of their scripts. They also needed support staff: musicians, one or more scribes, property men, wardrobe keepers, doormen (or women), and stage-keepers who did anything from sweeping the stage, clearing up refuse in the auditorium, appearing as extras in crowd scenes and posting playbills.[34]

Henslowe tells us much about the conditions in which actors worked. In 1597 he contracted a number of new players for the Rose, including one William Kendall who agreed to work for him for a period of two years at the rate of ten shillings for each week he played in London, and five shillings a week on tour, with the condition that he should be 'ready at all times to play in the house of the said Philip, and in no other during the said term'.[35] These were not bad rates at a time when an artisan would receive no more than one shilling a week, but then as now theatre was a risky profession. Some actors' contracts were more detailed and stringent than Kendall's. An agreement of 1614 between Henslowe and the actor Robert Dawes is illuminating about theatre practice. Dawes had to agree to a sliding scale of penalties for a variety of foreseeable misdemeanours. If he was late for a rehearsal 'which shall the night before the rehearsal be given publicly out', he would forfeit twelve pence; if he failed to turn up for the rehearsal at all, it would cost him two shillings; if he was not 'ready apparelled . . . to begin the play at the hour of three of the clock in the afternoon' he would pay three shillings; and if he should 'happen to be overcome with drink at the time when he [ought to] play, by the judgement of four of the said company' it would cost him ten shillings. If he failed to turn up at all, with no reasonable excuse, the penalty was a pound. And if he left the playhouse with any of the proprietors' costumes on his body, or took away any of their property, or even helped anyone else to do so, he would suffer the crippling penalty of £40.[36] Prosecution might have been more acceptable – except that theft was a capital offence.

Running a company was an expensive business, subject to unforeseeable hazards such as riots, bad weather and outbreaks of sickness, especially plague, which could close theatres for long periods of time. When this happened the companies' regular tours of the provinces would be indefinitely extended. Touring was arduous. Costumes, properties and musical instruments had to be transported by hand and by cart. Actors would travel by foot, on horseback or on mules, their entrance into towns heralded by trumpet and drum. They found accommodation where they could. City authorities had to give permission for playing, and not all of them were welcoming. The actors would carry a letter from their patron as evidence that they were authorized (an example of such a letter is reproduced in Documents, p. 238 below). It was usual to give the first performance in any town free for the mayor and his guests. There were virtually no purpose-built playhouses outside London; performances took place in guildhalls, great and not-so-great houses, schoolrooms and even in churches. This required flexibility of staging. If there was no trapdoor, the graveyard scene in *Hamlet* would have to be adapted or left out. If there was no upper level, the balcony scene in *Romeo and Juliet* would suffer. Texts had to be adjusted at short notice to suit the shifting circumstances. Shakespeare provides an entertaining illustration of this in the drastic alterations made by the mechanicals in *A Midsummer Night's Dream* to fit the tragedy of Pyramus and Thisbe for performance before Duke Theseus and his court.

Hazardous though the business was, the rewards of running a theatre and of performing in it could be great. As we have seen, Shakespeare became a rich man, able to buy a fine house in Stratford, by the time he was in his mid-thirties; Edward Alleyn (1566–1626), the leading actor of the Lord Admiral's Men who was also an astute businessman, became one of the leading educational philanthropists of his time and founded Dulwich College. And Henslowe, owner and manager of the Rose theatre (but also the owner of other playhouses, inns, brothels and bear-baiting arenas), amassed wealth. On his death he left money for mourning gowns for forty poor men to accompany his body to the grave.

As well as actors and support staff, the companies had a desperate need of a stream of new plays to satisfy the demands of both the court and the general public. London had a population of around 200,000 people. Theatregoing was immensely popular: around one in ten persons regularly saw plays. So when *Hamlet* was first performed at the Globe that theatre was competing for business with at least the Rose and the Fortune, as well as with the boys' companies of whom Hamlet complains. And the theatres were competing too for the services of writers. Each company performed a different play every weekday afternoon, which meant that they needed up to forty or so different plays a year. It is because Henslowe's son-in-law Edward Alleyn made enough money to found Dulwich College – and because he was so public-spirited as to do so – that we know as much as we do about the Rose theatre and its repertory. We should be even more grateful if we knew as much about Shakespeare's playhouse, the Globe. It is because the Henslowe papers survive that we know, for instance, that on successive days in January 1593 playgoers at the Rose were offered performances of plays called *The Comedy of Cosmo* and *Sir John Mandeville* (both of unknown authorship and now lost), *A Knack to Know a Knave* (anonymous), *Titus Andronicus* by Shakespeare, *Harry the Sixth* (presumably the first part of *Henry VI* by Shakespeare), *Friar Bacon and Friar Bungay* by Robert Greene, who had recently died, *The Jew of Malta* by Marlowe, one of the two parts of the anonymous *Tamar Cham*, and *Mulomuloc* (probably an alternative title for George Peele's *The Battle of Alcazar*, which the company had acted thirteen times during the previous year). The strain on the actors and support staff in putting on so large and varied a repertory within so short a space of time can only be imagined. Rehearsal time must have been minimal; actors had to have fast-working and phenomenally capacious memories. Only at the end of the afternoon, as either applause or catcalls filled their ears, would they know which play the bills should announce for the following day. In that particular January they were called upon for only one performance each of *The Jealous Comedy*, *Tamar Cham*, *The Tragedy of the Guise* (Marlowe's *Massacre at Paris*, which appears to have been new), two performances of Shakespeare's *Harry the Sixth*, *The Comedy of Cosmo*, *Jeronimo* (Kyd's *The Spanish Tragedy*) and *Mulomuloc*, and three each of *A Knack to Know a Knave*, *Sir John Mandeville*, Shakespeare's *Titus Andronicus*, Greene's *Friar Bacon and Friar Bungay*, and Marlowe's popular *The Jew of Malta*. The highest receipts were for the two plays by Marlowe. The company were unwise to give three performances each of *Friar Bacon and Friar Bungay*, which was several years old, and *Sir John Mandeville*, presumably based on the fourteenth-century account of the fantastical travels of the mythical traveller Sir John Mandeville, which, however, had done quite well for them in previous performances; both plays did poor business. During this month Shakespeare and Marlowe must have spent much time together in the playhouse where each of them was having such success. And though Marlowe was not an actor, Shakespeare may well have appeared in some of the Rose plays, perhaps including some by Marlowe.

Although a few writers were contracted to write exclusively for a single company for several years, most of them worked freelance, offering their services to any company that would employ them. Shakespeare is exceptional in having written solely for the Lord Chamberlain's, later the King's, Men from their beginnings to the end of his career nearly twenty years later. The money a freelance playwright could earn for a single play was not great, and some of them worked hard to keep up a phenomenal output. Before the end of a career that lasted for close on half a century, Thomas Heywood (*c.* 1573–1641) claimed to have had an entire hand, or at least a 'main finger', in some two hundred and twenty plays; in addition he wrote in many other literary forms. A standard fee during the 1590s for one single-authored play was £6 – less than the cost of some of the more expensive individual costumes. And there was no royalty system to give authors a continuing financial interest in their work.

It was customary for writers to receive part payment in advance, before the play was completed – or even before they started it – and some of them desperately needed it. At the beginning of December 1597 Henslowe advanced Ben Jonson £1 'in ready money' for a play that was to be completed before Christmas. Jonson had already shown an outline to the company, so Henslowe had an idea of what he would be getting. And towards the end of the same month Henslowe paid £3 to Anthony Munday and Michael Drayton for 'a book' – play script – called *Mother Redcap*; six days later Munday received an additional five shillings 'toward his book', and on 5 January a final payment of £4. 7s.

During the early part of the seventeenth century fees increased. Surviving correspondence between Philip Henslowe and the playwright Robert Daborne shows something of the hectic conditions of the theatre world. On 17 April 1613 Henslowe agreed to pay Daborne £20 in all for a tragedy to be called *Machiavel and the Devil*; after an initial advance of £6 Daborne was to receive a further £4 on handing in the play's first three acts, and a final £10 'upon delivery of the last scene perfected'. This was to be by 31 May, allowing six weeks for the entire task. But eleven days after the agreement Daborne, finding himself in urgent need because his servant – it is interesting that he could afford a servant – had been 'committed to Newgate' prison, implored Henslowe for a further advance of £2.[37] Five days after this he begged for another £1, promising to deliver the first three acts 'fair written' within four days. He managed some pages, 'though not so fair written all as I could wish', and though he acknowledged that he could not deliver the full script by the due date, still it would arrive 'upon the neck of this new play they are now studying', and if Henslowe would cough up the final instalment of his fee Daborne would read what he had written to Alleyn and lose no time 'till it be concluded'. But he was 'unwilling to read to the general company till all be finished'. This was on 16 May. On the 19th Daborne signed a receipt for his final payment, noting: 'This play to be delivered [presumably his servant was now out of prison] in to Mr Henslowe with all speed.' It has not survived, and we do not even know if it was acted.

Reading a newly written play to the company was a regular practice (and continued to be so at least until the twentieth century[38]), and could be an occasion for conviviality; in 1598 Henslowe lent the company five shillings to spend at a tavern called the Sun in New Fish Street on the occasion of the reading of 'the book called *The Famous Wars of Henry the First and the Prince of Wales*'.[39] The writers were Drayton, Dekker and Chettle. Whether Henslowe got his money back we know not.

Between four and six weeks seems to have been the standard timescale for writing a play. The six weeks of Lent, during which performances were prohibited by law, would have provided a convenient writing opportunity for an actor-dramatist such as Shakespeare, who may have ridden home to Stratford for the purpose. But urgent need sometimes imposed tighter deadlines. Michael Drayton promised to complete a play in a fortnight, and, as we have seen, Ben Jonson hoped to work up a plot within the same length of time. Shakespeare's rate of production seems not to have been so rapid. His output, which averaged around two plays a year, with an attempt to satisfy his company's needs by alternating tragedy and comedy, was steady rather than phenomenal, partly no doubt because his standards were high, but also because he had other duties as both actor and shareholder.

It has been estimated that almost half of the plays written for the public theatres were of joint authorship, partly no doubt to keep up with the demand.[40] The prevalence of collaboration as a working method is liable to be underestimated because most of the finest plays of the period that survive are single-authored. A play is, we may feel, more likely to achieve artistic coherence and unity of vision if it is the product of a single imagination. Nevertheless some great plays are collaborative: the comedy of *Eastward Ho* (1605) came from the joint pens of George Chapman, Ben Jonson and John Marston; the composition of *The Changeling* was the joint product of Thomas Middleton and the far less famous William Rowley; and the names of Beaumont and Fletcher are as inseparable as Gilbert and Sullivan or Rodgers and Hammerstein, even though many of the plays collected in 1647 under their joint names were written either by one of them working independently, or in collaboration with one or more other writers, or by someone entirely other.

Most of Shakespeare's best plays are single-authored, but he collaborated with other writers at times, especially early and late in his career. Scholars have been reluctant to acknowledge this, but there is now fairly general agreement that in his early years he worked with George Peele on *Titus Andronicus* and with Thomas Nashe on *Henry VI, Part One*. He also seems likely to have written some scenes of *Edward III*, printed anonymously in 1596. Towards the end of his career he apparently worked with Thomas Middleton on *Timon of Athens*, with John Fletcher on the play known in its own time as *All is True*, retitled *Henry VIII* for its publication in the First Folio, on *The Two Noble Kinsmen*, and on a lost play, *Cardenio*, which to judge by its title was based on episodes from *Don Quixote*. *Pericles* is now agreed to be a collaboration with George Wilkins, and Middleton apparently had a share in both *Measure for Measure* and *Macbeth*, but as an adapter rather than as a collaborator. Shakespeare's collaborative activities will loom large in later chapters of this book.

In his early years Shakespeare was more of a loner than Ben Jonson, most of whose early collaborations are lost. Jonson worked with Henry Chettle and Henry Porter on *Hot Anger Soon Cold* in 1598, with Thomas Dekker on *Page of Plymouth* the following year, and with Chettle, Dekker, 'and other gentleman' [*sic*] in 1599. But all we know of Jonson's personality suggests that he would not have been an easy creative bedfellow. As his career developed he took pride in his independence, even when he was working speedily. In the Prologue to *Volpone* (1606), he claims that

> five weeks fully penned it –
> From his own hand, without a co-adjutor,
> Novice, journeyman or tutor.
>
> (lines 16–18)

Those four nouns usefully define a range of the roles that a collaborator might enact. A coadjutor would be an equal collaborator, a novice a kind of apprentice, a journeyman a hack brought in perhaps to supply a comic subplot, and a tutor a master craftsman guiding a novice. Shakespeare, for example, may have started as tutor to John Fletcher, but they ended up as coadjutors – equal collaborators. Divisions of labour varied from play to play, and are often difficult to discern. In *The Two Noble Kinsmen*, discussed in more detail in Chapter 7, it seems clear that Shakespeare wrote the whole of the first and last acts, some intervening scenes and speeches, and perhaps added touches here and there. Presumably he and Fletcher had discussed the overall design of the play in relation to its principal source, Chaucer's *The Knight's Tale*. Sometimes new writers were brought in to revise an existing manuscript. As we shall see in Chapter 4, Shakespeare was not above helping to rework the play of *Sir Thomas More*, written originally by Anthony Munday, after it had fallen foul of the censor. It was not uncommon even for successful plays to be adapted after their initial composition. In 1601 Henslowe 'lent' Edward Alleyn £4 which he in turn was to 'lend' to Ben Jonson for writing additional scenes for Thomas Kyd's *The Spanish Tragedy*, originally written around 1587, and the surviving version of *Macbeth* is almost certainly Middleton's revision of Shakespeare's play.

Clearly then the conditions in which the greatest plays of the English drama were produced did not make for an easy life for those who wrote and performed them. Yet it was a system that worked, perhaps because rather than in spite of its improvisatory and tumultuous nature. Though theatre design was simple, it was flexible and effective. Speed of production seems to have acted as an inspiration rather than a deterrent to ambition and achievement. Collaboration may have evolved as a means of throwing plays together in a hurry, but at its best it could act as an imaginative stimulus, a pooling of diverse talents conducive to a wider range of dramatic style than individual authors might have achieved on their own. Rapid advances in humanistic education created receptive audiences. The intellectual excitement and rapid development of the expressive qualities of the English language were as apparent in the drama as in any other literary forms: there is no other period in which so much of the finest writing, in both verse and prose, is to be found in plays written for the popular theatre. This is the environment in which Shakespeare and his fellows flourished. In the chapters that follow I seek to describe some of their interactions and of their individual achievements. But first, let us look at the acting profession in Shakespeare's time, and at some of its most conspicuous practitioners.

2

William Shakespeare and the Actors

In Sonnet 23 Shakespeare compares himself to 'an unperfect actor on the stage / Who with his fear is put besides his part'. And Coriolanus, overwhelmed by emotion as his womenfolk come to plead with him for their lives and for Rome, says: 'Like a dull actor now / I have forgot my part, and I am out / Even to a full disgrace' (5.3.40–41). Shakespeare knew and understood the tensions inherent in the acting profession, and he knew them from personal experience. He was aware that actors depend on the good will of their patrons, that even the best of them are, as Theseus puts it in *A Midsummer Night's Dream*, 'but shadows' (5.1.210), and that the entire fabric of a play can be destroyed by unruly playgoers just as Prospero's vision dissolves 'into air, into thin air' as he remembers Caliban's conspiracy (*The Tempest*, 4.1.150).

Shakespeare earned his living partly as an actor. Indeed, though the beginnings of his association with the theatre are shrouded in mystery, it is quite likely that he began his career in the mid-1580s as an actor rather than as a writer. After that facts are few, but he is listed as one of the 'principal comedians' in Jonson's *Every Man in His Humour* of 1598, and as one of the 'principal tragedians' in *Sejanus*, first performed at the Globe in 1603, also by Ben Jonson. How long after this he continued to combine acting with his other responsibilities to the company is anyone's guess. The fact that his name does not occur in the actor list for Jonson's *Volpone* in 1605 may indicate that his acting career had come to an end by then. His name heads the list of 'The Names of the Principal Actors in all these Plays' printed in the First Folio, but the pre-eminence accorded him there may be a gesture of deference to his authorship. We do not need to believe that he literally acted in 'all these Plays', but the Jonson evidence is strong; actor lists are few and far between, and we may be sure that Shakespeare performed in plays by many other writers.

It would be good to know precisely what roles he played. In a short poem headed 'To our English Terence, Mr Will. Shakespeare', published in 1610, the poet John Davies of Hereford (c. 1565–1618 – not the Sir John Davies quoted on p. 10) implies that he specialized in regal roles: 'Hadst thou not played some kingly parts in sport, / Thou hadst been a companion for a king.'[1] Tradition first recorded in the eighteenth century gives him the Ghost in *Hamlet* and Old Adam in *As You Like It*.[2] These are not star roles (though Bernard Shaw, writing that 'the Ghost's part is one of the wonders of the play', declared this to be 'the reason why Shakespear [*sic*] would not trust anyone else with it'[3]). It is natural to conjecture that Shakespeare may have played some of the roles in which his own voice seems to sound most clearly. At the opening of *Henry V*, for instance, the Chorus, in calling upon 'a muse of fire', identifies himself with the author, and in his final speech he refers to 'Our bending author' as if Shakespeare himself were pleading for the audience's indulgence (Prologue, 1 and Epilogue, 2). Some characters in the plays reflect the function of the playwright in devising and controlling the unfolding action. We may think of Oberon in *A Midsummer Night's Dream*, the Duke in *Measure for Measure* and above all Prospero in *The Tempest*, all of whom have been identified to some degree or another with Shakespeare; but the idea that he himself played these roles is supported by nothing but guesswork.

If he had been as outstanding an actor as the finest of his contemporaries, such as Edward Alleyn and Richard Burbage, we should expect more evidence of the fact to survive; but whatever his abilities as a performer, there is no question that his plays are imbued with knowledge and understanding of the profession. In their immense practicality, they are written from inside, as it were. Shakespeare knows how many actors are available, how long it will take for them to change from one costume to another and to get from the lower to the upper stage, how many of them will be boys – very few of the plays call for more than four actors to play women's and boys' parts – and how much doubling he can impose.

It was a fine company. For around twenty years, through most of Shakespeare's career, the Lord Chamberlain's, later the King's, Men achieved a status that ranks it with the great theatre companies of later ages such as David Garrick's at Drury Lane in the mid-eighteenth century, the Duke of Saxe-Meiningen's in the 1870s, Henry Irving's at the Lyceum at the end of the nineteenth century and the Old Vic during the 1920s. And Shakespeare knew its members intimately. Clear evidence that he was creating parts with specific members of his company in mind exists in early texts of certain plays. In the 1599 edition of *Romeo and Juliet*, almost certainly printed from Shakespeare's own manuscript, one of the directions for the entry of the Nurse's servant Peter, identified generically in an earlier direction as '*the Clowne*', reads '*Enter Will Kemp*' (4.4.127.1). And in the first, 1600 quarto of *Much Ado About Nothing*, also printed direct from Shakespeare's own papers, it is clear that as he was writing the names of the comic actors Will Kemp and Richard Cowley, who were to play Dogberry and Verges, rose to the surface of his mind, supplanting those of the characters.[4] Inevitably the personalities of the actors contributed to the characterization. Their characters and talents are part of the source materials of his plays. Dogberry would not be the Dogberry we know and love if Shakespeare had not intended that the immensely popular Kemp would play the role.

If we knew more about the talents of other individual members of Shakespeare's company we should probably be able to identify more of the parts that he wrote for them. The presence of a boy actor from Wales is suggested by the requirement in *Henry IV*, Part One that Lady Percy should improvise speeches in Welsh. It seems significant that *As You Like It* and *Twelfth Night*, written within a year or so of each other, contain prominent and nicely differentiated parts for a pair of boy actors. And towards the end of Shakespeare's career his creation of the roles of Lady Macbeth, Volumnia and Cleopatra suggests that he could rely on an exceptionally talented boy to portray these mature women.

At all stages of theatre history, comedians have been the actors who have made the greatest impact on the general public. The first star of the English theatre is Richard Tarlton, a multi-talented man who worked his way up from humble beginnings in the provinces to become a legend in his lifetime and beyond. He emerges during the 1570s as a stand-up comic, a tavern-keeper in London who would entertain his customers by improvising scurrilous, often rhymed responses to quips and taunts. He became a professional actor, probably with the Lord Sussex's Men, and in 1583 was among those selected from existing companies to form the Queen's Men. Shakespeare may later have worked with this company, and have enjoyed Tarlton's talents at first hand. They shone most brightly in the jigs performed at the end of plays. These farcical afterpieces were not simply lively dances, but satirical, often bawdy verse playlets sung and danced by up to five members of the company; they may often have been improvised. They developed into a regular feature of the theatre of Shakespeare's age, but the graceful dance that Platter saw at the end of a performance of *Julius Caesar* in 1599 shows that jigs did not, as is too often said, form the inevitable conclusion to an afternoon's performance. Hamlet suggests that they were popular with less fastidious members of the audience: Polonius, he says, is 'for a jig or a tale of bawdry' (*Hamlet*, 2.2.503–4). At times and in some playhouses they became so scurrilous and obscene that they were banned: in 1612 the Middlesex Justices made an 'Order for Suppressing Jigs at the End of Plays' as the result of complaints about 'certain lewd jigs, songs, and dances' at the Fortune playhouse which were alleged to attract 'cut-purses and other lewd and ill-disposed persons in great multitudes'.[5]

Comic actor, singer and dancer, Tarlton was also an accomplished fencer and a writer of ballads and plays. His celebrity was so great that Sir Philip Sidney stood godfather to his son. His features appeared on inn-signs and the doors of privies. He died in 1588, probably just too early to appear in any of Shakespeare's plays, and for a couple of decades after that books about him and reprinting his jests were popular.

Tarlton had the natural comedian's ability to provoke mirth by his very appearance. Thomas Nashe writes that, as the Queen's Men 'were now entering into their first merriment as they call it, the people began exceedingly to laugh when Tarlton first peeped out his head'.[6] His legendary comic techniques and routines must have influenced Shakespeare. It is not too fanciful to see a reflection of Tarlton's genius in Falstaff's skills in improvising himself out of a tight situation, as displayed in the first tavern scene (2.5) of *Henry IV*, Part One, and while it may be sentimental to suppose that Shakespeare was 'portraying' Tarlton as he made Hamlet speak of Yorick's gibes, gambols, songs, and 'flashes of merriment that were wont to set the table on a roar' (*Hamlet*, 5.1.185–7), many members of his audience must have remembered Tarlton when they heard these words.

Tarlton's natural successor was Will Kemp, born probably around the same time as Shakespeare;[7] indeed the first printed reference to Kemp, in Thomas Nashe's tract named *An Almond for a Parrot* published in 1590, two years after Tarlton died, calls him 'that most comical and conceited Cavalier Monsieur du Kemp, jest-monger and vice-gerent general to the Ghost of Dick Tarlton'.[8] And some twenty years later the prolific playwright, actor and poet Thomas Heywood, in his *Apology for Actors* published in 1612, says that Kemp 'succeeded' Tarlton 'as well in the favour of her Majesty as in the opinion and good thoughts of the general audience' (sig. E2v).

Like Tarlton, Kemp was a freelance entertainer before joining a theatre company, but unlike Tarlton he worked much on the Continent, travelling in the entourage of the Earl of Leicester to the Netherlands in 1585 both as a member of the Earl's fifteen-strong acting company and as a solo entertainer; in the following year he was one of a group of five English musicians and tumblers who worked for three months at the court of Elsinore. Two other members of this group, like Kemp, were to join the Lord Chamberlain's Men; Shakespeare – who so far as we know never travelled overseas – could easily have talked with them about the Danish court before he wrote *Hamlet*.

Also like Tarlton, Kemp achieved fame as what Hamlet calls a 'jig-maker' (3.2.119). Four of Kemp's jigs survive, two of them in German translation – an indication of his renown on the Continent. An example is 'Singing Simpkin', printed in 1595 as 'a ballad called Kemp's new jig betwixt a soldier and a miser and Sim the Clown'. Using the age-old comic theme of cuckoldry, and based on an episode from Boccaccio's *Decameron*, it dramatizes a simple tale of a wife who, in her aged husband's absence, seduces a servant, Bluster, who seeks to hide in a chest in case the husband interrupts their love-

2. Richard Tarlton. This decorative drawing by John Scottowe cannot be regarded as a faithful likeness, but it shows him with the pipe and tabor – small drum – that were hallmarks of his trade.

making, but Simpkin is there before him, and keeps up a running commentary from his hiding place:

> BLUSTER Within this chest I'll hide myself,
>   If it chance he should come.
> WIFE O no, my love, that cannot be –
> SIMPKIN I have bespoke the room.
> WIFE I have a place behind here,
>   Which yet is known to no man.
> SIMPKIN She has a place before, too,
>   But that is all too common.

The husband is heard off stage:

> OLD MAN Wife, wherefore is the door thus barred?
>   What mean you, pray, by this?
> WIFE Alas, it is my husband!
> SIMPKIN I laugh now till I piss.
> BLUSTER Open the chest, I'll into it;
>   My life else it may cost.

WIFE Alas, I cannot open it.

SIMPKIN I believe the key is lost.

(lines 65–80)

In Shakespeare's *The Merry Wives of Windsor*, written a couple of years later, Falstaff too – who may have been played by Kemp – hides, this time in a clothes basket, to escape detection by a jealous husband; but he is genuinely (if comically) fearful of discovery. The fame of Kemp's jigs as bawdy entertainments is clear from a remark in Everard Guilpin's no less bawdy collection of satirical verses *Skialethia*, of 1598: 'Whores, beadles, bawds, and sergeants filthily / Chant Kemp's Jig . . .'[9]

Kemp's links with Shakespeare date from his founder-membership of the Lord Chamberlain's Men, in 1594. Like Shakespeare, as well as being a performer he took partial responsibility for the company's business affairs. No roles in Shakespeare's plays other than Peter and Dogberry can certainly be ascribed to him, but others that have been suggested include the Clown in *Titus Andronicus*, Costard in *Love's Labour's Lost*, Bottom in *A Midsummer Night's Dream* and, less confidently, Falstaff in both parts of *Henry IV* and in *The Merry Wives of Windsor*. In February 1599 Kemp bought a share in the Lord Chamberlain's Men to help to finance the building of the Globe, but later that year, for some reason, he sold his interest in the company and resumed his freelance career.

Kemp's national celebrity is evident from his account of his most famous exploit, the morris dance from London to Norwich which he undertook partly, no doubt, as a publicity stunt, partly to raise money, and partly for fun. He publicized this after the event in a pamphlet taking the form of a letter addressed to the Queen's Maid of Honour, Anne Fitton, who, he knows, would expect to see nothing 'but blunt mirth in a morris dancer, especially such a one as Will Kemp, that hath spent his life in mad jigs and merry jests'.[10] The title of his little book, *Kemp's Nine Days' Wonder*, draws on an already proverbial expression, roughly equivalent to 'a flash in the pan'. But when in *As You Like It* – assuming that, as seems probable, it was first acted shortly after Kemp's exploit – Rosalind says she is already 'seven of the nine days out of the wonder' (3.2.170), Shakespeare must have expected his audience to remember Kemp who, if he had stayed with the company, might well have been playing Touchstone.

Kemp set off early in the morning of the first day of Lent, 11 February 1600, amidst a throng of onlookers at the Lord Mayor of London's house. He was accompanied by his servant, William Bee, a drummer, Thomas Sly, and a minder named George Sprat, whose duty it was to ensure that Kemp didn't cheat – that he 'should take no other ease but [his] prescribed order'. They seem to have taken a horse with them. The nine days of their journey of around 110 miles were spread over a month, and by Kemp's lively account it attracted as much attention as a modern marathon. News of his coming spread ahead of him, onlookers cheered him on, and he constantly had to refuse tempting offers of drink for fear of slowing himself down. In Brentwood, constables (who may have reminded him of the role of Dogberry that he had played in *Much Ado About Nothing*) brought to the inn in which he was lodging two rogues who had followed him from London and claimed to have made bets on his journey. Kemp said he did not know them personally but he remembered one of them as 'a noted cut-purse' – and then he told the story about tying thieves to a stage post quoted on p. 11. At Chelmsford, it took him an hour to push his way through the throng to get to his inn, where he locked himself into his room and addressed the onlookers from a window, telling them that he was too tired to perform any more. As he danced along the lanes, country youths, hearing his pipe from far off in the still morning or evening air, would try to dance along with him for a while. On one muddy lane a lad competing with him got stuck in a pothole, cried out to his companion, 'Come, George, call ye this dancing, I'll go no further', and had to be rescued. Kemp 'could not choose but laugh to see how like two frogs they laboured'. And in Sudbury, 'a lusty tall fellow, a butcher by his profession', managed to dance beside him for no more than half a mile, when he gave up, saying that he couldn't go any further even if he was offered a hundred pounds to do so. But 'a lusty country lass', calling the butcher a 'faint-hearted lout', declared that she could have held out for a mile. So Kemp fitted her up with bells, summoned the taborer to play, and the pair of them 'footed it merrily to Melford, being a long mile'. The lass was in 'a piteous heat', but he rewarded her with 'her skinful of drink' and an English crown to buy more drink to cool her down. Kemp and his companions were royally received when they reached Norwich, the citizens paid all their expenses, and the Mayor awarded him an annuity of forty shillings.

In the following year Kemp visited Italy and Germany. His meeting in Rome in 1601 with the English traveller Sir Anthony Shirley is dramatized in a comic episode in a curious play, *The Travels of the Three English Brothers*, by William Rowley, John Day and George Wilkins, of 1607, several years after Kemp died. In it Kemp has a mildly bawdy conversation with an Italian Harlequin and his wife; Thomas Nashe, in *An Almond for a Parrot*, also associates Kemp with Harlequin, suggesting that contemporaries, like scholars later, saw affinities between the techniques of English clowns and the Italian *commedia dell'arte*. By March 1602 Kemp had become a senior member of the Earl of Worcester's Men; he is mentioned in a payment for a costume in Henslowe's papers in September 1602, and he may be the 'Kemp, a man' buried in St Saviour's, Southwark, at a time of plague on 2 November 1603.

The fact that Peter in *Romeo and Juliet* is not a star role though Kemp was a leading member of the company raises the question of the extent to which the comedians, or clowns, in plays of the period might have been in the habit of fattening their parts with improvisation. Does Hamlet's injunction that 'those that play your clowns speak no more than is set down for them' (3.2.38–9) imply that actors in Shakespeare's own company were accustomed to do this? Is this even an implied criticism of Kemp himself? The question has implications for modern performance. It is not unusual for the actor playing the Porter in *Macbeth* to improvise topicalities. But the Porter's principal speech is tightly written. Shakespeare leaves no obvious gaps in it or in comic speeches in any other of his plays; there is no sign that he expected or desired his comic actors to improvise, except possibly in post-performance jigs, which he did not script.

Kemp's departure from the Lord Chamberlain's Men left a gap that had to be filled, though his successor would not necessarily have taken over all his roles: redistribution among several different actors is likely. An obvious candidate is Robert Armin, who probably joined the company in 1599. Born around 1563 – one year before Shakespeare

– he was apprenticed in 1581 to a distinguished goldsmith. According to an anecdote in the anonymously written *Tarlton's Jests* of 1600, Tarlton, recognizing Armin's talents, adopted him (although they were of around the same age), prophesying that he would inherit his clown's costume. Armin would have served his full term as an apprentice goldsmith by 1592, and by the mid-1590s he had joined a provincial acting company, Lord Chandos's Men. But like many actors of the period he maintained at least a nominal alternative allegiance: he became a freeman of the Goldsmiths' Company in 1604. His popularity is witnessed by a verse tribute headed 'To honest-gamesome Robin Armin, / That tickles the spleen like an harmless vermin'. Written by John Davies of Hereford, it was printed in his collection of satires *The Scourge of Folly* (1611) and praises Armin in terms that link him with the wise fools of Shakespeare's later comedies. He addresses Armin as one who

> with harmless mirth
> Dost please the world, and so amongst [enjoy'st?] the earth,
> That others but possess with care that stings;
> So, mak'st thy life more happy far than kings.

And Davies looks forward to the eternal rewards that Armin will reap:

> . . . So, play thy part, be honest still, with mirth;
> Then, when thou'rt in the tiring-house of Earth,
> Thou, being His servant whom all kings do serve,
> Mayst, for thy part well played, like praise deserve:
> For in that tiring-house when either be,
> You're one man's men, and equal in degree.
> So thou, in sport, the happiest men dost school
> To do as thou dost: wisely play the fool.[11]

Whereas Kemp seems to have specialized in extrovert roles of robust comic humour, Armin, probably slighter in build, was more intellectual. He was not a jig-maker, but wrote ballads, a collection of tales called *Fool upon Fool* (1600, reprinted in 1605 and, as *A Nest of Ninnies*, in 1609), and an intricately plotted full-length play, *The Two Maids of More-clacke*, printed in 1609. After Armin's recruitment Shakespeare began to create clowns who are more wistful, introverted, and musical: semi-choric commentators on the action rather than active participants.

At least, this is the general view. But Touchstone, in *As You Like It*, of around 1600, just after Kemp's departure, is not all that different

3. *William Kemp. This drawing of Will Kemp, based on the title page of* Kemp's Nine Days' Wonder, *shows him dancing his way to Norwich, accompanied by his drummer, Thomas Sly.*

in style from the earlier clowns. He has no songs (unless he sings the few lines beginning 'O, sweet Oliver . . .' (3.3.89–95)); indeed, none of the characters Shakespeare is most likely to have created for Kemp has any songs worth speaking of (Bottom's 'The ousel cock' scarcely counts), whereas the two roles most confidently associated with Armin, the wise fools Feste in *Twelfth Night* and the Fool in *King Lear*, are among the most musical in the canon. It must be said, however, that the evidence that Armin played these roles has to be inferred, mainly from the associated facts that these are the roles most likely to have been played by the company's leading comic actor, and that the company's leading comic actor during this period was Armin. Other roles written after Armin joined the company which seem likely to have been played by the company clown, even if they were not tailor-made for Armin, include the First Gravedigger in *Hamlet*,

Lavatch or even Paroles in *All's Well That Ends Well*, Thersites – or possibly Pandarus – in *Troilus and Cressida*, the Porter in *Macbeth*, and, most musically, Autolycus in *The Winter's Tale*.

What of the tragedians? Two of them stand head and shoulders above the rest – one of them literally so. Edward Alleyn, to judge by his portrait at Dulwich College, must have been one of the tallest men of his time. Born in 1566, he was two years younger than Shakespeare and Marlowe, second son of an innkeeper who among other posts served as porter to the Queen and as head of Bethlem Hospital, London's main establishment for the confinement and treatment of the insane. Edward was acting with the Earl of Worcester's Men by the time he was 17; six years later, in 1589, he joined his elder brother John, also an actor, in buying 'playing apparel, playbooks, instruments, and other commodities', presumably on behalf of the Lord Admiral's Men, performing at the Rose. Edward not only went into business with the owner of the Rose, Philip Henslowe, but also, at the age of 26, married Henslowe's stepdaughter, Joan Woodward. Among his father-in-law's papers are affectionate letters which give us glimpses of rare intimacy into Elizabethan domestic life. They passed by carrier, and, through the good offices of travelling players, between Henslowe, Alleyn and Joan when the company was on tour during the plague of 1593 (one of the most charming of them is reproduced in full in Documents, pp. 236–7). On 1 August Edward was with Lord Strange's Men in Bristol. As he waited to go on stage in a play called *Harry of Cornwall*, now lost, he took the opportunity to write home, advising his wife on precautions she might take against the plague:

keep your house fair and clean, which I know you will, and every evening throw water before your door and in our backside [backyard], and have in your windows good store of rue and herb of grace and withal the grace of God which must be obtained by prayers, and so doing no doubt but the Lord will mercifully defend you.[12]

Alleyn had been married for only ten months, and was homesick; in a postscript he gently chides his wife for sending him no news 'of your domestical matters, such things as happens at home as how your distilled water proves or this or that or anything, what you will'. He wants to know how his garden is doing, and tells his wife (whom he

4. *Edward Alleyn. In this oil painting, Alleyn has removed his glove to show his signet ring, which remains in the custody of the Master of Dulwich College.*

playfully calls his 'mouse') that in September she should turn the parsley bed over to spinach 'for then is the time'; he would do it himself if he could, 'but we shall not come home till AllHolland tide' – that is, All Saints' Day, 1 November, two long months ahead – 'and so sweet mouse farewell and brook our long journey with patience'. He is sending back his white waistcoat, 'because it is a trouble to me to carry it', and asks Joan to have his orange-tawny stockings dyed 'very good black' for him to wear in the winter. Henslowe replied on Joan's behalf – probably she could not write – with a mixture of good and sombre news: 'we are all at this time in good health in our house', the stockings are duly dyed, the spinach bed is 'not forgotten', 'your poor mouse hath not been sick since you went'; but the sickness 'hath been almost in every house about us and whole households died', including the wife of a fellow actor, Robert Browne, who was at that time in Germany, along with 'all her children and household';[13] during that week 1,603 Londoners had died.

As an actor, Alleyn's name is for ever associated with the plays of Christopher Marlowe (discussed in the next chapter), especially

Tamburlaine and *Dr Faustus*. Marlowe may even have had him in mind as he described Tamburlaine:

> Of stature tall, and straightly fashionèd,
> Like his desire, lift upwards and divine;
> So large of limbs, his joints so strongly knit,
> Such breadth of shoulders as might mainly bear
> Old Atlas's burden . . .
> His arms and fingers long and sinewy,
> Betokening valour and excess of strength;
> In every part proportioned like the man
> Should make the world subdued to Tamburlaine.
>
> (Part One, 2.1.7–11, 27–30)

Alleyn seems to have been primarily a heroic actor, notable for grandeur of demeanour and powerful declamation. But he must also have had comic talents to play the Jew of Malta. He won the admiration of many distinguished contemporaries. Writing as early as 1592, the year of Alleyn's marriage, Thomas Nashe implied that his acting skills were already so well developed that they could make even a poor play seem better than it really was: Nashe describes a character as one whose 'very name – as the name of Ned Alleyn on the common stage – was able to make an ill matter good'.[14] He compares him to the great Roman tragedian, Roscius: 'Not Roscius nor Aesop, those admired tragedians that have lived ever since Christ was born, could ever perform more in action than famous Ned Alleyn.'[15] Ben Jonson, not an easy man to please, praised Alleyn in a poem published in 1616, declaring it to be just that a man 'who did give / So many poets life, by one should live'.[16] And the long-lived playwright Thomas Heywood, in a Prologue written for a 1632 revival of Marlowe's play *The Jew of Malta*, described Alleyn – dead then for six years – as 'the best of actors' at the time the play was written, one who won the attribute of 'peerless' in many roles, including Barabas (the Jew) and Tamburlaine, and praising him for both versatility and for eloquence.[17]

Alleyn's acting career was relatively short. Increasingly from about 1597 he devoted his energies to theatrical management and other business matters in collaboration with his father-in-law, but he made occasional appearances in special shows such as the *Magnificent Enter-*

tainment Given to King James on his formal entry into the City of London in 1604, and in a royal performance in 1608 for which he was paid the flatteringly large sum of £20. In 1623, six months after his wife Joan died, he married the poet John Donne's daughter Constance, thirty-seven years younger than he. He died, in 1626, a wealthy man.

As Edward Alleyn stands to the Lord Admiral's Men and to the plays of Christopher Marlowe, so Richard Burbage stands in relation to the Lord Chamberlain's Men and the plays of William Shakespeare. They were 'two such actors that no age must look to see the like', wrote Sir Richard Baker in his *Chronicles of the Kings of England* (1643).

Burbage's father, James, was one of the pioneers of the Elizabethan stage. Like Jonson, Armin and many other actors of the period, James began his working life as an apprentice to another trade: he was a joiner, possessor of a skill which he put to excellent use after he had become an actor with the Earl of Leicester's Men by initiating the construction of England's first major theatre – named 'the Theatre' after its Roman prototypes – in 1576. It was a troubled enterprise, and after performances had started James was accused of having used a secret key over a period of two years to filch from 'the common box where the money gathered at the said plays was put in'; it was alleged that he would 'thrust some of the money divident [due to be shared] between him and his said fellows in his bosom, or otherwhere about his body'.[18]

Like Alleyn, James Burbage's son Richard, born in 1568, was involved with the theatrical profession from an early age. He displayed his loyalty to his father in a brawl at the Theatre in 1590 resulting from a dispute over the 'moiety' or half-share of the takings which was due to them. In the ensuing court case, John Alleyn – Edward's elder brother – deposed that he had found Richard 'with a broom staff in his hand, of whom when [Alleyn] asked what stir was there, he answered in laughing phrase "how [originally 'hew': Phew?] they come for a moiety", but, quoth he, holding up the said broom's staff, "I have, I think, delivered him a moiety with this and sent them packing."' A witness added that Richard, 'scornfully and disdainfully playing with this deponent's nose, said that if he dealt in the matter he would beat him also and did challenge the field of him at that time'.[19] Burbage may already have been acting with the Lord Admiral's

5. Richard Burbage. Burbage was a painter as well as an actor. We have a reference to a portrait, 'a woman's head done on board by Mr Burbage', and the portrait of him now at Dulwich may be his own work – experts differ on the attribution.

Men, but we know for certain that he joined the Lord Chamberlain's company when they were formed, because he is recorded as payee, along with Kemp and Shakespeare, for performances of unnamed plays that they gave before the Queen at Greenwich during the Christmas season of 1594. He was then 26 years old, and like Shakespeare he was to remain with the same acting company for the rest of his life – in his case, for a quarter of a century.

Shakespeare, Burbage's senior by only four years, must have known him intimately, and the actor's special talents undoubtedly did much to influence Shakespeare's choice of material for plays and his characterization of many leading roles. Among those we can definitely identify, the range is in itself a guide to Burbage's versatility. An unknown obituarist, whose verses circulated in manuscript, was to write:

> He's gone, and with him what a world are dead,
> Which he revived, to be revivèd so
> No more. Young Hamlet, old Hieronimo,

Kind Lear, the grievèd Moor, and more beside
That lived in him have now for ever died.[20]

An even pithier epitaph was 'Exit Burbage'. The contrast between 'young' Hamlet and 'old' Hieronimo (in Thomas Kyd's *The Spanish Tragedy*) emphasizes the actor's ability to portray widely differing characters; and it is worth remembering that Burbage was under 40 when he first played the octogenarian Lear in the play written about seven years after *Hamlet*.

This same obituarist also praises Burbage for naturalism:

> Oft have I seen him leap into the grave,
> Suiting the person, which he seemed to have,
> Of a sad lover with so true an eye
> That there I would have sworn he meant to die.
> Oft have I seen him play this part in jest
> So lively that spectators and the rest
> Of his sad crew, whilst he but seemed to bleed,
> Amazed, thought even then he died indeed.

These lines seem to refer either to Romeo or to Hamlet, a role in which Burbage would have had to instruct the players visiting Elsinore to depict even passionate emotions with restraint:

... do not saw the air too much with your hand, thus, but use all gently; for in the very torrent, tempest, and as I may say the whirlwind of your passion, you must acquire and beget a temperance that may give it smoothness. O, it offends me to the soul to hear a robustious, periwig-pated fellow tear a passion to tatters, to very rags, to split the ears of the groundlings ... I would have such a fellow whipped for o'erdoing Termagant. It out-Herods Herod. (*Hamlet*, 3.2.4–14)

The tyrant Herod was a character in the obsolescent mystery plays, performed by amateurs, and Hamlet's satire is directed in part against ham-acting thespians like Bottom in *A Midsummer Night's Dream*, but Shakespeare may also have had in mind the huffing and puffing required of, and no doubt supplied by, Edward Alleyn in characters such as Marlowe's Tamburlaine.[21] Burbage's first words in this scene, 'Speak the speech, I pray you, as I pronounced it to you – trippingly on the tongue', may also suggest a contrast with Alleyn in speed of speaking.

A rare eyewitness description of Burbage's acting is provided by the physician and astrologer Simon Forman in notes written when he saw *Macbeth* at the Globe in 1611. Forman wrote:

The next night, being at supper with his noblemen whom he had bid to a feast to the which also Banquo should have come, he began to speak of 'noble Banquo', and to wish that he were there. And as he thus did, standing up to drink a carouse to him, the ghost of Banquo came and sat down in his chair behind him, and he turning about to sit down again saw the ghost of Banquo, which fronted him so that he fell into a great passion of fear and fury, uttering many words about his murder by which, when they heard that Banquo was murdered, they suspected Macbeth. [The whole entry is reproduced in Documents, pp. 240–41 below.]

Forman's observation that Macbeth 'fell into a great passion of fear and fury' sounds like a subliminal recollection of the character's description of life as 'a walking shadow' – the word was used for an actor – 'a poor player / That struts and frets his hour upon the stage, / And then is heard no more', a tale 'Told by an idiot, full of sound and fury, / Signifying nothing' (5.5.23–7). And Forman's description, besides giving precise information about the staging of the scene, gives an impression of Burbage's acting style. It has sometimes been supposed that he and his colleagues employed stylized gestures as a kind of semaphore for the emotions they sought to convey, but Forman's description suggests rather that Burbage actually seemed to be experiencing the character's fluctuating emotions.

Impressions of Burbage's qualities may be gleaned not only from the demands that his roles made upon him, but also by some of what Shakespeare and his contemporaries said about the profession both within plays and in other writings. 'Come, cousin', says Richard III to the Duke of Buckingham,

> canst thou quake and change thy colour?
> Murder thy breath in middle of a word?
> And then begin again, and stop again,
> As if thou wert distraught and mad with terror?

To which Buckingham replies:

> Tut, I can counterfeit the deep tragedian,
> Tremble and start at wagging of a straw,
> Speak, and look back, and pry on every side,
> Intending deep suspicion; ghastly looks
> Are at my service, like enforcèd smiles,
> And both are ready in their offices
> At any time to grace my stratagems.
>
> (3.5.1–11)

These are the techniques of the bravura actor, and we can be sure that Burbage possessed them. In 1615 appeared an essay descriptive of 'An Excellent Actor', possibly written by the author of two of the greatest tragedies of the period, John Webster; Burbage had played Ferdinand in his *The Duchess of Malfi*. This writer's astute description of how the performer can draw all eyes towards him could apply to great actors of all periods, now as well as then: 'by a full and significant action of body he charms our attention: sit in a full theatre and you will think so many lines drawn from the circumference of so many ears, whiles the *actor* is the *centre*.' Whether or not this writer had Burbage directly in mind – and it is likely, since he was the greatest actor performing at the time the essay appeared – this must characterize Burbage's genius. And part of what is said anticipates reactions to Burbage's death. When 'a worthy actor ... dies we cannot be persuaded any man can do his parts like him'.[22] Burbage died suddenly, on 12 March 1619, at a time when the theatres were closed because Queen Anne, too, had died a few days earlier. Among the many tributes paid to him, the only one known to have come from a playwright is some lines by Thomas Middleton, who implied that the actor was more deeply mourned than the Queen:

> Astronomers and stargazers this year
> Write but of four eclipses; five appear:
> Death interposing Burbage and there staying,
> Hath made a visible eclipse of playing.[23]

Two months later the Earl of Pembroke, who with his brother was to be a dedicatee of the First Folio, was still so distressed that he could not bring himself to join in the after-dinner festivities at a great banquet which was to be followed by a performance of *Pericles*, in which Burbage had probably created the leading role; the Earl wrote that 'I being tender-hearted, could not endure to see [the play] so soon after the loss of my old acquaintance Burbage'.

Actors then, as now, had a reputation for loose living; and then, as now, it was sometimes deserved. In the second part of the Cambridge University play *The Return from Parnassus*, written anonymously around the turn of the century, the admiration of young women is counted among the rewards of the profession: Kemp, speaking to students who have ambitions to go on the stage, says: 'There's not a country wench that can dance Sellenger's Round [probably a euphemism for 'engage in sexual activity'] but can talk of Dick Burbage and Will Kemp.'[24] And the ballad on the burning of the Globe (Documents, pp. 242–3 below) advises the actors to save the money they would otherwise have spent on whores to buy tiles in place of thatch for the new theatre.

Lewd speculation about what actors did after the play was over seems to have been common. In Middleton's comedy *A Mad World, My Masters* (1605), after an actor has spoken a prologue to a play, a courtesan says 'O'my troth, an I were not married, I could find in my heart to fall in love with that player now and send for him to a supper' (5.2.33–5). We do not have a lot of evidence about Shakespeare's personal behaviour, but an anecdote of 1602 suggests that he, like most of his fellow playwrights – though not Marlowe – may have been a womanizer: in 1602 John Manningham recorded the gossip that

Upon a time, when Burbage played Richard III, there was a citizen grew so far in liking with him that before she went from the play she appointed him to come that night unto her by the name of Richard the Third. Shakespeare, overhearing their conclusion, went before, was entertained, and at his game ere Burbage came. Then, message being brought that Richard the Third was at the door, Shakespeare caused return to be made that William the Conqueror was before Richard the Third.[25]

This anecdote anticipates one recounted in another essay, this time describing 'a virtuous player', published in 1628: 'He is tragical on the stage, but rampant in the tiring house, and swears oaths there which he never conned. The waiting-women spectators are over ears in love with him, and ladies send for him to act in their chambers.'

Circumstantial evidence of more serious lewd behaviour is provided by a court case involving Christopher Beeston, born about 1580, who seems to have begun his career during the 1590s as a boy player with the Lord Chamberlain's Men, and who had a long and influential career as a theatre manager until he died in 1638. He married in September 1602, and only a few weeks later a woman imprisoned in Bridewell for 'having a child in whoredom' accused him of raping her. Beeston, she said, boasting of having 'lain with a hundred wenches in my time', had 'committed with her the abominable sin of adultery in most filthy and brutish manner in one Winter's house in an alley without Bishopsgate on Midsummer Eve last'. Beeston denied the charges but he 'and others his confederate players did very unreverently demean themselves to certain governors and much abused the place'. The charges appear to have been dropped.[26] A modern commentator makes an interesting link between these events and Shakespeare's composition of *Measure for Measure*, which takes place partly in a prison:

The case provides a striking context for *Measure For Measure*, performed in December 1604, in which Angelo threatens Isabella with rape, Lucio vehemently demeans himself to the Duke, and Barnardine refuses to leave his cell. *Measure For Measure* seems to have enabled the company (now the King's men) to acknowledge the controversy and parody the Bridewell court at the same time, resolving the risks of legal procedure into an uneasy fiction. Shakespeare used a variety of literary sources to compose that play, but it is hard to imagine that he did not have in mind Beeston's experience too.[27]

Great companies do not rely on stars alone, but inevitably we know less about Shakespeare's middle-rank actors. Still, some of the information we have can help us to understand the state of the profession at the time, and perhaps to dispel some of the more misleading superstitions about the behaviour and status of actors – or players, as they were more usually known. As we have seen, strolling players who lacked aristocratic patronage were officially classed as rogues and vagabonds in Poor Law legislation designed to prevent them from becoming a burden on communities they visited. But actors with the major companies could gain a respected place in society. Many of them appear, so far as we can tell, to have lived blameless lives and to have been respectable citizens.

Like Shakespeare, Beeston's mentor Augustine Phillips had aspirations to gentility: he applied for, and may have been granted, a coat of arms.[28] Probably a founder-member of the Lord Chamberlain's Men, he was one of five actors to buy a 10 per cent share in the Globe in 1599, and he was the company's spokesman two years later when they were hauled before the authorities over a performance of *Richard II* commissioned by the Earl of Essex's supporters in the attempt to raise support for his rebellion against Queen Elizabeth. We know little of Phillips's acting career, but bequests of musical instruments, along with his authorship of 'Phillips's Jig of the Slippers', published in 1595, suggest that he was musically accomplished. He became wealthy enough to buy a country home in Mortlake, at that time a small village a few miles outside the City of London, and, in 1604, to lend £100 on interest. He died in 1605, and his will bears witness to the high degree of fellowship among the actors. His bequests include £5 to be distributed equally among the company's hired men at the time of his death, thirty-shilling pieces in gold to his 'fellows' William Shakespeare and Henry Condell and to his 'servant' Christopher Beeston (who had named a son Augustine), and twenty shillings each to five other fellow actors (including Armin). To his 'late apprentice' Samuel Gilborne he left forty shillings, various items of clothing, and his sword and dagger, and to 'James Sandes my apprentice' forty shillings and three musical instruments – a cittern, a bandore and a lute – at the expiration of his apprenticeship. John Heminges, Burbage and two others are named as overseers of the will, each of them to be rewarded with a silver bowl worth £5.

It is tempting to suggest that the stability of membership of the company – leading actors growing older together – may have something to do with the fact that principal characters in Shakespeare's later plays tend to be older than those in his earlier plays. But actors were skilled enough to play characters of a different age from their own. Burbage, we must suppose, progressed within a few years from first playing the youthful Romeo when he was about 27, through the slightly older Hamlet when he was about 32, Othello – 'declined / Into the vale of years – yet that's not much' (*Othello*, 3.3.269–70) – only a year or so later, and suddenly ageing as the octogenarian Lear when he was about 38. He got somewhat younger as Macbeth a year or so after that, and then aged from a relatively young man to a much older one during the course of the plays as Pericles and as Leontes when he was in his early forties; he probably played Prospero – whose age, as with many of Shakespeare's characters, is indeterminate, but who has a teenage daughter – when he was about 42.

One of the company's stalwarts was John Heminges, whose name is eternally linked with that of his lifelong colleague Henry Condell, with whom he put together the First Folio. Along with Burbage, who died four years before the Folio appeared, these are the only colleagues mentioned in Shakespeare's will. He left each of them money to buy a mourning ring, possibly knowing already of plans to publish the Folio. Both Heminges and Condell were actors, and both became men of substance, occupying a respected place in the community; they lived for much of their lives in the London parish of St Mary Aldermanbury, where both served as churchwardens. They are remembered there to the present day in a memorial garden with a monument commemorating especially their share in producing the Folio.

Condell's wife, whom he married when he was about 20, in 1596, was the daughter of a gentleman and man of property; like Phillips, Condell became wealthy enough to buy a country house – in Fulham, now a London suburb, but at that time a rural village on the banks of the River Thames. In his will, dated 13 December 1627, he appoints his colleagues and 'very loving friends' Heminges and Cuthbert, brother of Richard Burbage, as executors, and, very much like Phillips, leaves them £5 each to buy a piece of silver. Heminges, who served an apprenticeship with the Grocers' Company and became a freeman of the City, had special talents as a businessman and seems to have given up acting in his later years but to have continued to work for the King's Men as its business manager. Judging by the ballad on the burning of the Globe, he was afflicted with a stutter, an unfortunate handicap for an actor. His will of 1630 shows him, too, to have been a man of substance. He leaves ten shillings to all the fellows and sharers of the King's Men 'to make them rings for remembrance of me'. His bequests also include framed portraits of two of his daughters, which he leaves to their husbands. Actors who could make bequests like these were no rogues and vagabonds.

Understandably we know even less about hired men than about the leading actors, but it is possible to piece together something of the career of the minor actor variously known as John Sinclo, Sinklo, Sincklo and Sincler, all of which appear to be forerunners or variants of the name now standardized as Sinclair. He crops up in a number of places from the early 1590s to around 1604. In the Induction to *The Taming of the Shrew*, as printed in the First Folio, a speech which should obviously be spoken by one of the players who trick Christopher Sly into believing that he is a gentleman is headed '*Sincklo*' (Induction, 1.86); modern editors call him 'Another Player'. In another early play, *Richard Duke of York* (3 *Henry VI*), the name occurs in a stage direction at the opening of 3.1, as if the writer – whether author or theatre annotator – were writing an actor's in place of a character's name: '*Enter Sinklo, and Humfrey, with Crosse-bowes in their hands*'. It is also found in a document known as a 'plot' or 'platt' of a lost play called *The Seven Deadly Sins*, Part Two, in which the names of characters are mixed up with those of actors. This lists 'A Keeper J sincler', along with the names of actors known to have belonged to the King's Men, including Richard Burbage. These plots, incidentally, are curious documents whose function is uncertain. Seven of them, dating mostly from the 1590s, survive in various states of preservation, one only in a late transcript. They are scene-by-scene outlines of the plots of plays written on large sheets of paper and naming actors and properties. Each of them has a hole in the top, as if they were to be hung up, perhaps in the area behind the stage known as the tiring (attiring, dressing) house of the theatre where the play was to be performed. It has been assumed that they were intended as guides for the actors during a performance, showing when they should ready themselves to go on stage, but they would have been very inefficient guides, and it is more likely that they were drawn up during, or for, rehearsals.[29]

These references to Sinklo tell us little. More intriguingly, in the 1600 quarto of *Henry IV*, Part Two we have the stage direction '*Enter Sinkclo and three or foure officers*' (5.4.0), which is replaced in the

First Folio by '*Enter Hostesse Quickly, Dol Tear-sheete, and Beadles*'. It seems likely that, as he wrote, Shakespeare had Sinklo in mind for the role of one of the beadles, and that when the script was tidied up for later publication the name of the actor, who in any case was probably no longer available, was replaced by that of the character. Why should Shakespeare have envisaged a particular actor for so tiny a role? He has only four short speeches. The answer probably lies in his appearance, since Doll and Mistress Quickly apply to him a variety of colourful and inventive insults, including 'nut-hook' and 'tripe-visaged'. They call him a 'thin man in a censer', a 'filthy famished correctioner', a 'starved bloodhound', 'Goodman Bones', 'thou atomy', and 'you thin thing'. All this suggests that Shakespeare was capitalizing on the distinctive appearance of a member of his company in order to bring a minor functionary to vivid life. Sinklo turns up in 1596 under the alias 'Dinckenclo' as a strolling player in Germany, when he is described as 'der kleine englelender' – the little Englishman.[30] He appears too in John Webster's Induction of 1604 to John Marston's play *The Malcontent*, in which he plays the significantly named role of Doomsday; when a theatre patron invites him to sit between his legs, he fears that 'the audience will then take me for a viol de gamba [a long and narrow stringed instrument resembling a cello, held between the player's legs] and think that you play upon me'. In *Twelfth Night*, we learn that Sir Andrew Aguecheek 'plays o'th' viol-de-gamboys' (1.3.23–4), and he may well have looked like one. Could this have been one of Sinklo's parts too?[31]

From these scraps of evidence we might be tempted to identify other roles in which Shakespeare might have exploited Sinklo's peculiar physique. In *Henry IV*, Part Two he would have been especially eligible to double the First Beadle with the even tinier role of the 'half-faced fellow Shadow' who, says Falstaff, 'presents no mark to the enemy; the foeman may with as great aim level at the edge of a penknife' (3.2.261–3). In *The Comedy of Errors*, who better to play Master Pinch,

> a hungry lean-faced villain,
> A mere anatomy, a mountebank,
> A threadbare juggler, and a fortune-teller,

> A needy, hollow-eyed, sharp-looking wretch,
> A living dead man.
>
> $$(5.1.238-42)$$

And in *Romeo and Juliet* he would have been a natural for the Apothecary:

> Meagre were his looks.
> Sharp misery had worn him to the bones . . .
>
> $$(5.1.40-41)$$

says Romeo, and

> Famine is in thy cheeks,
> Need and oppression starveth in thy eyes,
> Contempt and beggary hangs upon thy back.
>
> $$(5.1.69-71)$$

Sinklo, one might fancy, must have been an amiable, long-suffering man, well accustomed to tolerating jokes about his appearance. It was, after all, his living.

Boy actors made an enormous and indispensable contribution to the theatres of the time. They fall into two distinct categories. On the one hand are those who belonged to the companies in which all the actors were boys, and on the other hand are those who worked for the adult groups. The popularity of the boy-only companies at times reached such heights as to constitute a serious threat to the adult companies, as Shakespeare makes clear in an unusual and lengthy digression in *Hamlet* which has far more to do with the theatres of his own time than with the matter of the play. The 'tragedians of the city', says Rosencrantz, are less followed than when Hamlet was 'in the city' – fictionally Wittenberg, though with an obvious application to London. They have been forced to go on tour (to Elsinore in this case) because of an 'eyrie of children' who 'are now the fashion, and so berattle the common stages – so they call them – that many wearing rapiers are afraid of goose-quills, and dare scarce come thither' (*Hamlet*, 2.2.340–45). Shakespeare was writing *Hamlet* around 1600, a year after the company known as Paul's Boys resumed playing after being in abeyance for nine years. And it was in 1600 that the Children of the Chapel Royal, who had stopped playing in 1584, began again at the Blackfriars.

The boys' service was not always voluntary. Royal choirmasters had the right to impress boys for the Queen's service, very much as men could be pressed into the army. A writ of 1585, signed by Elizabeth and addressed to 'all and singular Deans, Provosts, Masters and Wardens of Colleges, and all ecclesiastical persons and ministers, and to all other our officers, ministers, and subjects to whom in this case it shall appertain', empowers 'our servant Thomas Giles, Master of the Children of the Cathedral Choir of Saint Paul's' and his deputies

to take up such apt and meet children as are most fit to be instructed and framed in the art and science of music and singing as may be had and found out within any place of this our realm of England or Wales, to be by his education and bringing-up made meet and able to serve us on that behalf when our pleasure is to call for them.[32]

A similar writ was issued in 1597 to Nathaniel Giles, Master of the Children at Windsor; it goes into more detail about the process. This time the Master and his deputy had authority to take 'horses, boats, barges, carts, cars [carriages], and wagons for the conveyance of the said children from any place, with all manner of necessaries appertaining to the said children by land or water at such reasonable prices as by the discretion of him or his said deputy shall be thought sufficient'.[33] It would be interesting to know what the parents of children conscripted in this way thought about it all.

These writs refer specifically to the training of boy choristers singing in the Chapels Royal. Trouble arose when the choirmasters attempted to extend their authority to the recruitment of boy actors, and here we have ample information about the views of one parent. In 1601 Henry Clifton, from Toftrees in Norfolk, accused Nathaniel Giles and his deputies of acting illegally in recruiting several boys to act at the Blackfriars, using methods that amounted to kidnapping.[34] Behind the formal but by no means unimpassioned legalese of his bill of complaint, addressed to the Queen, lies a serio-comic tale of accusation and counter-accusation, of bitter recrimination and brutal high-handedness. Clifton lived in a house near Great St Bartholomew's, London, with his 'only son and heir' Thomas, who was about 13. Thomas went every day to a grammar school in Christ Church, London, where for some years he had 'been taught and instructed in the grounds of learning and the Latin tongue'; he had 'no manner of sight in song nor skill in music'. Nevertheless on 13 December 1600 Giles and his confederates waylaid the boy as he was walking quietly from home to school and 'with great force and violence did seize and surprise him', and 'with like force and violence did, to the great terror and hurt of him the said Thomas Clifton, haul, pull, drag and carry' him 'to the said playhouse in the Blackfriars'. One of them had the audacity to threaten him that if he did not do as he was told, they would report him to the constable. The lad was committed to the playhouse 'amongst a company of lewd and dissolute mercenary players', intending to 'use and exercise him . . . in acting of parts in base plays and interludes', to their 'mercenary gain'. On hearing what had happened, the boy's father took himself to the playhouse and repeatedly demanded his son's release. The kidnappers 'utterly and scornfully' refused to let him go, whereupon Clifton told them that if he complained to the Privy Council they would be in serious trouble ('would hardly answer it'). But they retorted that he could complain to whoever he liked, and added that if the Queen would not support them, she could get someone else to do her dirty work for her ('get another to execute her commission for them'), and 'then and there' they 'used divers other contemptuous speeches, manifesting a very slight regard in them towards your majesty's service'. After more argy-bargy, they had the audacity to hand the boy 'a scroll or paper containing part of one of their said plays or interludes' and to tell him to learn it by heart. And one of them took him into custody, threatening him with a whipping if he did not do as he was told. This went on for some twenty-four hours – 'the space of a day and a night' – until the father succeeded in getting a member of the Privy Council to issue a warrant for the boy's release. Clifton demanded that the confederates be called 'before your highness and the lords of your majesty's honourable council in your majesty's court of Star Chamber', to await trial and due punishment.

We do not know what eventually happened, but Giles and his associates seem to have got their way with at least some of their victims. Clifton alleged that they had abducted not only his son, but also seven other grammar school boys and apprentices, among whom were 'Nathan Field, a scholar of a grammar school in London kept by one Mr Mulcaster' – a famous educationalist, former headmaster of Merchant Taylors' School – and 'Salomon Pavy, apprentice to one Peerce'.[35] Field, 14 years old at this time, was to become one of the best actors of the age. After working with the boys' company at the Blackfriars, and later at the Whitefriars, where he appeared in plays including Jonson's *Bartholomew Fair* (1614), he joined the King's Men, apparently in 1615, and was also a playwright of some distinction, working partly on his own and also in collaboration with Fletcher and Massinger. Young Salomon Pavy, also very talented, especially at playing old men's roles, was less fortunate. He died after only three years with the company, and received the tribute of a touching elegy from Jonson:

> Weep with me all you that read
> This little story,
> And know, for whom a tear you shed,
> Death's self is sorry.
> 'Twas a child that so did thrive
> In grace and feature,
> As heaven and nature seemed to strive
> Which owned the creature.
> Years he numbered scarce thirteen
> When fates turned cruel,
> Yet three filled zodiacs had he been
> The stage's jewel,
> And did act (what now we moan)
> Old men so duly
> As, sooth, the Parcae thought him one,
> He played so truly.
> So, by error, to his fate
> They all consented;
> But, viewing him since (alas, too late)
> They have repented;
> And have sought (to give new birth),
> In baths to steep him;
> But being so much too good for earth,
> Heaven vows to keep him.[36]

Whereas some boys, like Field, graduated from private to public companies, others, like Beeston and many of his colleagues, started their working lives with primarily adult companies. No doubt the boys in the company – no more than four or five of them at any one time – started, perhaps from as early as 8 years old, by playing pageboys such as Mote in *Love's Labour's Lost* and boys such as Brutus's page Lucius in *Julius Caesar* and Leontes's son Mamillius in *The Winter's Tale*, going on to play waiting maids such as Lucetta in *The Two Gentlemen of Verona* and Nerissa in *The Merchant of Venice*, before graduating to romantic heroines such as Portia and Viola, and more mature figures such as Mistress Quickly, Lady Macbeth and Volumnia. There is no reason to suppose that Shakespeare or any other dramatist of his time expected female roles of any age to be taken by male adult players.

The boys had no formal training but learnt their trade through a system of mentorship.[37] When Augustine Phillips names 'apprentices' in his will he is using the term loosely. There was no formal acting guild – like the Grocers' Company, to which Heminges belonged – so there could be no formal apprenticeship.[38] Nevertheless a number of leading actors had trainees in their care, and Phillips is not the only one to have treated them as members of his family. Indeed it is likely that the boys lived in their masters' households, like regular apprentices, receiving no remuneration for their work beyond board and lodging.[39] When Edward Pyk, or Pig, was touring with his master Edward Alleyn, probably in 1593, he got Alleyn to write on his behalf a jokey letter to Mrs Alleyn, in London. His intimate familiarity with the household is revealed by the way he signs it: 'your petty, pretty, prattling parleying Pig.'[40]

The best of the boy actors must have had remarkable powers of female impersonation. Richard Robinson (*c.* 1595–1648) started as a boy player, probably as an apprentice to Richard Burbage, whose will he witnessed and whose widow he was to marry, and then had a successful career as an adult actor. In a metatheatrical passage of *The Devil is an Ass*, Jonson works in a tribute to the plausibility with which Robinson could imitate a woman. Merecraft, wanting someone to impersonate a Spanish lady, says:

There's Dick Robinson,
A very pretty fellow, and comes often
To a gentleman's chamber, a friend of mine. We had
The merriest supper of it there one night –
The gentleman's landlady invited him
To a gossip's feast. Now he, sir, brought Dick Robinson,
Dressed like a lawyer's wife amongst 'em all
(I lent him clothes), but to see him behave it,
And lay the law, and carve, and drink unto 'em,
And then talk bawdy, and send frolics! Oh!
It would have burst your buttons, or not left you
A seam.

(2.8.64–74)

It is understandable that actors suffered much from the diatribes of Puritans and other opponents of their profession. But they had their defenders. Heywood, in his *Apology for Actors*, writes with dignity, learning and eloquence of the qualifications that actors need; they

should be men picked out personable, according to the parts they present; they should be rather scholars, that though they cannot speak well, know how to speak, or else to have that volubility that they can speak well, though they understand not what, and so both imperfections may by instructions be helped and amended; but where a good tongue and a good conceit both fail, there cannot be a good actor. (1612, sig. E3)

Heywood's style here is not translucent, but he appears to be saying that though actors need not be scholars in their own right, they must at least be able to speak learned words convincingly. Some actors, too (including Heywood himself, a Cambridge man), were educated at grammar schools and went on to university. Indeed, the second part of *The Return from Parnassus* shows Will Kemp and Burbage auditioning Cambridge students ambitious for a stage career – their audition speeches are one of the most famous soliloquies from *The Spanish Tragedy* and the opening soliloquy of *Richard III*. Kemp speaks glowingly of the rewards to be earned in the profession: 'You have happened upon the most excellent vocation in the world: for money, they come north and south to bring it to our playhouse, and

for honour, who of more report than Dick Burbage and Will Kemp?'
(But when the actors have left, one of the students speaks scornfully
of them and of their 'trade':

> And must the basest trade bring us relief?
> Must we be practised [prenticed?] to those leaden spouts
> That nought do vent but what they do receive?)

Heywood deplores those who by bad behaviour bring the profession
into ill repute, and wishes that they 'might by a general consent be
quite excluded from our society'. And he writes, in terms that might
be applied to what we know of Heminges and Condell, for instance,
and indeed of Shakespeare, that 'Many amongst us I know to be of
substance, of government, of sober lives and temperate carriages,
housekeepers, and contributory to all duties enjoined them equally
with them that are ranked with the most bountiful'. He writes too of
the fame that English players enjoy overseas: 'Playing is an ornament
to the City, which strangers of all nations, repairing hither, report of
in their countries, beholding them here with some admiration: for
what variety of entertainment can there be in any city of Christendom
more than in London?' (sig. F3). He even praises the actors and those
who write for them for the refinement of the English language: 'Our
English tongue, which hath been the most harsh, uneven and broken
language of the world, part Dutch, part Irish, Saxon, Scotch, Welsh,
and indeed a gallimaufry of many, but perfect in none, is now, by this
secondary means of playing, continually refined, every writer striving
in himself to add a new flourish unto it; so that in process, from the
most rude and unpolished tongue, it is grown to a most perfect and
composed language' (ibid.).

In Shakespeare's time, as in ours, acting was a hazardous profession.
Plague closed theatres sometimes for many months in succession,
sending actors on tour or casting them out of work. And their work
was very demanding. They had to learn their parts and to rehearse
quickly, to carry many roles in their heads at once, to adjust rapidly
to the shifting requirements of touring, playing often in buildings
very different from the custom-built playhouses of London which, as
we have seen, would have required changes to both text and stage

movement. They had to be physically fit, and many of them needed to be able to fence, to fight, to sing, to dance, to play musical instruments. They had to speak highly wrought, rhetorically complex language, to give at least an impression of understanding classical allusions, and quite often to speak in languages other than English.

Though the actors of Shakespeare's time are inadequately memorialized, the drama would not have reached the heights that we admire without them.

3

Christopher Marlowe and Shakespeare's Other Early Contemporaries

6. Christopher Marlowe. This painting, discovered in a dilapidated condition at Corpus Christi College, Cambridge, in 1952, has been claimed as the only surviving portrait of Marlowe. It is dated 1585, when Marlowe was 21.

A useful source of information – and of gossip – about Shakespeare and many of his fellow playwrights is a relatively small part of a lengthy book published in 1598, much of which is cribbed from other writings in both Latin and English. This is *Palladis Tamia*, which translates in its subtitle as *Wit's Treasury*. Its author, Francis Meres (1565–1647),[1] was a graduate of both Cambridge and Oxford, where he knew many writers and intellectuals. Before writing *Palladis Tamia* he had translated two substantial Spanish religious treatises, and in 1599 he became a clergyman and schoolteacher, continuing in these professions for the rest of his long life, mostly in the village of Wing, in Rutland. For posterity, the most interesting part of *Palladis Tamia* is the chapter called 'A Comparative Discourse of Our English Poets with the Greek, Latin, and Italian Poets', above all because it provides us with invaluable information about Shakespeare's reputation halfway through his career, and, by naming twelve of his plays, gives us the dates by which they must have been written. Meres knew more about Shakespeare than he could have read in printed sources, and he may well have been personally acquainted with some of the other writers he mentions.

For all its usefulness, the chapter is a vacuous and highly derivative chronicle, in which Meres makes many empty comparisons between classical and Continental writers and his English contemporaries. To some extent these seem designed, like other literary criticism of the period, to show that English writers can hold their own with, or excel, those of the past and of other nations; at other times they seem more like answers in a parlour game: 'What has such-and-such a classical writer, however obscure, in common with such-and-such an English one?' Some of Meres's parallels are trivial and unedifying: so, for example, we learn that 'As Anacreon died by the pot, so George Peele by the pox.' This may be no more than idle gossip, but Meres probably picked up some of the stories that he purveys at first hand from those involved: 'As Archesilaus Prytanaeus perished by wine at a drunken feast (as Hermippus testifieth in Diogenes), so Robert Greene died of a surfeit taken at pickled herrings and Rhenish wine, as witnesseth Thomas Nashe, who was at the fatal banquet.' And Meres, writing five years after the event, passes on a story about the death of Christopher Marlowe: 'Christopher Marlowe was stabbed to death by a bawdy serving-man, a rival of his in his lewd love.'[2] It has often been assumed that 'lewd love' means a female prostitute, but there is nothing in the records of Marlowe's life to show that he had any sexual interest in women, and much in contemporary gossip to suggest that he was more interested in men. Meres's remark probably implies a homosexual affair, but, as we shall see, mention of the 'bawdy serving-man' does not accord with more reliable evidence about Marlowe's death.

Marlowe was the greatest, the most colourful and the most influential of Shakespeare's immediate precursors and early contemporaries, the one of whose personality we know most and whose plays and poems have had most impact on later ages; he will provide the main focus of this chapter. But there were others, successful in their time, and all also mentioned by Meres, who helped to pave the way for Shakespeare, whose work interacted with his, and who still have much to offer. Those discussed here are John Lyly, Robert Greene, Thomas Lodge, George Peele, Thomas Nashe and Thomas Kyd. All, like both Shakespeare and Marlowe, were men of letters whose writings extended beyond the drama. And all but Kyd had a university education – unlike Shakespeare – with the result that they have become known as the University Wits. They were thought of as a group: Thomas Dekker, in his pamphlet *A Knight's Conjuring* (1607), imagines a merry posthumous meeting in the Elysian Fields where 'Marlowe, Greene and Peele had got under the shades of a large vine, laughing to see Nashe, that was but newly come to their college'.[3] Some of these dramatists – certainly Lyly, probably Marlowe – started writing for the stage before Shakespeare. He must have known all of them, whether as friends, rivals, fellow actors or collaborators. He learnt from them in dramatic characterization, structure and style. He quoted them and parodied them. Probably he drank with them, talked with them and quarrelled with them. All of them contributed to his development as a dramatist.

The eldest, John Lyly (1554–1606), grandson of the William Lilly whose Latin grammar was prescribed by royal decree for study in all grammar schools, was, like Marlowe, a Canterbury man. After taking his MA at Magdalen College, Oxford, in 1575, and then (as was common) another MA at Cambridge in 1579, he sprang to fame a year later with the publication of his prose narrative *Euphues: The Anatomy of Wit*, an immediate best-seller which went through four editions in its first year. A second part, *Euphues and his England*, followed two years later. The name of its central character was suggested by a passage in a book called *The Schoolmaster*, by Roger Ascham (1515–68), who had been tutor to the Queen when she was a teenager, where he writes that he who is called by the Greek word '"Euphues" is he, that is apt by goodness of wit, and appliable by readiness of will to learning'.[4] Lyly's book, short on narrative but rich in dialogue, argument and debate, had a colossal if brief impact on the development of English prose. Coming when it did, it provided a model for writers in search of a prose style which would enable them to deploy rhetorical skills learned in the grammar schools and universities which were more commonly used in Latin prose and verse, and in English verse, than in English prose. *Euphues* is a work of extreme elegance and artificiality, the prose equivalent of the elaborate jewellery and fantasticated costumes worn by Elizabeth's courtiers. It makes unremitting use of alliteration, antitheses, puns, carefully balanced clauses, similes derived especially from natural history, and many other rhetorical figures of speech commonly used in classical literature. Here is a brief example:

Though the camomile, the more it is trodden and pressed down, the more it spreadeth, yet the violet, the oftener it is handled and touched, the sooner it withereth and decayeth.[5]

In later times the compulsory reading of *Euphues* and its sequel came to be used as a form of punishment suitable for uppish under-graduates, but for a decade or so the books were widely read for pleasure and influenced many prose writers, especially Robert Greene and Thomas Lodge. Within a few years, however, euphuism had delighted readers long enough. Like any style when pushed to extremes it dated rapidly and was easily imitated and parodied; Shakespeare certainly had *Euphues*, and perhaps the passage printed above, in mind when, wanting to cause Sir John Falstaff to sound comically bombastic and pompous while speaking to Prince Harry in the person of the King, he caused him to say

though the camomile, the more it is trodden on, the faster it grows, yet youth, the more it is wasted, the sooner it wears. That thou art my son I have partly thy mother's word, partly my own opinion, but chiefly a villainous trick of thine eye, and a foolish hanging of thy nether lip, that doth warrant me. If then thou be son to me, here lies the point. Why, being son to me, art thou so pointed at? Shall the blessed son of heaven prove a micher, and eat blackberries? – A question not to be asked. Shall the son of England prove a thief, and take purses? – A question to be asked.

And so on (*1 Henry IV*, 2.5.403–14).

Lyly became secretary to Edward de Vere, 17th Earl of Oxford (1550–1604), who has been absurdly touted as a candidate for the authorship of Shakespeare's plays. Under his aegis during the 1580s Lyly ran a company at the Blackfriars, producing entertainments designed with a keen eye on Elizabeth's court. Lyly is the only major dramatist to have composed exclusively for a boys' company, and this fact has kept him out of the mainstream of dramatic history.[6] It is unfortunate that the reputation of *Euphues* as one of the world's least readable books – not entirely deserved – has infected views about its author's eight comedies. They have many of the same qualities as *Euphues* – elegance, symmetry, an emphasis on ideas and debate – but the dramatic form enlivens the tone, and Lyly's witty dialogue, almost always in prose, is eminently speakable. At times it is Wildean in its delight in paradox – and it requires the same kind of stylish and stylized delivery as Wilde's. Mostly Lyly plays fantasies on classical themes. In *Alexander and Campaspe* (1583?), the emperor returns from conquering Thebes with a beautiful prisoner, Campaspe, and calls together a group of great philosophers, including Aristotle, Plato and others. Alexander falls in love with Campaspe and commissions Apelles to paint her portrait; she falls in love with the painter, and Alexander magnanimously orders them to marry, which they are pleased to do. The cynic philosopher Diogenes, refusing to join his colleagues, sulks in his tub:

ALEXANDER ... How happened it that you would not come out of your tub to my palace?

DIOGENES Because it was as far from my tub to your palace as from your palace to my tub.

ALEXANDER Why, then, dost thou owe no reverence to kings?

DIOGENES No.

ALEXANDER Why so?

DIOGENES Because they be no gods.

ALEXANDER They be gods of the earth.

DIOGENES Yea, gods of earth.

ALEXANDER Plato is not of thy mind.

DIOGENES I am glad of it.

ALEXANDER Why?

DIOGENES Because I would have none of Diogenes' mind but Diogenes.
  (2.2.140–54)

This kind of comic catechism is taken up by Shakespeare in dialogues such as those of Lance and Speed in *The Two Gentlemen of Verona* (e.g. 3.1.276–end), Armado and Mote in *Love's Labour's Lost* (e.g. 1.2.1–117) and, more briefly, Feste and Olivia in *Twelfth Night* (e.g. 1.5.62–7).

Lyly stopped writing plays in the early 1590s; he became a Member of Parliament and maintained connections at court. He repeatedly begged to succeed Edmund Tilney in the office of Master of the Revels, and became increasingly bitter about his failure to get a promise that he should do so, as we see in the second of two petitions he addressed to the Queen, in which his mastery of rhetoric is fully at the service of his feelings:

Thirteen years your Highness' servant, and yet nothing; twenty friends that though they say they will be sure, I find them sure to be slow; a thousand hopes, but all nothing; a hundred promises, but yet nothing. Thus casting up the inventory of my friends, hopes, promises and time the *summa totalis* amounteth in all to just nothing. (*c.* 1601)[7]

Lyly died, a disappointed man, in 1606.

Robert Greene (*c.* 1558–92), another of Marlowe's companions under Dekker's imaginary vine, was like Meres an MA of both Cambridge and Oxford. Born in Norwich, he is best known as the supposed author of a deathbed attack on Shakespeare as one who thought himself 'the only Shake-scene in a country', the first allusion to Shakespeare in print. This is in *Greene's Groatsworth of Wit* (1592), which may actually have been written by Henry Chettle, and in which Shakespeare is attacked as 'an upstart crow, beautified with our feathers, that with his "tiger's heart wrapped in a player's hide" supposes he is as well able to bombast out a blank verse as the best of you'.[8] The quotation parodies a memorable line from *Henry VI*, Part Three: 'O tiger's heart wrapped in a woman's hide!' (1.4.138), and helps to date that play.

But there is more to Greene than that. He has claims to be our first fully professional writer – or literary hack. 'Glad was that printer', wrote Thomas Nashe, in a vivid pen portrait, 'that might be so blest to pay him dear for the very dregs of his wit.'[9] Greene was so much a master of the journalistic skill of turning anything that happened to him into copy for the printers that it is difficult to distinguish between fact and fiction in his writings, but to judge by the increasingly confessional tone of his later, allegedly autobiographical pamphlets, he led a dishonest and dissolute, if convivial, life.

Greene churned out a constant stream of short books in prose, some of them (like Sir Philip Sidney's far superior *Arcadia*) with interpolated lyrics, usually referred to under the portmanteau label of pamphlets. Best known is *Pandosto, or The Triumph of Time*, of 1588, mainly because some twenty years later Shakespeare was to transform it into *The Winter's Tale*. Greene also wrote ostensibly realistic accounts of petty criminality, the coney-catching pamphlets – 'coneys' are rabbits, here characterizing gullible young men up from the country who are 'caught', or preyed upon and tricked into parting with their money by rogues. Greene was himself an unscrupulous thief of other men's wit, and indeed of his own, since he repeatedly transfers whole paragraphs and more from one work to another. Although he tries to give the impression that he is writing from observation of the London scene, in fact he often plagiarizes and paraphrases writings of an earlier period. Shakespeare does his share of borrowing in the coney-catcher Autolycus, also of *The Winter's Tale*.

Greene's best work comes in his lyrics and his plays. It is not surprising that Benjamin Britten, in his song cycle *A Charm of Lullabies* (1947), set the lullaby, Blakean in its innocence, from Greene's pastoral novella *Menaphon* (1589), where a princess, separated in a shipwreck from her husband and believing him to be dead, sings it to their baby son:

> Weep not, my wanton [darling], smile upon my knee;
> When thou art old there's grief enough for thee.
>> Mother's wag, pretty boy,
>> Father's sorrow, father's joy.
>> When thy father first did see
>> Such a boy by him and me,
>> He was glad, I was woe:
>> Fortune changed made him so,
>> When he left his pretty boy,
>> Last his sorrow, first his joy.
> Weep not, my wanton, smile upon my knee;
> When thou art old there's grief enough for thee . . .[10]

The delicacy of sensibility revealed in this poem is a far cry from the often sordid aspects of Greene's life-story.

The plays of Greene that are best remembered, and studied if not often performed, are *The Scottish History of James the Fourth, Slain at Flodden* and *Friar Bacon and Friar Bungay*, both written probably between 1588 and 1592. Whereas it is only too easy to believe that many of Greene's pamphlets were, as Nashe alleges, 'yarked up' 'in a night and a day', the best of his plays show a lively imagination, mastery of dialogue in both prose and verse, and an original talent for dramatic construction.[11]

James IV, in spite of its title, is not a history play but a romantic drama of love and adultery with comic interludes, based on a tale by Giraldi Cinthio (1504–73), who was to provide Shakespeare with the raw material for *Othello*. *Friar Bacon*, too, is a romantic comedy, this time involving necromancy. This provides the occasion for striking stage effects, especially in the episodes in which Friar Bacon causes a brazen head to speak: first, it says to the hapless servant Miles, who has fallen asleep, 'Time is', then 'Time was'; climactically, *'the Head speaks; and a lightning flasheth forth, and a hand appears that breaketh down the Head with a hammer'*, just giving it time to utter: 'Time is past' (Scene 11, lines 53–74). The terms in which Prince Edward speaks of the beautiful Margaret of Fressingfield have a lyric grace that looks forward to Florizel's descriptions of the supposed shepherdess Perdita in *The Winter's Tale*:

> When as she swept like Venus through the house,
> And in her shape fast folded up my thoughts,
> Into the milkhouse went I with the maid,
> And there among the cream bowls she did shine
> As Pallas 'mongst her princely huswifery.
> She turn'd her smock over her lily arms
> And dived them into milk to run her cheese;
> But, whiter than the milk, her crystal skin,
> Checked with lines of azure, made her blush,
> That art or nature durst bring for compare.
>
> (Scene 1, lines 72–81)

Greene had a son, inaptly named Fortunatus, by his mistress, sister of a thief and cut-throat, Cutting Ball, who was hanged at Tyburn. Fortunatus died almost a year after his father, in 1593, still a child. Like Marlowe's, Greene's death is extensively if unreliably reported, partly by the malicious Gabriel Harvey. Greene appears to have been living in squalor with a shoemaker named Isam who had taken pity on him. He was ill for several weeks, consumed with repentance, and wrote a pitiful letter to the wife he had abandoned:

Sweet wife, as ever there was any good will or friendship between thee and me see this bearer, my host, satisfied of his debt. I owe him ten pound, and but for him I had perished in the streets. Forget and forgive my wrongs done unto thee, and almighty God have mercy on my soul. Farewell till we meet in heaven, for on earth thou shalt never see me more. This 2 of September, 1592, written by thy dying husband, Robert Greene.[12]

He died on the next day; by his own request his landlady, who 'loved him dearly', crowned his corpse with a garland of bays. While Nashe acknowledged Greene's faults, he wrote compassionately of him: 'He inherited more virtues than vices. A jolly long red peak [quiff] – like the spire of a steeple – he cherished continually without cutting, whereat a man might hang a jewel, it was so sharp and pendant.' Addressing his and Greene's enemy, the pedant Gabriel Harvey, Nashe writes: 'A good fellow he was, and would have drunk with thee for more angels than the lord thou libelledst on gave thee in Christ's College; and in one year he pissed as much against the walls as thou and thy two brothers spent in three.' Clearly Dekker was right to place both Nashe and Greene beneath the same vine in Elysium.

Though Thomas Lodge (1558–1625) collaborated with Greene early in his career, his later activities suggest that the two men would have been oddly sorted. An adventurer during the 1580s, after being cut out of his father's will, he sailed on voyages to the Azores, the Canary Islands and South America. It was at sea that he wrote his prose romance *Rosalynde* (1590), far superior in style and imagination to anything of the kind written by Greene, which became the main source for Shakespeare's *As You Like It*. In later life he studied medicine in France and practised as a physician in London, writing and translating religious works reflecting his conversion to Roman Catholicism, until he died of the plague in 1625.

George Peele (1556–96), an Oxford graduate whom Dekker also envisaged under the vine, doubtless because he too had a reputation for riotous living, was a translator from the Greek and an accomplished poet who wrote plays in an exceptional variety of genres, as well as Lord Mayors' shows. His first play, *The Arraignment of Paris* (1583), written before either Marlowe or Shakespeare had made his mark, is a gracefully composed comedy of ideas with numerous songs, designed as a one-off entertainment for the court. It appeared in print in 1594, however, as having been 'presented before the Queen's Majesty by the children of her chapel', and found a readership; Nashe justly praised it for its 'pregnant dexterity of wit and manifold variety of invention' in which, he considered, Peele 'goeth a step beyond all that write'.[13] It ends with an episode of direct address and, inevitably, obsequious flattery to the Queen – 'the noble phoenix of our age, / Our fair Eliza, our Zabeta fair!' – in which Diana presents her with 'the ball of gold' for which the goddesses Pallas, Venus and Juno have been competing but which they yield unhesitatingly as to an acknowledged superior.

Peele's *The Old Wife's Tale* (1588–94?), which gently satirizes chivalric romances, is an enchanting mixture of witchcraft and fairy-tale; its large number of characters, together with its brevity and its deliberately sophisticated naivety, help to suggest that it may have been intended initially for a children's company. It is a delicate and delightfully inconsequential fantasy that would bear revival and might appeal to an opera composer.

Peele's eclectic style has caused his name to be associated with many anonymous plays of the period and, conspicuously, with one that is not anonymous, Shakespeare's *Titus Andronicus*. There is no documentary evidence that Peele ever collaborated with anyone, but there are stylistic discrepancies in, especially, the first act of the play, and the suggestion that Peele was responsible for part of it, perhaps as a direct collaborator, perhaps as an original author whose work Shakespeare revised, goes back a long way and has been strongly supported in the early twenty-first century.[14]

Thomas Nashe (1567–c. 1601) was less important as a playwright than as a commentator. A Cambridge graduate, he was a central figure of London literary life from the time of his first appearance in print with the preface to Robert Greene's novella *Menaphon*, in 1589, to the turn of the century. Nashe was a genius, a brilliant if eccentric prose stylist and satirist whose linguistic innovations vie with those of James Joyce but who never found a form that could adequately contain his talents. The result is that he is great by fits and starts. He dabbled in various literary kinds. *The Anatomy of Absurdity*, published in 1589, is a euphuistic literary satire. He made a hit in 1592 with *Pierce Penniless his Supplication to the Devil*, a comic piece of social satire which like much of his work flits inconsequentially from topic to topic while scoring many hits along the way. His longest and most serious work, the pamphlet *Christ's Tears over Jerusalem* (1593), is a bizarre, surreal indictment of the society of his time, a pseudo-sermon of extreme, exaggerated stylistic sophistication. He came nearer to finding his own voice in what is now his best-known work, *The Unfortunate Traveller* (1594), an episodically brilliant precursor of the picaresque novels of Henry Fielding and Tobias Smollett. His later works include much direct comment on literary controversies of the period, which inevitably makes them difficult for modern readers, and we shall encounter him briefly as an associate of Ben Jonson.

Nashe's only surviving play, *Summer's Last Will and Testament* (1592), written for a private performance in time of plague, and in extreme consciousness of its ravages, is a pageant-like piece, as the actor who speaks its Prologue confesses: 'Nay, 'tis no play neither, but a show.' Representing Will Summers, Henry VIII's jester, he stays on stage throughout the performance, anticipating Shakespeare's use of the fool as a character standing apart from the main action. In spite of its leisurely, digressive structure the play has episodes of both wit and beauty, not least in the song 'Adieu, farewell earth's bliss', a dirge for humanity which has become famous in its own right:

> Beauty is but a flower,
> Which wrinkles will devour.
> Brightness falls from the air;
> Queens have died young and fair;
> Dust hath closed Helen's eye:
> I am sick, I must die.[15]

In complete contrast is the long poem 'The Choice of Valentines', otherwise known as 'Nashe's Dildo', which circulated furtively in manuscript and was not printed until 1899, and then only privately. In a curious species of selective censorship, the great standard edition of Nashe's works, edited by R. B. McKerrow in 1904–10, includes it only in subscribers' copies, with the apologetic remark: 'There can, I fear, be little doubt that this poem is the work of Nashe.' Jauntily pornographic, somewhat Chaucerian in style, indebted to Ovid, and looking forward to the shameless obscenities of the Earl of Rochester, it recounts a visit to a brothel by a young man who loses his erection at the crucial moment:

> O gods, that ever anything so sweet
> So suddenly should fade away and fleet!
> Her arms are spread, and I am all unarmed,
> Like one with Ovid's cursèd hemlock charmed.
> So are my limbs unwieldy for the fight,
> That spend their strength in thought of her delight.
> What shall I do to show myself a man?
> It will not be, for aught that beauty can.
> I kiss, I clap, I feel, I view at will,
> Yet dead he lies not thinking good or ill.
> 'Unhappy me', quoth she, 'and will't not stand?
> Come, let me rub and chafe it with my hand.
> Perhaps the silly worm is laboured sore,
> And wearièd that it can do no more.'

Before long, after having 'rolled it on her thigh . . . And dandled it, and danced it up and down . . . she raised it from his swoun [its swoon]', and all was well.[16]

Like Peele, Nashe may have collaborated with Shakespeare. Stylistic studies suggest he may have written most of Act 1 of *Henry VI*, Part One.[17] If this is so, it adds piquancy to Nashe's praise in *Pierce Penniless* of that play in performance:

How would it have joyed brave Talbot, the terror of the French, to think that after he had lien two hundred years in his tomb he should triumph again on the stage, and have his bones new-embalmed with the tears of ten thousand spectators at least, at several times, who in the tragedian that represents his person imagine they behold him fresh bleeding![18]

The episode of Talbot's death, however, is not in the part of the play attributed to Nashe.

Shakespeare certainly read Nashe: traces of his influence are particularly apparent in the Falstaff scenes of *Henry IV*, Part One. So, as Nashe writes in *Pierce Penniless* of Newgate as 'a common name for all prisons, as "homo" is a common name for a man or woman', Gadshill says 'Go to, *"homo"* is a common name to all men' (*1 Henry IV*, 2.1.95); in *The Unfortunate Traveller*, Nashe writes: 'heavens will not always come to witness when they are called', and after Glyndŵr has boasted 'I can call spirits from the vasty deep', Hotspur asks: 'But will they come when you do call for them?' (*1 Henry IV*, 3.1.51, 53); and as Prince Harry calls Sir John a 'roasted Manningtree ox with the pudding in his belly' (*1 Henry IV*, 2.5.457–8), so in *Christ's Tears over Jerusalem* Nashe writes of 'an ox with a pudding in his belly, not fit for anything else save only to feast the dull ears of ironmongers, ploughmen, carpenters, and porters'.[19]

Thomas Kyd (1558–94) was the son of a London scrivener, a profession especially relevant to the theatre, where copyists were much in demand. Like Shakespeare, Kyd had a grammar school education – at the Merchant Taylors' School in London – but did not go to university; also like Shakespeare, he was learned enough to write in a highly literary, classically influenced style that nevertheless was of great appeal to audiences in the popular theatres. He became a professional dramatist – Francis Meres listed him among those 'best for tragedy' – but little of his work has survived; indeed he is partly remembered for a play that has not. There is some reason to believe that he wrote a lost tragedy about Hamlet – referred to as the 'Ur-*Hamlet*' – to which there are several references during the 1590s and which may be a ghostly presence behind Shakespeare's play.

But Kyd's major surviving work is *The Spanish Tragedy*, of around 1587. This was to prove a seminal play, the first great example of a line of revenge tragedies, influenced by the Roman dramatist Seneca, which extends well into the seventeenth century. In Kyd's play the personified figure of Revenge (impersonated by Tamora in Shakespeare's *Titus Andronicus*) oversees the play's action in a series of inter-act conversations with the ghost of the murdered Andrea which turns the main action into a play within a play. *The Spanish Tragedy* shares with the greatest of its progeny, Shakespeare's *Hamlet*, such features as a revenge plot, a ghost (of Andrea, a Spanish courtier), mad scenes, a thwarted love affair, a drama staged by the revenger, a philosophical concern with the afterlife, and episodes of violence culminating in a maelstrom of murder for revenge.

In style, Kyd's verse is rhetorical rather than poetical, powerful if self-conscious in its patterning, as in the opening lines of Hieronimo's long soliloquy after discovering the hanged body of his son, Horatio:

> O eyes, no eyes, but fountains fraught with tears;
> O life, no life, but lively form of death;
> O world, no world, but mass of public wrongs,
> Confused and filled with murder and misdeeds;
> O sacred heavens! If this unhallowed deed,
> If this inhuman and barbarous attempt,
> If this incomparable murder thus
> Of mine, but now no more, my son,
> Shall unrevealed and unrevengèd pass,
> How should we term your dealings to be just,
> If you unjustly deal with those that in your justice trust?
>
> (3.2.1–11)

It would be easy to find parallels to this kind of writing in Shakespeare's early history plays. We may compare, for instance, Young Clifford's rhetorical outburst on seeing his father's dead body in *The First Part of the Contention* (*2 Henry VI*):

> O, let the vile world end,
> And the premisèd flames of the last day
> Knit earth and heaven together.
> Now let the general trumpet blow his blast,
> Particularities and petty sounds
> To cease! Wast thou ordainèd, dear father,
> To lose thy youth in peace, and to achieve
> The silver livery of advisèd age,
> And in thy reverence and thy chair-days, thus
> To die in ruffian battle? Even at this sight
> My heart is turned to stone, and while 'tis mine

> It shall be stony. York not our old men spares;
> No more will I their babes.

$$(5.3.40-52)$$

The Spanish Tragedy was immensely popular; there were ten printed editions between 1592 and 1633, Henslowe records numerous performances at the Rose, and it was frequently imitated and parodied. The line 'Hieronimo, go by, go by' became, like Tamburlaine's 'Holla, ye pampered jades of Asia', a catchphrase of the Elizabethan theatre. Shakespeare may well have written *Titus Andronicus* in direct emulation of this play, which combines tragedy with black comedy and sensational horror.

Henslowe's payment to Ben Jonson for writing additional passages for *The Spanish Tragedy* in 1601 did not stop Jonson from lumping it and *Titus Andronicus* together in 1614 as works that were popular only among theatregoers whose taste had not moved on for a quarter of a century: 'He that will swear *Jeronimo* or *Andronicus* are the best plays yet shall pass unexcepted at, here, as a man whose judgement shows it is constant, and hath stood still these five and twenty or thirty years' (*Bartholomew Fair*, Induction, 94–7). In more recent times the play had been regarded as of mainly academic interest until a revival at the National Theatre in London in 1982 showed that it can exert a chilling hold over audiences. The episode in which the revenger, Hieronimo, bites out his own tongue, which may seem ridiculous on the page, became a terrifyingly real climax to the play's horrors.

As we have seen, Shakespeare learnt from the plays of Lyly and Greene, Kyd, Nashe and Peele, and adapted prose fictions by Greene and Lodge. All these writers have their independent and significant places in the dramatic pantheon. But the brightest star among his early contemporaries, and the only one who might have developed as a serious competitor to his pre-eminence, was Marlowe. And he is the only writer of his time to whom Shakespeare makes direct reference. This is in *As You Like It*, written probably in 1599, when Phoebe, having fallen in love even more hopelessly than she knows with Rosalind disguised as Ganymede, bemoans her lovelorn plight with the words

Dead shepherd, now I find thy saw of might:
'Who ever loved that loved not at first sight?'
(3.5.82–3)

The saw, or saying, that Phoebe quotes is a line from Marlowe's narrative poem *Hero and Leander*, first printed in 1598,[20] in which Leander, young, beautiful and innocent, falls in love with the beautiful but chaste Hero as soon as their eyes meet. 'Where both deliberate, the love is slight,' the worldly-wise narrator opines; 'Who ever loved, that loved not at first sight?' (Sestiad 1, line 176). The 'dead shepherd' is Marlowe, murdered six years previously. *As You Like It*, then, was written shortly after *Hero and Leander* appeared in print; Marlowe's poem would have been fresh in Shakespeare's and in theatregoers' and readers' minds when the play was first performed.

But Shakespeare was well acquainted with Marlowe's writings long before this; Marlowe may have allowed him to read *Hero and Leander* in manuscript, and his own first published work, *Venus and Adonis*, of 1593, belongs to the same newly fashionable literary genre of the amorous epic. Indeed the two erotic poems as a pair acquired a reputation as soft porn; a character in Thomas Middleton's play *A Mad World, My Masters* (1608) was to boast that he has 'conveyed away' from his wife 'all her wanton pamphlets, as *Hero and Leander*, *Venus and Adonis*; oh, two luscious mary-bone pies for a young married wife' (1.2.44–6).

Phoebe calls Marlowe a shepherd partly because she herself is a shepherdess living in a forest, and possibly because Marlowe – by no means shepherd-like in many of his activities – was the author of the pastoral poem beginning 'Come, live with me and be my love' and known as 'The Passionate Shepherd to his Love'. But Shakespeare had quoted from this poem, without mentioning who wrote it, a couple of years earlier, in *The Merry Wives of Windsor*, where Parson Evans sings two of its stanzas in an effort to keep up his spirits as he waits to fight a duel with Dr Caius (3.1.16–25). This play was probably first performed in 1597, at which time Marlowe's poem had still not reached print; and when it did so, two years later, in a four-stanza version, it was in the pirated volume *The Passionate Pilgrim*, ascribed to Shakespeare, as if whoever compiled that collection supposed that

Shakespeare had written the poem. A longer version appeared in 1600, in an anthology called *England's Helicon*, where it is said to be by Marlowe, but it is quite possible that many contemporaries thought of Shakespeare as the author of these immensely popular lines.

Another phrase in *As You Like It*, 'it strikes a man more dead than a great reckoning in a little room' (3.3.11–12), has been thought to allude to the manner and place of Marlowe's death, especially since, though the expression has ancient origins, it resembles a memorable line from Marlowe's play *The Jew of Malta*, where Barabas speaks of 'Infinite riches in a little room' (1.1.37). 'Dead shepherd' suggests affection, and it is quite likely that Marlowe and Shakespeare were friends. At the very least, they must have been well known to each other both professionally and personally. As we have seen, plays by each of them were performed during the same week at the Rose. That theatre was home to the acting company with which Marlowe was most closely associated, and it put on many plays that Shakespeare, as a rising dramatist, could not have afforded to miss.

There are enough resemblances in the circumstances of Marlowe's and Shakespeare's lives to have appealed to Francis Meres's passion for parallelism. Both were baptized in 1564, Marlowe on 6 February, Shakespeare on 26 April. Both were born of relatively humble parents in the provinces: Marlowe's father was a shoemaker in Canterbury, Shakespeare's a glover in Stratford-upon-Avon. Both attended good grammar schools. Marlowe went to the King's School, Canterbury (he did not win a scholarship until his fifteenth year, but may have attended as a fee-payer before then), and Shakespeare went to the King's New School, Stratford-upon-Avon. At these institutions – which still flourish – both boys received and profited from excellent and rigorous educations in, primarily, Latin, classical literature, rhetoric and oratory.

After school the parallels stop, at least for a while. We know virtually nothing of how Shakespeare lived between leaving school, presumably around the age of 15, in 1579, and his emergence on the London theatrical scene in 1592, though the absence of his name from their records suggests that he did not attend either university. Unlike Shakespeare, Marlowe was an early starter in the theatrical profession. His genius emerges full-blown even in his earliest surviving writings, and he engaged in many extra-professional activities. If he had died a natural death, it would have been tempting to suggest that he burnt himself out. Though the dates and sequence of Shakespeare's early plays are problematic, it seems certain that if Shakespeare had died when Marlowe did, we should now regard Marlowe as the greater writer.

Of Marlowe during the great hiatus in Shakespeare's life story, the so-called 'lost years' – from 1585, the date of the birth in Stratford-upon-Avon of his last child, to 1592, when he turns up in London – we know much, and some of it is distinctly unsavoury. His intellectual brilliance was apparent from an early age. In 1580, at the age of 16, he won a scholarship (designed, ironically in view of his later career, to prepare candidates for Holy Orders) to Corpus Christi College, Cambridge. He must have worked hard for the BA that he was awarded four years later, but his subversive and dissident tendencies soon found outlets. It may have been while he was still at Cambridge that he embarked on the first English translation of Ovid's *Amores*. Marlowe's versions, unpublished during his lifetime, are best regarded as free variations on their Ovidian models. The earliest surviving edition of some of the poems appeared surreptitiously as *Epigrams and Elegies by I. M.* [John Davies] *and C. M.* [Christopher Marlowe], without date but probably around 1595, two years after he died, with the claim that they had been printed in Holland, probably a device to evade censorship. In fact, they suffered the ultimate censorship in 1599, when Archbishop Whitgift and his ecclesiastical colleagues required that all copies of this book, along with satirical writings by Thomas Nashe and others, should be called in and publicly burned, though as the ban was primarily aimed at satire Marlowe's poems probably suffered in part because of Sir John Davies's bawdy and libellous epigrams.

Marlowe's very decision to translate Ovid's *Amores* was itself a characteristically transgressive act, a cocking of a snook against the religious and moral establishment. These poems, written while Ovid was a young man, celebrate the delights and excitements of, especially, illicit heterosexual love, of promiscuity, seduction and adultery. With their racy, joyful, sensual and comic abandon, the rhyming couplets of Marlowe's version anticipate Byron, not least in their imitation of the diction and rhythms of ordinary speech:

> What arms and shoulders did I touch and see,
> How apt her breasts were to be pressed by me!
> How smooth a belly under her waist saw I,
> How large a leg, and what a lusty thigh!
> To leave the rest, all liked me passing well;
> I clinged her naked body, down she fell.
> Judge you the rest: being tired, she bade me kiss;
> Jove send me more such afternoons as this.[21]

After taking his first degree in 1584, Marlowe registered for an MA, but he frequently took leave of absence from Cambridge. His scholarship allowance was meagre, and he found a profitable if hazardous way of supplementing it. Since this was apparently by performing undercover work for the government, it is unsurprising that the details of his activities are murky. They were thought important enough to warrant the attention of the Queen's Privy Council, whose members at the time included her chief minister, Lord Burghley, her Lord Chamberlain, Lord Hunsdon, Archbishop Whitgift, and – most significantly – Francis Walsingham, head of Elizabeth's secret service and espionage system. In June 1587 the Council wrote to the university authorities defending Marlowe against a rumour that he 'was determined to have gone beyond the seas to Rheims and there to remain', and to deflect them from their intention of withholding his MA. It looks as if Marlowe's frequent absences from Cambridge had aroused suspicion that he was, or was in danger of becoming, a Catholic. Though Catholics could study at the university, they were not permitted to take degrees. Many young members of English Catholic families and others crossed the Channel to study in the English seminary at Rheims, some with the intention of returning to serve covertly as missionaries or as priests in Catholic households. The implication of the Privy Council's statement is that, though Marlowe had indeed absented himself, he had done so for some reason which, though laudable, could not be disclosed: for example, by posing as a secret Catholic in order to gather information that would be useful to the government in its ongoing battle with secret and half-concealed Catholicism. As if to excuse his absences, the Council reported that he 'had done her majesty good service, and deserved to be rewarded for his faithful dealing'. They requested that 'he should be furthered in the degree he was to take this next Commencement because it was not her majesty's pleasure that anyone employed, as he had been, in matters touching the benefit of his country should be defamed by those that are ignorant in th'affairs he went about'. Something had to be hushed up: 'Their lordships' request was that the rumour thereof should be allayed by all possible means.'[22]

The university withheld Marlowe's grant while he was away, but the college accounts show that his spending increased when he came back, no doubt because he had been well rewarded during his absence. It may have been during Marlowe's late days as a student that he wrote *Dido, Queen of Carthage*, which would make it his first play. Composed entirely in verse, mostly blank but with a few passages of rhyme, it contains long speeches of direct narrative. *Dido* is heavily, perhaps excessively, dependent on Virgil's *Aeneid*, even to the extent of quoting eight lines of the epic poem in Latin in the last act; Dido throws herself into the flaming pyre (difficult to stage) with Virgil on her lips. Many passages are directly if freely translated from the original.

At the same time *Dido* anticipates specifically Marlovian character-istics of later works, not least in the homoeroticism of the invented early episodes between Jupiter and Ganymede. The play begins with a typical challenge to orthodoxy: Jupiter is revealed '*dandling Ganymede upon his knee*', and addresses him with 'Come, gentle Ganymede, and play with me: / I love thee well, say Juno what she will'. Nevertheless, this is Marlowe's only play to centre on heterosexual love relation-ships. Although it ends, as in Virgil, with Dido's suicide – to which Marlowe adds those of her sister Anna and Dido's suitor Iarbas – for much of the play's length its tone incorporates ironic comedy, contrasting the heroic and divine status of its legendary protagonists with their all-too-worldly desires. When it was published in 1594, the year after Marlowe died, it was said on its title page to have been played by the Children of the Chapel Royal and to have been written by Marlowe and Nashe. It is understandable that so learned a play should have been acted by, and probably written for, one of the children's companies, catering to minority audiences; and the juvenility of the actors would have enhanced its mock-heroics. As for

Nashe, it is impossible to determine the extent of his involvement with the play.

Marlowe's university career came to an end sometime soon after March 1587, at which point he made the kind of transition he was to write of in his play *Edward II*, where Spenser Junior says:

> . . . you must cast the scholar off
> And learn to court it like a gentleman.
> 'Tis not a black coat and a little band,
> A velvet-caped cloak faced before with serge,
> And smelling to a nosegay all the day,
> Or holding of a napkin in your hand,
> Or saying a long grace at a table's end,
> Or making low legs to a nobleman,
> Or looking downwards with your eyelids close,
> And saying 'Truly, an't may please your honour',
> Can get you any favour with great men;
> You must be proud, bold, pleasant, resolute,
> And now and then stab as occasion serves.
>
> $(2.1.31-43)^{23}$

Like many characters in his plays – including the hero of his first great public success, *Tamburlaine the Great*, performed soon after he left Cambridge at the age of 23, and rapidly followed by a sequel – Marlowe was intensely ambitious; and like many of them, he could stab as occasion served. On the afternoon of 18 September 1589, in a Shoreditch street, for reasons unknown he became involved in a violent encounter with an innkeeper's son named William Bradley. By good fortune Marlowe's friend, neighbour and fellow poet Thomas Watson came upon the combatants and drew his sword in an attempt to separate them and calm them down. Marlowe withdrew, but Bradley, seeing Watson with his sword drawn, 'leapt upon' him with the words 'Art thou now come? Then I will have a bout with thee.' 'Then and there,' it was reported, 'with a sword and dagger of iron and steel he struck, wounded, and maltreated the said Thomas Watson so that there was fear for his life.' Bradley cornered the poet, who retaliated by stabbing his sword six inches into his chest, killing him instantly. Both Marlowe and Watson were hauled off to Newgate prison and charged with homicide. On the following day an inquest found that Watson had acted in self-defence, but he was held in prison to await trial, and Marlowe too remained a prisoner for almost two weeks before bail could be arranged. At the Old Bailey on 3 December Marlowe was discharged, but Watson remained in prison until he received the Queen's pardon on 10 February 1590.

This incident shows how – as in the Verona of Shakespeare's *Romeo and Juliet*, written four or five years later – violence could erupt suddenly and irrationally on the streets of Elizabethan London, and how even the most civilized poets could become embroiled in sordid disputes. Watson (?1557–92) was no nonentity. A well-travelled writer and translator, he studied briefly at Oxford and was regarded as the best Latin poet of the age, in which Latin was still a common language. Surprisingly to us, when he translated from other languages he was liable to do so into Latin, not English. Also, like Marlowe, he had the capacity, rare in his time, to read Greek: he achieved the intellectual feat of translating Sophocles' *Antigone* from Greek into Latin. For all his fame in his own time, he is best remembered now, if at all, for his *Hekatompathia* of 1582, a collection of a hundred love poems described as sonnets, though each is actually made up of three six-line stanzas. These poems draw on themes made popular by the Italian poet Francesco Petrarch (1304–74) – understandably, since Watson had translated his collection of love poems, the *Canzoniere*, from Italian into Latin. *Hekatompathia* is a significant forerunner of the English sonnet sequences of the 1590s; indeed Shakespeare may well have had one of its poems in mind when he wrote his anti-Petrarchan parody Sonnet 130. Watson, in his Sonnet 7, writes that the 'sparkling eyes' of the 'saint' he serves deserve a place in heaven; for Shakespeare, on the other hand, 'My mistress' eyes are nothing like the sun'. On Watson's death one of his friends and admirers, Thomas Nashe, wrote of him as 'a man that I dearly loved and honoured' who 'for all things hath left few his equals in England'.[24]

Marlowe's fight with Bradley was not an isolated act of violence. In May 1592 he was bound over in the large sum of £20 to keep the peace, and required to appear at the next General Sessions of Justices of the Peace, for an unspecified offence committed in Shoreditch. In September of the same year, on a street corner of his home town of

Canterbury, he fought 'with staff and dagger' a musical tailor named Corkine, who sang daily in the Cathedral choir. Marlowe later counter-claimed that the tailor did 'beat, wound, and maltreat' him to his 'grave damage'. In the end the men were reconciled and the case dismissed. A rather charming footnote to this episode is that in 1612 a composer called William Corkine, who was probably the tailor's son and had inherited his musical interests, published a setting of Marlowe's 'Come live with me and be my love'.[25]

Dido, Queen of Carthage was composed for minority audiences, and has only ever achieved a minority readership, but apparent echoes in the First Player's speeches in *Hamlet* suggest that Shakespeare knew it, and certainly no one in the theatre world could have avoided familiarity with Marlowe's first big hit, *Tamburlaine the Great*, whose sensational success gave Marlowe his breakthrough into the public arena. It is difficult not to read Marlowe's own ruthless ambitions into his dramatization of the career of the Scythian shepherd whom we see, as the Prologue puts it,

> Threat'ning the world with high astounding terms
> And scourging kingdoms with his conquering sword.

With Kyd's *The Spanish Tragedy*, *Tamburlaine* was to have a seminal effect on the drama of its time, above all for the magnificence and grandiloquence of its language. The joint influence of Marlowe and Kyd was to change the entire course of English drama by establishing blank (unrhymed) verse, instead of rhymed lines, as its principal medium.

The best-known characterization of Marlowe's style was written by Ben Jonson, in his elegy on Shakespeare printed in the First Folio. Addressing Shakespeare, Jonson says he would

> tell how far thou didst our Lyly outshine,
> Or sporting Kyd, or Marlowe's mighty line.

Though the compliment to Marlowe is backhanded, there is justice in the implication that Marlowe displays more limited skill in his versification than Shakespeare; but when Marlowe is mighty he is mighty indeed, and it is in *Tamburlaine* that this quality is first fully displayed.

> Our souls, whose faculties can comprehend
> The wondrous architecture of the world
> And measure every wand'ring planet's course,
> Still climbing after knowledge infinite
> And always moving as the restless spheres,
> Wills us to wear ourselves and never rest
> Until we reach the ripest fruit of all,
> That perfect bliss and sole felicity,
> The sweet fruition of an earthly crown.
>
> (Part One, 2.7.21–9)

When Marlowe is writing like this he bears comparison with Shakespeare in his finest flights of rhetoric – the battle speeches of Henry V, the eloquence of Mark Antony in *Julius Caesar* or of Cleopatra in *Antony and Cleopatra*. Marlowe must have thought himself lucky to have in Edward Alleyn a heroic actor superbly well equipped to portray his hero, and in later times some of the finest heroic actors, such as Donald Wolfit, Albert Finney and Antony Sher, have revelled in the role.

Marlowe's verse is capable too of an almost surreal beauty, as in Tamburlaine's declaration of love to Zenocrate:

> With milk-white harts upon an ivory sled
> Thou shalt be drawn amidst the frozen pools
> And scale the icy mountains' lofty tops,
> Which with thy beauty will be soon resolved [i.e. dissolved, melted].
>
> (Part One, 1.2.98–101)

And he can prick his own bubbles. When Techelles responds to these words with 'What now? In love?', Tamburlaine replies: 'Techelles, women must be flatterèd. / But this is she with whom I am in love.'

Marlowe is not simply a poet working in the theatre, but a dramatist capable of creating awesome stage pictures. In Part Two (4.3), Tamburlaine enters with a band of followers in a chariot drawn by the Kings of Trebizond and Soria, '*with bits in their mouths, reins in his left hand, in his right hand a whip, with which he scourgeth them*'. Shakespeare echoes this image in Titus Andronicus's first entry (1.1.69.5–6). Marlowe's wild imagination results sometimes in bizarre happenings that present as much of a challenge to modern interpreters as they must have done in his time. In *Tamburlaine*, Bajazeth, Emperor of Turkey, after being imprisoned and pulled around in a cage, commits suicide by braining himself against its bars, provoking his wife, Zabina, to exclaim:

> What do mine eyes behold? My husband dead!
> His skull all riven in twain, his brains dashed out!
> The brains of Bajazeth, my lord and sovereign!
>
> (Part One, 5.1.305–7)

Shakespeare may have been remembering this with amusement when he made Bottom, in the role of Pyramus in *A Midsummer Night's Dream*, react to the sight of Thisbe's blood-stained mantle with 'Eyes, do you see? / How can it be? / O dainty duck, O dear!' (5.1.274–6). After this Zabina lapses, understandably, into incoherent prose that anticipates the mad Ophelia: 'Hell, death, Tamburlaine, hell! Make ready my coach, my chair, my jewels. I come, I come, I come!' – 'Come, my coach! Good night, sweet ladies, good night, sweet ladies, good night, good night,' says Ophelia (*Hamlet*, 4.5.70–72).

Master though he rapidly became of the 'mighty line', Marlowe was capable too of a piercing irony that can devastatingly expose moral hypocrisy, as he demonstrated in what may have been his next play, *The Jew of Malta*. Though written around 1589, it did not appear in print until 1633, when it was described on its title page as *The Famous Tragedy of the Rich Jew of Malta*. And the Prologue, spoken in the person of Machiavelli, tells of the intention 'to present the tragedy of a Jew'. At least to audiences accustomed to the tone and conventions of Shakespearian tragedy, wide-ranging though these are, the term 'tragedy' is seriously misleading. The great actor Edmund Kean (1787–1833) – a famous Shylock – played its central character, Barabas, in the early nineteenth century, but after that the play was neglected until a revival by the Royal Shakespeare Company in 1964. Critics had felt uncertain about its tone, which is often far from what is usually understood as tragic, and so did the actors who were to perform it. With no traditions to follow or even to disagree with, they were working in a void, and it was not until they moved from rehearsal into performance before an audience that they discovered the play's true nature. Even then, the performer of the Prologue, Tony Church, said that unless he gave the word 'tragedy', in 'the *tragedy* of a Jew', an ironic inflection, the audience was bewildered for the first half-hour. T. S. Eliot had read the play correctly in 1920, writing that if we take it 'as a farce, the concluding act becomes intelligible . . . it is the farce of the old English humour, the terribly serious, even savage comic humour'.[26] (Even here, however, the term 'terribly serious' could be questioned.) Misunderstandings arise partly from Marlowe's technique of presenting episodes in a foreshortened style so that on the page they seem underwritten. Take for example the opening of Act 3, Scene 2. Mathias is the favoured suitor of the heroine, Abigail; Lodowick, the Governor of Malta's son, is his rival. Lodowick enters reading a letter from Mathias:

> LODOWICK What, dares the villain write in such base terms?
> MATHIAS I did it, and revenge it if thou dar'st.
>   [*They*] *fight. Enter Barabas above.*
> BARABAS O, bravely fought, and yet they thrust not home.
>   Now, Lodowick! Now, Mathias! So.
>   [*Both fall dead*]
>   So, now they have showed themselves to be tall fellows.
> VOICES WITHIN Part 'em, part 'em!
> BARABAS Ay, part 'em now they are dead. Farewell, farewell.
>
>   (3.2.3–9)

Any attempt to play that seriously would be bound to fail. This is sardonic, black comedy; the characters are manipulated like puppets, as in a melodrama. The pace is rapid, almost breathless, leaving the audience with neither time nor inclination to reflect on the events they are witnessing. There is little place for real emotion in a play in which the central character, disapproving of his daughter's choice of suitor and of her conversion to Christianity, cheerfully kills her, along with all the other inmates of the convent in which she has taken refuge, with a pot of poisoned rice-porridge. The play's characters delight in villainy. Ithamore, Barabas's slave, is entranced by his master's device to cause Mathias and Lodowick to kill each other: 'O, mistress, I have the bravest, gravest, secret, subtle, bottle-nosed knave to my master that ever gentleman had' (3.3.9–10). Reactions to horrific happenings are callously comic. Cynicism is rife: 'have not the nuns fine sport with the friars now and then?' (3.3.32–3), Ithamore asks Abigail after she has entered the convent; Abigail's last words are: 'witness that I die a Christian' (3.6.40); 'Ay and a virgin, too, that grieves me most,' responds Friar Barnardine. 'O brother, all the nuns are dead! Let's bury them' (3.6.44), says Friar Jacomo; and, most famously, in response to the accusation that he has committed fornication, Barabas says 'But that was in another country; and besides, the wench is dead' (4.1.42–3).

A climax of farcical brutality comes when Barabas and Ithamore, having strangled Friar Barnardine, prop his body up against a wall and put a staff in his hand; 'So, let him lean upon his staff. Excellent! He stands as if he were begging of bacon,' exults Ithamore (4.1.158). Friar Jacomo, coming upon the body and supposing that Barnardine is deliberately standing in his way, takes the staff and swinges the dead man with it, whereupon Barabas and Ithamore make Jacomo believe he has killed his friend. 'Ay, master, he's slain,' says Ithamore, with ghastly particularity. 'Look how his brains drop out on's nose' (4.1.180–81). Let us hope that this macabre detail does not reflect Marlowe's personal experience.

There is cynicism, too, even in the play's ostensible morality. Marlowe skilfully counterpoises the villainy of the Jews with that of the Turks, and though the Christians, whose prime representative is Ferneze, governor of Malta, may seem to occupy the moral high ground, both their actions and the governor's words at the end of the play take this ground from under their feet in a manner that may well reflect Marlowe's own views about religious hypocrisy. Barabas has told Ferneze of his 'policy' – a key word of the play, meaning 'cunning strategy' – to blow up the entire Turkish army by placing underneath the monastery 'whole barrels full of gunpowder, / That on the sudden shall dissever it / And batter all the stones about their ears' (5.5.28–30 – did Guy Fawkes and his associates know this play?). In addition we see Barabas, 'very busy', as the direction has it, constructing 'a dainty gallery' with a false floor which, 'this cable being cut, / Doth fall asunder, so that it doth sink / Into a deep pit past recovery' (5.5.34–6). But the Christian Ferneze is no less politic than the Jewish Barabas. He prevents the Turkish leader from mounting to the gallery and gives the signal for the cable to be cut while Barabas is still standing there, precipitating him into a cauldron of water which is merrily boiling below (another little challenge to the stage managers). Barabas's pleas to the Christians – the word is several times repeated, with increasing possibilities for irony – fall on deaf ears and he dies defiantly boasting of his sins:

> Know, governor, 'twas I that slew thy son;
> I framed the challenge that did make them meet.
> Know, Calymath, I aimed thy overthrow,
> And had I but escaped this stratagem,
> I would have brought confusion on you all,
> Damned Christians, dogs, and Turkish infidels!
> But now begins the extremity of heat
> To pinch me with intolerable pangs.
> Die, life! Fly, soul! Tongue, curse thy fill and die!
>
> (5.5.80–88)

(It is tempting to imagine that Richard Burbage playing Bottom in *A Midsummer Night's Dream* may have imitated Alleyn playing Barabas as he died with similar words on his lips:

> My soul is in the sky.
> Tongue, lose thy light;
> Moon, take thy flight.
> Now die, die, die, die, die!)

The governor closes the play with a couplet that either betrays extreme lack of self-knowledge or is cynically hypocritical:

> So, march away, and let due praise be given
> Neither to fate nor fortune, but to heaven.

The Machiavellian delight in villainy displayed by Barabas and Ithamore as they vie in boasting of their villainy in Act 2, Scene 3 of *The Jew of Malta* is close to that of Aaron, in Act 5, Scene 1 of Shakespeare's *Titus Andronicus*, written probably at around the same time. But the more obvious Shakespeare play for comparison with *The Jew of Malta* is *The Merchant of Venice*, of a few years later, and it is a paradox – and a measure of the essential difference between the two writers – that whereas Marlowe's tragedy is comic in its effect, Shakespeare's comedy has often proved tragic. Like Barabas, Shylock appears to hold his daughter and his money at equal value. As Abigail throws down the bags of money that she has retrieved from under the floorboards of their house which has become a nunnery, Barabas, hugging the bags to his breast, exults:

> O my girl,
> My gold, my fortune, my felicity . . .
> O girl, O gold, O beauty, O my bliss!
>
> (2.1.47–54)

Shylock, who dreams of money-bags (2.5.18), also has a daughter, Jessica, who throws valuables down from a window, but hers go to her suitor, Lorenzo, and her father's laments are reported to us satirically by the Christian, Solanio:

> I never heard a passion so confused,
> So strange, outrageous, and so variable
> As the dog Jew did utter in the streets.
> 'My daughter! O, my ducats! O, my daughter!
> Fled with a Christian! O, my Christian ducats!'
>
> (2.8.12–16)

Shakespeare's play is greater in stylistic range and in emotional depth than Marlowe's, and gentler in its morality. Though Shakespeare's Jew, like Marlowe's, seeks blood, his villainy is more rounded than Barabas's, and although Shakespeare's Christians are not without blame, they are let off far more lightly than Ferneze.

Marlowe's other play with strong Shakespearian connections is *Edward II*, of around 1590–92, which must have influenced Shakespeare's *Richard II*, written three or four years later. Both are early examples of plays about English history centring on the life and death of a king and cast into the form of dramatic tragedy, but by the time Shakespeare wrote *Richard II* he had also written the three plays about the life of Henry VI – another weak king – and *Richard III*, all of which display Marlovian elements. It is easy to feel that Edward II had special appeal for Marlowe because of the king's homoerotic relationship with his favourite, Gaveston. In the year of Marlowe's death, 1593, Michael Drayton was to publish a poem, *Piers Gaveston, Earl of Cornwall*, on the same topic; in it Gaveston compares his relationship with the king with that between Jove and Ganymede, directly portrayed in *Dido, Queen of Carthage* (it was of course a commonplace in this context).

Marlowe is perfectly explicit about the nature of the love that Edward feels for his favourite, though we have more sense in this play than in Marlowe's other writings of ways in which homoeroticism may lead to morally dubious actions. In his opening speech Gaveston, reading a love letter from Edward, compares himself to Leander in his willingness to swim the Channel to reach the King:

> Sweet prince, I come; these, these thy amorous lines
> Might have enforced me to have swum from France
> And like Leander gasped upon the sand,
> So thou wouldst smile and take me in thy arms.
>
> (1.1.6–9)

Though his physical desire is unquestionable, there is at least a hint that Gaveston is willing to exploit the King's love for him:

> I must have wanton poets, pleasant wits,
> Musicians that with touching of a string
> May draw the pliant king which way I please.
>
> (1.1.50–52)

He will devise an entertainment in which

> a lovely boy in Dian's shape,
> With hair that gilds the water as it glides,
> Crownets of pearl about his naked arms,
> And in his sportful hands an olive tree
> To hide those parts which men delight to see,
> Shall bathe him in a spring . . .
>
> (1.1.60–65)

(There is a nice ambiguity about the concealed 'parts', since though they grace a boy he is personating a goddess.)

Marlowe's play has risen in popularity since the relaxing of moral attitudes to homosexuality. Ian McKellen played both Edward II and

Richard II for the Prospect Players in 1969, and since then the plays have not infrequently been paired, for instance at the Globe in 2003. Derek Jarman's film of 1991 is open and touching in its portrayal of the King's relationship with his lover, and powerful in acceptance of the play's cruel aspects, even if it becomes too much of a gay polemic in its later part.

Like Edward II, Shakespeare's Richard, too, has his favourites, Bushy, Bagot and Green, but (as so often with Shakespeare) the exact nature of their relationship with the King is indeterminate. They are said, in an otherwise unexplained phrase, to have 'Made a divorce betwixt the Queen and him, / Broke the possession of a royal bed', yet later the love between the King and Queen is movingly expressed both in the garden scene (3.4), where she defends Richard against what she sees as the Gardener's calumnies, and in the scene of parting as Richard is taken to the Tower. 'Doubly divorced!' says Richard to Bolingbroke and his men.

> Bad men, you violate
> A twofold marriage: 'twixt my crown and me,
> And then betwixt me and my married wife . . .
> One kiss shall stop our mouths, and dumbly part.
> Thus give I mine, and thus take I thy heart. (*They kiss*.)
> (5.1.71–3, 95–6)

Richard changes in the course of the play; it is possible to imagine scenes in which husband and wife were reconciled, but Shakespeare did not write them.

Marlowe's most enduringly successful play over the centuries has been *Dr Faustus*,[27] partly no doubt because of the appeal of the myth that it dramatizes, and also because it contains some of the best-known lines of amorous verse ever written:

> Was this the face that launched a thousand ships
> And burnt the topless towers of Ilium?
> Sweet Helen, make me immortal with a kiss.
> [*They kiss*]
> Her lips sucks forth my soul. See where it flies!
> Come, Helen, come, give me my soul again.

[*They kiss again*]
Here will I dwell, for heaven be in these lips,
And all is dross that is not Helena . . .
O, thou art fairer than the evening air,
Clad in the beauty of a thousand stars . . .

(5.1.90–96, 103–4)

Poetry of love and longing does not come much finer than this, and the opening lines clearly made a deep impression on Shakespeare. After the deposed Richard II calls for a looking glass, he asks:

Was this face the face
That every day under his household roof
Did keep ten thousand men? Was this the face
That like the sun did make beholders wink?

(*Richard II*, 4.1.271–4)

And memory of Marlowe's lines seems too to lie behind the alleged ballad sung by the Clown Lavatch in *All's Well That Ends Well*:

'Was this fair face the cause', quoth she,
'Why the Grecians sackèd Troy?'

(1.3.69–70)

The most seminally innovative passage in *Dr Faustus* is the great speech in which Faustus takes his leave of the earth. It is an extraordinary speech to have been written by a self-professed atheist, showing that Marlowe, whatever his personal beliefs, had the imaginative power to project a profoundly religious state of mind:

Ah Faustus,
Now hast thou but one bare hour to live,
And then thou must be damned perpetually.
Stand still, you ever-moving spheres of heaven,
That time may cease and midnight never come! . . .
O lente, lente currite noctis equi!
The stars move still; time runs; the clock will strike;
The devil will come, and Faustus must be damned.
O, I'll leap up to my God! Who pulls me down?
See, see where Christ's blood streams in the firmament!

One drop would save my soul, half a drop. Ah, my Christ!
Ah, rend not my heart for naming of my Christ!
Yet will I call on him.

(5.2.57–61, 66–73)

This speech is 'literary' in so far, for example, as it quotes a line from Ovid's *Amores* in Latin and does so with special irony since the words are a lover's plea that night's horses will delay the coming of the dawn: 'run slowly, slowly, you horses of the night.' (Marlowe had translated it freely as 'Whither runn'st thou that men and women love not? / Hold in thy rosy horses that they move not.') But the soliloquy is colloquial and familiar in its vocabulary, its elisions and its unsignalled shifts of address. It is also superbly actable, not least in its silences, the unwritten but vital transitions between one exclamation and another. In this speech Marlowe's mastery of the mighty line merges into a new flexibility, a calculated irregularity of rhythm and of thought patterns that creates within a verse structure an impression of spontaneous and passionate utterance unique up to this date in English drama, and which, I believe, is not taken up again until Shakespeare uses it first comically, in the Nurse's description of Juliet's childhood, and then in Hamlet's emotional soliloquies.

As we have seen, Shakespeare's only direct, acknowledged quotation from Marlowe's writings comes not from a play but from a poem, *Hero and Leander*. This tender, witty and immensely accomplished poem tells the lovers' story only up to the point at which they consummate their passion, but no one knows whether that is because Marlowe had no interest in taking it any further, or whether he was prevented from completing it by death. The first surviving edition, of 1598, was followed in the same year by one that included George Chapman's continuation of the tale to its tragic conclusion. For all its sensuous celebration of adolescent, heterosexual love, like many of its author's works *Hero and Leander* reveals also his fascination with the desire of man for man. Lingering over the beauty of Leander's body, in phrasing that anticipates the androgynous attraction of the 'mastermistress' of Shakespeare's Sonnet 20, the narrator remarks how Leander might have been desired by even the most brutish of menlovers in classical times:

Had wild Hippolytus Leander seen,
Enamoured of his beauty had he been;
His presence made the rudest peasant melt,
That in the vast uplandish country dwelt.
The barbarous Thracian soldier, moved with nought,
Was moved with him, and for his favour sought.
Some swore he was a maid in man's attire,
For in his looks were all that men desire . . .

(Sestiad 1, lines 77–84)

And as Leander swims the Hellespont the god Neptune seductively threads his way around and between his naked limbs:

He watched his arms, and as they opened wide
At every stroke, betwixt them would he slide
And steal a kiss, and then run out and dance,
And as he turned, cast many a lustful glance,
And threw him gaudy toys to please his eye,
And dive into the water, and there pry
Upon his breast, his thighs, and every limb,
And up again, and close beside him swim,
And talk of love. Leander made reply,
'You are deceived, I am no woman, I.'

(Sestiad 2, lines 183–92)

There is only one poet of the 1590s whose interest in homoeroticism is comparable to Marlowe's. He is Richard Barnfield (1574–1620) – not a dramatist – whose writings link him directly with both Marlowe and Shakespeare. Francis Meres mentions him in the same sentence as Sir Philip Sidney and Edmund Spenser as 'amongst us the best in their kind for pastoral', a measure, for all Barnfield's merits, of Meres's lack of critical discrimination, or of his uncritical loyalty to a friend, rather than of Barnfield's true distinction; elsewhere Meres refers to him as 'my friend Master Richard Barnfield'. And it is an interesting (and little-observed) curiosity that in writing of Shakespeare's 'sugared sonnets among his private friends' (so giving us a date by which some at least of these poems had been written), Meres is repeating a phrase, 'sugared sonnets', that had appeared in Barnfield's poem *Greene's*

Funerals, of 1594 (Sonnet 9, line 15). Barnfield echoes both *Venus and Adonis* and *The Rape of Lucrece* in poems published within a year or two of Shakespeare's, and then does something to repay his debt by praising Shakespeare – as a poet, not as a playwright – in his lines headed 'A Remembrance of Some English Poets', of 1598:

> And Shakespeare thou, whose honey-flowing vein,
> Pleasing the world, thy praises doth obtain;
> Whose *Venus* and whose *Lucrece* – sweet and chaste –
> Thy name in fame's immortal book have placed;
>
> > Live ever you, at least in fame live ever.
> > Well may the body die, but fame dies never.
>
> (Barnfield, *Poems*, p. 182)

Barnfield is the author of poetry which in some ways anticipates and probably influenced Shakespeare's Sonnets.[28] His own fine sonnet beginning 'If music and sweet poetry agree', like Marlowe's 'Come live with me and be my love', was printed as Shakespeare's in *The Passionate Pilgrim*, of 1599. And among all the many sonneteers of the 1590s, Barnfield and Shakespeare are the only two to defy convention by writing sonnets addressed to a male object. Barnfield's are more explicitly erotic, if more playful and less intense in their expressions of love. In his skilful and often charming, if derivative, verse – long ignored because of its content, and still underrated – Barnfield not merely reveals a homoerotic sensibility akin to Marlowe's but actually borrows from him to express it. This is in one of Barnfield's longer poems, 'The Tears of an Affectionate Shepherd Sick for Love; or The Complaint of Daphnis for the Love of Ganymede', published in 1594 when he was around 20 years old, and written in the same stanza form as *Venus and Adonis*, from which it also borrows. Barnfield's poem is sensuously erotic in a manner that far exceeds any of the sonnet sequences of the 1590s addressed to women, more conspicuously resembling Marlowe's homoeroticism in *Hero and Leander* and *Edward II*. Barnfield takes over an entire line from the play: as the King's favourite, Gaveston, imagines entertaining Edward with a lovely boy 'in Dian's shape' adorned with 'Crownets of pearl about his naked arms', so Barnfield (personified as Daphnis) says to the man he loves that he would like to put 'Crownets of pearl about thy naked arms' (Barnfield, *Poems*, p. 82, line 104; *Edward II*, 1.1.60, 62). *Edward II* had appeared in print very shortly before Barnfield wrote his poem. Unless he remembered the line from performance, he must have been one of the first to buy a copy.

The interest in homoeroticism evident in Marlowe's writings conspired with charges that he was an atheist to make him notorious in his own time as well as later. Atheism was very much in the air, especially among aristocratic and intellectual circles, and it was linked in many people's minds with sexual transgression of various kinds.[29] Notably, the Earl of Oxford, who converted to Roman Catholicism on a visit to Italy but nevertheless betrayed a number of fellow Catholic noblemen to the Protestant authorities on his return, and who was accused of sodomizing his pageboys and of trying to kill Sir Philip Sidney, confessed to at least one charge of atheism. Many of his alleged blasphemies anticipate those attributed to Marlowe. Like many people before and after him, he 'could never believe in such a God as dealt well with those that deserved evil, and evil with those that deserved well'.[30]

Some of the most revealing information about Marlowe's views on both religion and sexuality comes from Thomas Kyd.[31] In the summer of 1593, not long before Marlowe died, Kyd wrote of their having written 'in one chamber' (which seems to imply that they shared lodgings) 'two years since'. Kyd had been arrested, imprisoned and threatened with torture on suspicion of propagating heretical opinions. He claimed that papers found when his room was searched, and held to be incriminating, actually belonged to his one-time roommate; so far as Kyd was concerned they were Marlowe's 'waste and idle papers' which had become 'shuffled with some of mine own', and which he 'cared not for and which unasked I did deliver up'. This led to the immediate issue of a warrant for Marlowe's arrest, by force if necessary. In his letter of self-defence to the Lord Keeper of the Privy Seal, Sir John Puckering, Kyd goes so far as to declare that it is absurd to think that he 'should love or be familiar friend with one so irreligious' as Marlowe; 'besides, he was intemperate and of a cruel heart' – the very opposite of what even his greatest enemies would say of Kyd himself, he claims. He is anxious to clear himself 'of being thought an atheist, which some will swear he [Marlowe] was'. In another note to Puckering, Kyd expands on his accusations of Marlowe's alleged atheism; he would 'jest at the divine scriptures' and 'gibe at prayers'; moreover he accused Christ of homosexuality: 'He would report Saint John to be our saviour Christ's Alexis' (the male object of Corydon's desire in Virgil's homoerotic Second Eclogue), 'I cover it with reverence and trembling' (a way of saying 'I am not going to call a spade a spade') ' – that is, that Christ did love him with an extraordinary love.' Marlowe's blasphemies were such that Kyd 'left and did refrain his company'.

Kyd was writing under at least the threat, and possibly the effects, of bodily torture, but he is not the only witness to Marlowe's notoriety for atheistical and heretical opinions. A few weeks after Marlowe died, a subversive informer and government spy called Richard Cholmely, arrested on suspicion of treason, said 'that one Marlowe is able to show more sound reasons for atheism than any divine in England is able to give to prove divinity' and that Marlowe had 'read the atheist lecture to Sir Walter Raleigh and others'.[32] These and other allegations surface again in the famous 'Baines note', a report written by an informer, Richard Baines, around the time that Marlowe died and headed 'A note containing the opinion of one Christopher Marlowe concerning his damnable judgement of religion and scorn of God's word'.

Baines has been described as Marlowe's Judas – aptly enough, though the corollary that there was anything at all Christ-like about Marlowe is not justified. Baines had studied at Cambridge some years before Marlowe, had taken his MA in 1576, and then travelled to the seminary at Rheims as a candidate for the Catholic priesthood. In fact, however, he was – whether for profit or through genuine conviction – a secret heretic. Throughout his stay at the college he did all he could to undermine his fellow seminarians' morale and to stir up disaffection by propagating views resembling those of which he was later to accuse Marlowe, and with which indeed he may have indoctrinated him. More trivially, he was alleged to have tempted his colleagues to eat meat pies on fast days. He was said to have been reporting to the Privy Council daily, and to have intended to return to England as an informer, with the hope of lavish rewards. One contemporary reported that he had actually been sent as a spy to poison the college president,

Dr Allen; another that 'in the seminary he became a naughty spy, and was taken and punished there as a spy, by the uniform consent of all from the highest to the lowest'. At Rheims he was subjected to horrifying and prolonged tortures after a tip-off that he was an undercover agent, but he stoically refused to confess. His most bizarre plan, which happily was not put into action, was to kill off the entire community by injecting poison into the college's wells, or communal baths, a scheme echoed in the episode in *The Jew of Malta* in which Barabas declares: 'Sometimes I go about and poison wells' (2.3.177; as we have seen he does in fact 'spice' a 'pot of rice porridge' with fatal consequences for his own daughter, Abigail, 3.4, 3.6). In spite of everything Baines was ordained as a full priest in September 1581. Among the many heretical views he ascribed to Marlowe were the statements that 'all Protestants are hypocritical asses', that 'the first beginning of religion was only to keep men in awe', that 'Christ was a bastard and his mother dishonest' (i.e. unchaste), that 'Saint John the Evangelist was bedfellow to Christ, and leant always in his bosom, that he used him as the sinners of Sodoma', and that 'all they that love not tobacco and boys were fools'. And the aesthete in Marlowe may be discerned in his reported criticism that 'all the New Testament is filthily written'.

In January 1592 Marlowe lodged with Baines and a goldsmith named Gifford Gilbert in Flushing, a British-occupied town in the war-torn Netherlands. Their aim was, literally, to make money by coining, an enterprise in which the goldsmith's skills were indispensable. The three men were detected and Marlowe was arrested and deported, accompanied on the journey back to England by the counterfeit coins and a letter from the governor of the town, Sir Robert Sidney – brother of the late great Sir Philip – addressed to Lord Burghley revealing that the treacherous Baines, who also accompanied the party, had acted as informer, and saying that the men should 'take their trial as you [Burghley] think best'. The criminals admitted the crime to Sidney while claiming that 'what was done was only to see the goldsmith's cunning [skill]', and Sidney mercifully expressed his belief 'that the poor man was only brought in under that colour, whatever intent the other two had'. Only one Dutch coin had actually been put into circulation, and the coiners would have been unlikely to get away with many more since 'the metal is plain pewter, and with half an eye to be discovered'.

Marlowe and Baines fell out, accusing 'one another of intent to go to the enemy [i.e. the Catholic cause], or to Rome, both as they say of malice to one another'.[33] How Marlowe fared in his interview with Burghley is unknown, but he was free by May 1592 when he was bound over to keep the peace in Shoreditch. He retained his interest in coining; in his 'Note', Baines reported Marlowe as saying 'that he had as good right to coin as the Queen of England, and that he was acquainted with one Poole, a prisoner in Newgate, who hath great skill in mixture of metals and having learned some things of him meant, through help of a cunning stamp-maker, to coin French crowns, pistolets, and English shillings'.

On 20 May 1593, after Marlowe had been arrested as the result of Kyd's testimony, he was released but required to report daily to the Privy Council, 'until he shall be licensed to the contrary'. Ten days later he felt free to go to a boarding house kept by a widow named Eleanor Bull in Deptford, a district on the south bank of the Thames, now subsumed into Greater London. He arrived at about ten in the morning, and met three other men: Ingram Frizer, Nicholas Skeres and Robert Poley. All were of dubious character (but none was a 'bawdy serving-man', as Meres reported). The purpose of their meeting is unknown. They had a midday meal, apparently supplied by the widow, a woman of some social status, after which they 'were in quiet sort together' – which presumably means that they seemed to be getting on well with each other – and walked in the garden until six o'clock in the evening, then went back to the house for supper. Marlowe and Frizer argued about who should pay the bill, 'the sum of pence, *le recknynge*', as the coroner's report puts it. Marlowe was lying on 'a bed in the room where they supped' and Frizer sitting with his back towards the bed, with Skeres and Poley on either side of him in such a way that Frizer, trapped, 'in no wise could take flight' when Marlowe suddenly and 'maliciously' drew Frizer's dagger out of his back pocket and attacked Frizer, giving him 'two wounds on his head of the length of two inches, and of the depth of a quarter of an inch'. This wound was long but not deep, effected presumably with the pommel or hilt of the dagger, and not intended to kill. Frizer, fearful for his life and unable to escape, struggled with Marlowe and appears to have wrenched his dagger back into his own hands and to have held it by the hilt, since the wound he gave Marlowe was deep but not wide: 'a mortal wound over his right eye of the depth of two inches and of the width of one inch'. Marlowe died instantly, according to the coroner's report, though modern medical opinion holds that he is likely to have lingered for a few minutes.[34]

The coroner's inquest was held two days later before a jury of sixteen men, who inspected the corpse, examined the witnesses and found that Frizer killed Marlowe 'in the defence and saving of his own life'. This may be true, but the witnesses on whom the coroner would have to depend were not exactly unbiased. Many readers of the documents have speculated that Marlowe may have been the victim of an undisclosed conspiracy, even that his death was brought about by government agency impelled by the Queen, but there is no documentary evidence for this. What is perfectly clear is that he died. On the same day as the inquest Marlowe was buried in the churchyard of St Nicholas at Deptford, and on 28 June Frizer received a royal pardon.

The unimpugnable documentary evidence deriving from legal documents was discovered by Leslie Hotson, translated by him from the original Latin, and published in 1925.[35] It makes this one of the best recorded episodes in English literary history. Even before these papers turned up there was ample evidence that Marlowe had died a violent death in Deptford in 1593, and, as we have seen, he was a man who made his mark, as rioter, forger, heretic, blasphemer, secret agent or social dissident, wherever he went. All this compounds the initial and inherent ludicrousness of the idea that in fact he lived on to write the works of William Shakespeare while leaving not the slightest sign of his continuing existence for at least twenty years. During this period he is alleged to have produced a string of masterpieces which must be added to those he had already written, which no one in the busy and gossipy world of the theatre knew to be his, and for which he was willing to allow his Stratford contemporary to receive all the credit and to reap all the rewards. Yet since the late nineteenth century innumerable articles and many books have been published to this effect.

Calvin Hoffman, an American journalist who in the early 1970s had the Walsingham tomb opened in the attempt to find documentary proof, and who believed Marlowe and Thomas Walsingham to be lovers, left all his estate to the King's School, Canterbury to found an annual prize for contributions to the debate. Anyone proving the case outright was to win the jackpot. So far no one has satisfied this requirement, but among the prizewinners is Mike Rubbo, for a 2001 film called *Much Ado About Something* (which cheats by omitting the words 'Dead shepherd' when the passage from *As You Like It*, quoted earlier in this chapter, is read). Many members of the Marlowe Society dedicate themselves to the proposition, and numerous websites argue the case. Astonishingly, in 2002 the Dean and Chapter of Westminster Abbey, having accorded Marlowe long-overdue recognition in Poets' Corner in a stained-glass window which couples him with Oscar Wilde, flew in the face of the evidence of the coroner's jury who had seen Marlowe's body by permitting the placing of a question mark before the year of his death.

Variously inaccurate accounts of Marlowe's death that circulated in Elizabethan and early Jacobean times include a moralizing one in a book called *The Theatre of God's Judgements*, by Thomas Beard, of 1597, which sees it as a punishment for blasphemy. Meres refers to Beard in *Palladis Tamia*, written a year later, adding, as we have seen, the gossip that the murder was motivated by a quarrel over a 'lewd love', and for close on a century, up to the time of Anthony à Wood in his encyclopedia of Oxford authors, *Athenae Oxonienses* (1691), other writers seized upon and embroidered Beard's account. The idea that Marlowe had a 'lewd love' who was a woman became part of the legend, and informs for example Clemence Dane's once successful verse play *Will Shakespeare*, of 1922 (a terrible piece of fustian if ever there was one).

Although it is indisputable that Marlowe made many enemies, it is clear from contemporary reports that he could command both admiration and affection. An early disciple appears to have been a Mr Fineaux, of Dover, who in 1640 was said to have been 'a very good scholar, but would never have above one book at a time, and when he was perfect in it, he would sell it away and buy another. He learned all Marlowe by heart, and divers other books. Marlowe made him an atheist.' (Although writings undoubtedly circulated in manuscript, the report that Fineaux 'learned all Marlowe by heart' may need to be taken with a pinch of salt, since Marlowe's only work to be published in his own lifetime was *Tamburlaine*, and *The Jew of Malta* did not appear in print until as late as 1633.) A symptom of Fineaux's mixed-up disbelief was that 'he would go out at midnight into a wood, and fall down upon his knees, and pray heartily that the devil would come that he might see him (for he did not believe that there was a devil)'.[36]

Even colleagues who did not share Marlowe's heretical views did not necessarily let disapproval supplant admiration of his genius. Within weeks of his death his friend Thomas Nashe described him in his novel *The Unfortunate Traveller* as 'one of the wittiest knaves that ever God made'. George Peele lamented Marlowe's death in a poem, 'The Honour of the Garter', composed to celebrate the Duke of Northumberland's installation in the order:

> Unhappy in thy end,
> Marlowe, the Muses' darling, for thy verse
> Fit to write passions for the souls below!

Henry Petowe, who like George Chapman paid Marlowe the tribute of composing a continuation of *Hero and Leander*, addressed him as

> Marlowe, late Marlowe, now framèd all divine,
> What soul more happy than that soul of thine!
> Live still in heaven thy soul, thy fame on earth!

And he grieved that

> Marlowe, still-admirèd Marlowe's gone
> To live with Beauty in Elysium.

Chapman himself wrote of inscribing his part of the story of Hero and Leander to Marlowe's 'deathless memory'. The anonymous author of *The New Metamorphosis* (1600) writes – whether from personal knowledge we do not know – of 'kind Kit Marlowe', in opposition to Kyd's description of him as 'cruel'. Thomas Nashe, who was clearly a crony, wrote an elegy, now lost, on Marlowe's death, and, comparing him with the fifth-century AD Greek poet Musaeus whose work

Marlowe was adapting in *Hero and Leander*, writes in *Nashe's Lenten Stuff* (1599) of 'a diviner Muse than him, Kit Marlowe'. Perhaps the most eloquent of all tributes to Marlowe's poetic genius comes in a poem by Michael Drayton, 'To Henry Reynolds, of Poets and Poesy', published as late as 1627:

> Neat Marlowe, bathèd in the Thespian springs,
> Had in him those brave translunary things
> That your first poets had; his raptures were
> All air and fire, which made his verses clear;
> For that fine madness still he did retain
> Which rightly should possess a poet's brain.[37]

It is impossible not to apply the opening lines of the Epilogue to *Dr Faustus* to Marlowe himself:

> Cut is the branch that might have grown full straight,
> And burnèd is Apollo's laurel bough . . .

Though the notion that Marlowe wrote Shakespeare's plays is ludicrous, there are many resemblances between their writings, extending even to direct quotations, beyond those that we have seen from 'Come live with me and be my love' in *The Merry Wives of Windsor* and from *Hero and Leander* in *As You Like It*. In Shakespeare's *Henry IV*, Part Two the bombastically bragging Pistol quotes from *Tamburlaine* – 'hollow pampered jades of Asia' (2.4.161) – in a tavern scene along with scraps from Kyd's *The Spanish Tragedy*, Peele's *The Battle of Alcazar*, and the anonymous *Locrine*, bearing witness to the genuine popularity of these poetic dramas among the ordinary people of London. And Marlowe came in handy for writers lacking invention. The anonymous play *The Taming of a Shrew*, first printed in 1594 (most satisfactorily explained as a cobbled-up imitation based on performances of Shakespeare's *The Taming of the Shrew*, which would remain unpublished until 1623), contains close on twenty borrowings, some of them several lines long, from both parts of *Tamburlaine*, *Edward II* and *Dr Faustus*; as *Faustus* seems not to have been printed till 1604, the compiler must have had access to a manuscript, or have remembered passages from performance. The presence of two lines from *Henry VI*, Part Three (5.3.2 and 5.7.14) in Marlowe's late play *The Massacre at Paris*, which survives only in a short and corrupt version, is probably also a result of textual cobbling after Marlowe's death.

Though verbal parallels offer clues to the relationship between Marlowe and Shakespeare, evidence of intellectual and aesthetic interplay between the two dramatists is more interesting, though less easy to demonstrate. The university-educated Marlowe was a more accomplished classicist than Shakespeare, as we see in his translations from Ovid, Musaeus and Lucan as well as in *Dido, Queen of Carthage*. And Shakespeare's Sonnets suggest that he understood Marlowe's fascination with male beauty. Addressing Time, for instance, he writes:

> O carve not with thy hours my love's fair brow,
> Nor draw my lines there with thine antique pen.
> Him in thy course untainted do allow
> For Beauty's pattern to succeeding men.
>
> (Sonnet 19)

His beloved's cheek is 'the map of days outworn, / When beauty lived and died as flowers do now' (Sonnet 68), and he writes of 'my love's fair brow' (Sonnet 19), addressing him as 'Lord of my love' (Sonnet 26) and 'my lovely boy' (Sonnet 126).

But Shakespeare did not get into trouble as Marlowe did. In temperament he appears to have been at the respectable end of the scale; John Aubrey, writing around 1680, says that he was 'the more to be admired quia [because] he was not a company keeper . . . wouldn't be debauched and, if invited to, writ he was in pain'.[38] If Dekker had envisaged him in Elysium he would not have placed him underneath a vine. A mulberry tree beside a soft-flowing river might have been more apt.

For all the affinities between Marlowe and Shakespeare, their gifts were different. Shakespeare's range was much greater, even in his earliest plays, which include the lyrical comedy of *The Two Gentlemen of Verona*, the more intellectual comedy of *The Comedy of Errors*, the epic pageantry of the *Henry VI* plays, and the Senecan tragedy *Titus Andronicus*, not to mention the deliberately contrasted narrative poems, one comic, the other tragic. And the dominance of Shakespeare in the centuries since the dramatists' deaths has established his modes of writing as norms that have hindered the understanding of other modes that in themselves are equally valid.

The shape of English literature would have been very different had Marlowe not succumbed to Frizer's dagger in Deptford at the age of 29. But a new generation of dramatists was soon to emerge, writers who would also challenge Shakespeare's supremacy, with most of whom he would have close personal and professional relationships, whom he would influence and who in turn would influence him. He was not a solitary genius, though his creativity was of a distinct and special kind, and one which has made his work particularly attractive to later ages.

4

Thomas Dekker and London

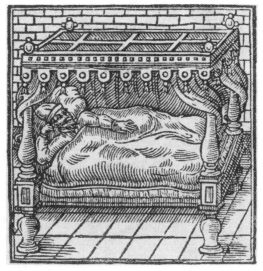

7. Thomas Dekker. This engraving of Dekker in bed, printed in his pamphlet Dekker his Dream *of 1620, is the nearest we can come to knowing what he looked like.*

Almost all the dramatists writing in the earlier part of Shakespeare's career died in their thirties or early forties. The exception is Thomas Lodge, and he had given up working in the theatre – except perhaps, since he was a surgeon by profession, in the operating theatre – before he was 40. More importantly, all of them concentrated in their plays on mythological, classical, historical, biblical and romantic subject matter. Drama related rather to literature than to day-to-day life. It is not until the later 1590s that Elizabethan London begins to figure at all prominently in the drama. Shakespeare draws upon London life in his English history plays, especially in the tavern scenes of the first and second parts of *Henry IV*, written around 1596 to 1598, but, nominally at least, they are set in the fourteenth and early fifteenth centuries. His only play with contemporary metropolitan associations is *The Merry Wives of Windsor*, probably dating from 1597, in which Falstaff brings historical associations along with him, and he and his followers are Londoners on a country outing. The first surviving city of London comedy is the little-known *Englishmen for My Money*, of 1598, by William Haughton. The first prominent dramatist whose work centres on the capital is Thomas Dekker (*c.* 1572–1632), who is also one of the longer lived, and who wrote prolifically throughout his adult life, except for the seven years that he spent in prison; even then he was not idle. A Londoner – possibly, his name suggests, of Dutch extraction – he was passionately dedicated to the City, which he apostrophized as 'O London! – thou mother of my life, nurse of my being!',[1] and his relationships to the London scene will be the burden of my song.

Dekker's year of birth can only be assumed, from a reference in 1632 to his 'three-score years'. We know nothing of his early life, which probably means that he, like Shakespeare, did not attend university, but his writings suggest that he had a grammar-school education. He was clearly fluent in Latin. His name first appears when he was in his mid-twenties; in January 1598 Henslowe lent the Lord Admiral's Men money 'to buy a book' – that is, a play script – 'of Mr Dekker'. But later that year Francis Meres was to list Dekker, along with George Chapman, Shakespeare and Jonson, among those he considered 'our best for tragedy', so Dekker may already have been working for Henslowe for several years. He was a freelance, ready to offer his services to any company that would pay for them. From 1598 until 1602 he contributed regularly and prolifically to the work of the Lord Admiral's Men. In 1602 he wrote for both the Earl of Worcester's Men (then coming to the end of its career) and, briefly, for the Lord Chamberlain's Men (Shakespeare's company). He worked for Prince Henry's – previously the Lord Admiral's – Men from 1604, and for other companies, including the boys of St Paul's, after that. He pressed himself hard. Henslowe's papers show that between 1598 and 1602 alone he had a hand in between forty and fifty plays, but only about six of those got into print. The fact that he could churn out work with what must seem to us to be extraordinary speed and efficiency does nothing to diminish the fact that some of it was of the highest quality. His published plays bear witness to his genius, and there is no strong reason to suppose that lost plays were necessarily less good than those that got into print, or than the few by any writer that survive in manuscript.

In his plays, Dekker almost always worked as a collaborator, often with as many as three other writers, some of them no less capable of first-class work than he, and always writing at top speed. Let us look at what he accomplished in a single year, 1599.

On 20 January he received £3 'in earnest of' – that is, as an advance payment for – 'his play called the first Introduction of the Civil Wars of France', which follows from a payment on the previous 30 December of £5 'to Mr [Michael] Drayton and Mr Dekker'[2] for 'the third part of the Civil Wars of France'. (Parts One and Two had been written by the same authors, and put into production, in the autumn of 1598.) Maybe 'the first Introduction' was some kind of supplementary play, to be given when the three parts were not performed together. There is no record of its completion. On 30 January he was in trouble; Henslowe had to lay out £3. 10s. to discharge him from 'the arrest of my Lord Chamberlain's Men'. It looks as if the principal rival company had some financial claim upon him which he had been unable to meet. Things go quiet for a few months; maybe his discharge was only temporary and he was in prison for debt in spite of Henslowe's help. But on 7 April Dekker, along with Henry Chettle, receives £3 in advance for a play about Troilus and Cressida. Work was in danger of being interrupted because this time it was Chettle who got into trouble. On 2 May Henslowe paid twenty shillings 'in ready money' to the two men 'to discharge Harry Chettle of his arrest from Ingram . . .'. But Dekker had come up with a new idea; on the same day Henslowe lent him the small sum of five shillings in earnest of a play called *Orestes Furens* (the term seems to have been foreign to Henslowe as he spells it 'orestes fvres'). No more is heard of this. Work on 'Troilus and Cressida' proceeded apace, and its working title changed. Henslowe lent the dramatists thirty shillings on 26 May, originally writing that it was for 'a book called Troilus and Cressida', but deleting that title and substituting 'the tragedy of Agamemnon'. Presumably the play changed shape as it evolved. Payment for it under its new title was

completed four days later with the sum of £3. 5s., and four days after
that Henslowe paid seven shillings to the Master of the Revels' man
for its licensing. The play was written, therefore, within two months,
and was immediately put into production. Shakespeare, too, was to
write a play about Troilus and Cressida some three years later. There
is no way of telling how it stood in relation to Dekker's except that
Shakespeare's is certainly not a 'tragedy of Agamemnon'.

Dekker was soon at work again, and within six weeks, on 15 July,
Henslowe laid out £3 to buy 'a book of Thomas Dekker's called *The
Gentle Craft*'. The sum seems small; maybe there had been earlier,
unrecorded payments. *The Gentle Craft* was a recently published
novella by Thomas Deloney which had appeared in two parts in 1598.
Dekker turned it into a play finally called *The Shoemaker's Holiday*,
which was to become his best-known work. It was printed in the
following year, 1600, with the boast that it had been 'acted before
the Queen's most excellent majesty on New Year's Day at night last
by the Right Honourable the Earl of Nottingham, Lord High Admiral
of England, his servants'. A week after Henslowe's payment, on
24 July, Dekker was working on a *Stepmother's Tragedy*, presumably
with Chettle who received £1 for it on 23 August and £4 in full
payment on 14 October.

Dekker's ability to keep several balls in the air at once is revealed
by the fact that one week after the initial payment for the *Stepmother's
Tragedy* he received £3 for a play called either *Better Late than Never*
or *Bear a Brain* (Henslowe deleted the first title and substituted the
second). Ten days after that Dekker and Ben Jonson received £4
'in earnest of their book which they be a-writing called *Page of
Plymouth*'. This play was completed by 2 September, and on the 12th
Henslowe paid out £10 'to buy women's gowns for it'. Meantime, on
the 3rd, Dekker, Jonson, Chettle 'and other gentlemen', apparently
forming a literary syndicate, had £4 'in earnest of a play called *Robert
the Second King of Scots' Tragedy*', which cost Henslowe another
twenty shillings on 15 September, ten shillings the next day, and
another twenty shillings paid to Jonson on 27 September. Dekker was
at it again on 9 November when he received £2 advance for *The
Whole History of Fortunatus*, for which he received a further £3 on
24 November and a final twenty shillings on the 30th. This appears

to be a redaction into a single play of a two-part work based on a German folk tale; *The First Part of Fortunatus* had been acted by the Admiral's Men in 1596. Revisions were needed; on '31 November' Dekker received £1 'for the altering of the book of *The Whole History of Fortunatus*', and then on 12 December £2 for an alternative ending for a court performance given as part of the Christmas season, on 27 December. The revision along with the epilogue is sycophantically laudatory of the Queen, addressed as 'Empress of heaven and earth' and as 'dear goddess'. In the meantime Henslowe had laid out £10 'for to buy things for *Fortunatus*'. Dekker soldiered on: on 19 December he along with Chettle and Haughton received £3 in advance for *Patient Grissel* which brought them further sums of £6 on the 26th, then five shillings on 28 December; Henslowe was paying a tailor £1 for 'a grey gown for Grissel' by the end of January.

Overall, then, Dekker was involved to some degree or other in the composition of no fewer than eleven plays in 1599. Assuming that payments were shared equally among the contributors, this means that he earned something like £30 during that year. It was a decent, though far from princely, income, half as much again as, for example, those of the vicar and the schoolmaster of Stratford-upon-Avon, though they received additional emoluments, including accommodation. Only two of Dekker's plays from this period, *The Shoemaker's Holiday* and *Old Fortunatus*, survive. *The Shoemaker's Holiday* is the work by which he is best known, and represents the culmination of the early part of his career. Initial performances would have been given at the Rose; its court performance on New Year's Day 1600 must have been a great occasion for Dekker and for the Lord Admiral's Men as a whole. For it he wrote a prologue spoken by one member of the cast while the remainder knelt facing the Queen:

> O grant, bright mirror of true chastity,
> From those life-breathing stars your sun-like eyes
> One gracious smile; for your celestial breath
> Must send us life, or sentence us to death.

This play is the richest expression of Dekker's love affair with London. The ebullient shoemaker of the title is Simon Eyre, a historical figure who became Lord Mayor in 1445, during the reign of King Henry VI.

But Dekker's play has more to do with romance than with history, which came to him second-hand from Deloney's charming novella. It is a romantic comedy centring on the Dick Whittington-like story of Eyre's progress – the reward for hard work assisted by wifely support – from humble shoemaker through the offices of alderman and sheriff to that of Lord Mayor of London. With this tale Dekker entwines two separate stories of young love, one in high life, the other among the lower classes, involving deception and disguise but issuing in happy endings. Pathos and contemporary relevance are provided by the plight of Ralph Damport, the young shoemaker who, required in the opening scene to leave his weeping bride, 'blubbered Jane', and to serve in the wars overseas, returns lame to find that Jane is the reluctant object of the attentions of a rich suitor, Hammon.

In this play Dekker's verse is mostly homespun, setting off the idiosyncratic and colloquial pungency of the prose. His linguistic exuberance and inventiveness create a strong sense of individual character, especially in the figures of the hard-working, hard-swearing and hard-drinking Eyre, his often-bemused wife Margery, and in the well-seasoned relationship between them.

Dekker's language is many-sourced. There is a degree of self-referentiality in the plays of Shakespeare's time, as we have already noticed in the way that a line from one play, or even a poem, is liable to pop up in another. Playgoers enjoyed being reminded of previous visits to the theatre. It is no surprise in *The Shoemaker's Holiday* to find the maid Sybil quoting *The Spanish Tragedy* as she tells her mistress she should not 'love him that loves not you. He thinks scorn to do as he's done to; but if I were as you, I'ld cry "Go by, Jeronimo, go by!"' (2.45–6). And later Eyre too suggests familiarity with the Elizabethan playhouse as he declares that he 'knows how to speak to a pope, to Sultan Soliman' (the central character of Thomas Kyd's *Soliman and Perseda*) and 'to Tamburlaine an he were here' (20.59–60). It is no doubt Dekker's own familiarity with Shakespeare that peeps through as he makes Rose, entering 'making a garland' at the opening of Scene 2, echo Titania's 'Come, sit thee down upon this flow'ry bed' (*A Midsummer Night's Dream*, 4.1.1); Rose says to herself 'Here sit thou down upon this flow'ry bank' (the substitution of 'bank' for 'bed' may be a subliminal echo of Oberon's 'bank where the wild thyme blows', 2.1.249). Oberon's 'Lovers, to bed' (5.1.357) is echoed in the King's 'At night, lovers to bed' (21.97). And Juliet's promise in the balcony scene to 'follow thee, my lord, throughout the world' (*Romeo and Juliet*, 2.1.190) underlies Rose's 'Invent the means, / And Rose will follow thee through all the world' (15.8).

But if there is an inherited literariness about some of the play's language, Dekker also shows great delight in re-creating (and, no doubt, improving upon) the everyday speech of the streets and the workshop. This is often cheerfully bawdy in a straightforwardly direct manner, appreciative of sexuality, less intellectual than the crackling wordplay of, for instance, both the servants and the gallants of *Romeo and Juliet*. 'Where's Cicely Bumtrinket, your maid?' asks Eyre of his wife. 'She has a privy fault: she farts in her sleep' (4.36–7; how does he know, we may ask – though it was common for servants to sleep in the same rooms as their employers). 'O heart, my codpiece point is ready to fly in pieces every time I think upon Mistress Rose,' says the shoemaker Firk, whose very name invites lewd interpretation. He continues: 'but let that pass, as my Lady Mayoress says' (18.181–3), drawing attention to Dekker's use of catchphrases as a source of the comedy of character, as in Eyre's repeated 'Prince am I none, yet am I princely born' and his wife's 'but let that pass' – often a source of double meanings of which she may or may not remain unconscious. Hearing that Ralph is wounded in the leg, she says, with an allusion to the 'malady of France' (syphilis), ''Twas a fair gift of God the infirmity took not hold a little higher, considering thou camest from France – but let that pass' (10.73–5). And Eyre has a nice line in insults and colourful nicknames, especially for his long-suffering wife:

Away, you Islington whitepot. Hence, you hopperarse, you barley pudding full of maggots, you broiled carbonado. Avaunt, avaunt, avoid, Mephistophilus! Shall Sim Eyre learn to speak of you, Lady Madgy? Vanish, Mother Miniver-Cap, vanish! Go, trip and go, meddle with your partlets and your pishery-pashery, your flews and your whirligigs! Go, rub out of mine alley! (20.51–8)

All this because Margery has told him to be careful how he speaks to the King.

The play's climax is a scene of high festivity with much to celebrate. The love plots are coming to a happy conclusion. Eyre has become

Lord Mayor. He has built Leadenhall as a gift to the city. He sets out his – and the playwright's – agenda for the day:

Soft, the King this day comes to dine with me, to see my new buildings. His Majesty is welcome. He shall have good cheer, delicate cheer, princely cheer. This day my fellow prentices of London come to dine with me too. They shall have fine cheer, gentlemanlike cheer. I promised the mad Cappadocians, when we all served at the conduit together, that if ever I came to be Mayor of London, I would feast them all; and I'll do it, I'll do it, by the life of Pharaoh, by this beard, Sim Eyre will be no flincher. Besides, I have procured that upon every Shrove Tuesday, at the sound of the pancake bell, my fine dapper Assyrian lads shall clap up their shop windows and away. This is the day, and this day they shall do't, they shall do't. (15.43–56)

The unnamed King who appears in the closing scenes is usually portrayed in modern productions as Henry V, though he has also appeared as Henry VIII. Dekker is avoiding specificity, more concerned to make connections between past and present, to involve the playgoers at the Rose in the play's joyous climax, than to be true to history. This is a celebration of London, of Londoners, and of patriotism. It creates a sense of holiday, of a time when wine is as 'plentiful as beer, and beer as water' (20.9–10), when a sovereign will confer favours and blessings upon his subjects and join in their revels. But at the very end there is just a passing shadow as the King declares that

> When all our sports and banquetings are done,
> Wars must right wrongs which Frenchmen have begun.

Theatregoers could have seen the French wars of Shakespeare's *Henry V* – another play that celebrates national identity – in its earliest performances at the Globe while *The Shoemaker's Holiday* was playing at the Rose.

From early in the nineteenth century *The Shoemaker's Holiday* has been one of the most popular and frequently performed of the plays written by Shakespeare's fellows. A series of amateur productions, including one in 1919 with an all-female cast, led up to more high-profile performances with distinguished actors in Birmingham in 1921 and at the Old Vic in London in 1926, where, understandably, an actor (Baliol Holloway) who had recently made a hit in the similar role of Falstaff was no less successful as Eyre. And the great Edith Evans triumphed as Madgy. In an illuminating review, the theatre critic James Agate wrote:

Miss Evans has this characteristic of all good acting – that she takes hold of her dramatist's conception, absorbs it, and then gives it out again re-created in terms of her own personality and delighted imagination, so that you get the twofold joy of one fine talent superimposed upon another. 'How shall I look in a hood?' asks the new-enriched dame, to be answered, 'Like a cat in the pillory.' Whereupon Margery has the astonishing, irrelevant, 'Indeed, all flesh is grass.' Hear Miss Evans say this . . . and you reflect, first, that Dekker was a good playwright, and, second, that the best wit in the world gains when it is delivered by a witty actress.[3]

Among numerous other productions have been one by Orson Welles in New York in 1938, an American musical version in 1959, a Marxist adaptation in Germany in 1967, and a National Theatre, London, production in 1981. In more recent times the play has been neglected, perhaps because Eyre can seem over-hearty and the play as a whole over-optimistic. But a director sensitive to the ambiguities of the text could bring it into touch with modern sensibilities.

Though *The Shoemaker's Holiday* shows Dekker's genius at his most individual, he was a jobbing playwright, not above revising and adding to his own or other men's work. On 12 January 1602(?) he composed a prologue and epilogue to the otherwise unknown *Pontius Pilate*, four days later he had £1 for 'altering of *Tasso*', and in September 1602 he wrote additions for *Sir John Oldcastle*. He wrote for money, and for some of his commissioned work he was quite highly paid. In 1612, for instance, he devised an elaborate Lord Mayor's Show called *Troia-Nova Triumphans*, adopting the ancient name for London, for which he and the actor John Heminges received £181.[4] But for all his hard work he often failed to keep his head above water. Soon after devising this show he was arrested for debt and committed to the King's Bench prison, where he was to spend seven years, from 1612 to 1619. Among his creditors during this period was John Webster senior, a coach-builder, father of the playwright with whom Dekker often collaborated, and to whom he owed £40, possibly for the cost in part of the pageant wagons.

Dekker did little work for the Lord Chamberlain's Men, the company with which Shakespeare was solely associated from 1594 onwards, but there is one play with which both men were involved, though to an unknown extent. They seem to have contributed to one of the more puzzling and tantalizing relics of the Elizabethan theatre, the play of *Sir Thomas More*, which survives only in an incomplete and undated manuscript offering only inferential information about who wrote it. The play presents loosely linked scenes from More's life. He quells the riots of Londoners against resident foreigners on the 'Ill May Day' of 1517, and is appointed Lord Chamberlain as a reward. He persuades the rebels to surrender to the King, Henry VIII. A sequence of serio-comic episodes dramatize his wit in attempting to reform minor offenders, his credentials as a humanist scholar, his practical joking and his love of plays. A picturesque scene in which he is visited at home by travelling players is illustrative of early sixteenth-century drama. More's downfall and passage to the scaffold begin when he refuses to sign unspecified articles. The closing scenes depict his saintly, almost light-hearted resolution to embrace death rather than yield to the King's demand.

The manuscript is a fascinating and enigmatic document which shows something of the operations of the Elizabethan censorship system and of the contortions that dramatists had to go through in their efforts to cope with its demands. It suggests, too, that even at the height of his career Shakespeare, like Dekker and his collaborators, could be called upon to work with fellow playwrights in what may well be thought of as a journeyman's task.

The surviving papers form a heavily revised text with contributions in six different hands along with annotations by the Master of the Revels, Sir Edmund Tilney. It is a messy document, with alterations, cancellations, evident omissions, and insertions written on added pages. Probably it started off as a fair copy by Anthony Munday of a play that he wrote in the early 1590s in collaboration with someone else, perhaps Henry Chettle. In the normal course of events this was submitted for approval to Tilney. Disturbed by the play's relevance to current events in London, where riots against foreign immigrants were common, he called for substantial revisions, writing: 'Leave out the insurrection wholly and the cause thereof, and begin with Sir

Thomas More at the Mayor's sessions, with a report afterwards of his good service done being Sheriff of London upon a mutiny against the Lombards – only by a short report, and not otherwise, at your own perils. E. Tilney.'

What happened next is unclear. The surviving alterations and additions do not appear to have been written in a direct attempt to meet Tilney's basic objections. It seems likely that the manuscript was laid aside in despair, but taken up again after the Queen died in 1603, in the hope that under the new regime it might form the basis of an acceptable drama. At this stage several writers were commissioned to effect a salvage operation. The result of their combined efforts is, understandably, an episodic, patchy and uneven piece of work which nevertheless has fine individual scenes and speeches.[5]

The episodes of *Sir Thomas More* that have attracted most attention are the 'Ill May Day' scenes. The leading rioters, outraged by what they see as the illegal activities of foreign groups in London, have planned to 'go forth a-Maying, but make it the worst May Day for the strangers' – foreigners – 'that ever they saw'. More, sent as a peacemaker, subdues the rioters with powerful and humane pleas for tolerance in the face of racial bigotry and jingoistic exclusiveness which were topical in their own time and continue to be so today.

> Imagine that you see the wretched strangers,
> Their babies at their backs, with their poor luggage,
> Plodding to th'ports and coasts for transportation,
> And that you sit as kings in your desires,
> Authority quite silenced by your brawl,
> And you in ruff of your opinions clothed:
> What had you got? I'll tell you: you had taught
> How insolence and strong hand should prevail,
> How order should be quelled. And by this pattern
> Not one of you should live an agèd man,
> For other ruffians, as their fancies wrought,
> With selfsame hand, self reasons, and self right
> Would shark on you, and men like ravenous fishes
> Would feed on one another.
>
> (6.84–97)

These episodes have been attributed to Shakespeare since the middle of the nineteenth century, as the result of study of handwriting, spelling, rhetoric, imagery and dramatic style, and are now usually printed in editions of his complete works, sometimes along with the rest of the play.[6] A lively passage of dialogue only about thirty lines long can confidently be ascribed to Dekker on the evidence of his handwriting, which survives elsewhere in greater abundance than Shakespeare's. It cannot, however, be claimed that Shakespeare genuinely collaborated with Dekker or with any of the other contributors: certain features of the scene Shakespeare is most likely to have written suggest that, for all his profound imaginative identification with the plight of the immigrants, he had only the vaguest idea of how the episode should be tied in with the rest of the play.[7]

The presumed date of the revision of *Sir Thomas More* places it towards the end of Dekker's most productive period as a playwright, at a time when theatre was suffering one of its most severe disruptions as the result of a prolonged outbreak of plague – the worst since 1592–3. Though King James I was crowned at Whitehall on 25 July 1603, he postponed until the following March his planned ceremonial progress through the City, for which elaborate triumphal arches had been erected and pageants prepared. The impact of the plague in London was devastating. During a hot August deaths averaged well over 2,000 a week, and in September totalled more than 10,000 – over 20,000 dead of the plague alone out of a total population in the capital of around 200,000 within two months.[8] Most of them were poor people whose squalid living conditions fostered the disease, which was transmitted by rat-fleas. The royal family, and many citizens including some of those, such as ministers and doctors, who were most needed in London, fled to the country, where they were liable to receive a frosty welcome. Some had left it too late, and died on the way. Among those who courageously remained at their posts was Thomas Lodge, playwright turned physician, who published a *Treatise on the Plague* at the height of the epidemic, in August.

The London theatres were closed for nearly a year from mid-May 1603, and though the companies were able to tour and, by October, when the plague had abated, to play at court, new plays were little in demand, and a number of dramatists turned to alternative employment.

But though Shakespeare had written his narrative poems during the even more severe outbreak of 1592–3, there is nothing to suggest that he was driven to abandon playwriting during the later outbreak. Maybe by this time he was more confident of his position as a dramatist, and glad of the opportunity to stock up more work for when the theatres reopened. He may have gone on tour, or retreated to Stratford, but he must have been keenly aware of what was happening in London, and perhaps had the effects of the plague in mind a few years later when in *Macbeth* he made Ross describe Scotland as a place

> Where sighs and groans and shrieks that rend the air
> Are made, not marked; where violent sorrow seems
> A modern ecstasy [commonplace emotion]. The dead man's knell
> Is there scarce asked for who, and good men's lives
> Expire before the flowers in their caps,
> Dying or ere they sicken.
>
> (4.3.169–74)[9]

The plague was grist to Dekker's mill. Always the professional, he turned a national disaster to his advantage by writing about it, embarking even while the plague was raging on the first of a series of pamphlets, written mostly in prose but including passages of verse, in the manner of Greene and Nashe, which were to help to sustain his livelihood over the next decade and more.

Dekker's close involvement with the plight of the capital is shown by the appearance in 1603 of his pamphlet *The Wonderful Year: Wherein is showed the picture of London lying sick of the plague*, published anonymously but claimed by Dekker as his in 1606. In the dedication he makes a claim for the therapeutic properties of laughter similar to that in the epistle to *The Shoemaker's Holiday*: 'If you read, you may haply laugh. 'Tis my desire you should, because mirth is both physical [medicinal] and wholesome against the plague.' He begins with a characteristically charming if hyperbolical picture of the joys of spring:

... the lark sung at his window every morning, the nightingale every night, the cuckoo – like a single-sole fiddler that reels from tavern to tavern – plied it all the day long, lambs frisked up and down in the valleys, kids and goats leaped to and fro on the mountains, shepherds sat piping, country wenches singing, lovers made sonnets for their lasses whilst they made garlands for their lovers. And as the country was frolic, so was the city merry.

But all this has been brought to an end, first because Death has made Sickness 'his herald, attired him like a courtier and, in his [Death's] name, charged him to go into the Privy Chamber of the English Queen to summon her to appear in the Star Chamber of Heaven'. If Dekker's eulogy of 'the great landlady' of England is at times over-heated, it can also rise to simple eloquence: 'She came in with the fall of the leaf and went away in the spring.'[10] Born in the autumn of 1533, on 7 September, Elizabeth had died on 24 March 1603. The year's second wonder is James's accession to the throne, by which, Dekker optimistically writes, 'in an hour two nations were made one' and even 'wild Ireland became tame on the sudden'. 'Upon Thursday it was treason to cry "God save King James, King of England!" and upon Friday high treason not to cry so.' And the third and last wonder is 'a most dreadful plague'.[11]

Dekker expounds his themes with unremitting elaboration which nevertheless can bring us close to the realities of the sufferings created by the epidemic:

For he that durst in the dead hour of gloomy midnight have been so valiant as to have walked through the still and melancholy streets – what think you should have been his music? Surely the loud groans of raving sick men, the struggling pangs of souls departing; in every house grief striking up an alarum – servants crying out for [mourning over] masters, wives for husbands, parents for children, children for their mothers ... How often hath the amazed husband, waking, found the comfort of his bed lying breathless by his side, his children at the same instant gasping for life, and his servants mortally wounded at the heart by sickness![12]

There is a pungency in Dekker's style that can entertain even as it horrifies, as when he describes men who have fortified themselves against infection by carrying herbs as being 'muffled up and down with rue and wormwood stuffed into their ears and nostrils, looking like so many boars' heads stuck with branches of rosemary to be served in for brawn at Christmas'. When he is writing like this Dekker may remind us of that other great celebrant of London – and of Christmas – Charles Dickens.

Dekker followed up *The Wonderful Year* with the punningly titled *News from Gravesend*, published in 1604 but apparently composed late in the previous year, before the plague had died down. The lengthy prose dedication addressed to Nobody is more obscure to modern readers in the topicality of its references and the forced ingenuity of its style than *The Wonderful Year*, but the remainder of the pamphlet, written entirely in rhymed couplets, is more accessible and vivid in its human evocations of suffering:

> Whole households and whole streets are stricken,
> The sick do die, the sound do sicken,
> And 'Lord have mercy upon us' crying,
> Ere Mercy can come forth, they're dying.
> No music now is heard but bells,
> And all their tunes are sick men's knells,
> And every stroke the bell does toll,
> Up to heaven it winds a soul.[13]

By way of conclusion, in a section headed 'The Necessity of a Plague', Dekker offers cold comfort in the claim that 'A plague's the purge to cleanse the city':

> Who amongst millions can deny
> – In rough prose or smooth poesy –
> Of evils, 'tis the lighter brood,
> A dearth of people than of food!
>
> And who knows not our land ran o'er
> With people, and was only poor
> In having too too many living,
> And wanting living.[14]

Grieving survivors cannot have thanked Dekker for this – maybe it is as well that this pamphlet, too, was first published anonymously.

As the plague abated Dekker, along with his fellow dramatists Jonson and Middleton – but not Shakespeare – composed pageants for the King's delayed entry into the City, and, wrote Dekker in his

Magnificent Entertainment Given to King James, 'he that should have compared the empty and untrodden walks of London which were to be seen in that late mortally destroying deluge with the thronged streets now might have believed that upon this day began a new creation'.[15] Dekker was able to resume his playwriting career, both independently and collaboratively. Among the more notable plays with which he was involved before his long imprisonment of 1612 to 1619 are two lively collaborations with Thomas Middleton: the two-part *The Honest Whore*, a romantic and comic drama ostensibly set in Milan, and the London-based drama *The Roaring Girl*. Dekker's portrayal of women is strong, and both plays have achieved modern performances under distinguished auspices and with a feminist slant: Helen Mirren played Moll for the Royal Shakespeare Company in 1983, and *The Honest Whore* was abbreviated into a single play at the Bankside Globe in 1998.

The Roaring Girl, written probably in 1611, is based on a real-life London character, Mary Frith, also known as Moll Cutpurse, a woman who dressed as a man and pursued a flamboyant and criminal lifestyle. In the play she is presented as a kind of female Robin Hood figure, doing good to others through her knowledge of the seamy side of London life. Reputedly the first woman to smoke tobacco, she admitted in a court statement of 1612 that she had regularly

resorted to alehouses, taverns, tobacco shops and also to playhouses there to see plays and . . . being at a play about three quarters of a year since at the Fortune in man's apparel and in her boots and with a sword by her side, she told the company there present that she thought many of them were of opinion that she was a man, but if any of them would come to her lodging they should find that she is a woman.[16]

Moll herself actually appeared on the stage at the Fortune, though not in a play: she 'sat there upon the stage in the public view of all the people there present in man's apparel and played upon her lute and sang a song'. It is natural to suppose that this was in association with a performance of Dekker and Middleton's play, in which she would have been personated by a boy actor.

In one of the more remarkable speeches in *The Roaring Girl* the room of a house that characters of the play enter is praised in terms of the Fortune theatre itself, as if the audience were invited to see themselves and their surroundings reflected through the eyes of the character:

> SIR ALEXANDER Nay, when you look into my galleries –
> How bravely they are trimmed up – you all shall swear
> You're highly pleased to see what's set down there:
> Stories of men and women, mixed together
> Fair ones with foul, like sunshine in wet weather –
> Within one square a thousand heads are laid
> So close that all of heads the room seems made;
> As many faces there, filled with blithe looks,
> Show like the promising titles of new books
> Writ merrily, the readers being their own eyes,
> Which seem to move and to give plaudities;
> And here and there, whilst with obsequious ears
> Thronged heaps do listen, a cutpurse thrusts and leers
> With hawk's eyes for his prey – I need not show him:
> By a hanging villainous look yourselves may know him,
> The face is drawn so rarely.
>
> (1.1.14–29)

(The words 'hanging villainous look' recall the description by Shakespeare's Falstaff, speaking in the person of King Henry, of the Prince: 'That thou art my son I have partly thy mother's word, partly my own opinion, but chiefly a villainous trick of thine eye, and a foolish hanging of thy nether lip, that doth warrant me'; *1 Henry IV*, 2.5.406–9).

In that passage Dekker is writing obliquely about a London theatre of his time. He wrote more directly, if satirically, about playgoing in the most entertaining of his prose pamphlets, *The Gull's Hornbook*, of 1609. A gull is a fashionable and foolish man-about-town – in *Twelfth Night*, Sir Toby Belch insults Sir Andrew Aguecheek by calling him 'an ass-head, and a coxcomb, and a knave; a thin-faced knave, a gull' (5.1.203–4) – and a hornbook is a sheet of paper printed with the alphabet and other elementary texts and mounted on a horn frame as a teaching aid for infants. In his Dedication, Dekker explains why he has written a hornbook for gulls: 'I know that most of you, O admirable gulls, can neither write nor read. A horn-book have

I invented because I would have you well schooled.' Each chapter advises the gull on how to behave in matters of greater and lesser importance: 'The praise of sleep and of going naked'; 'How a gallant should warm himself by the fire; how attire himself; . . . the praise of long hair'; 'How a gallant should behave himself in a tavern'; and so on. The objects of Dekker's satire, which looks back to Nashe and forward to Jonathan Swift, are entertainingly revealing about London society.

Dekker's chapter called 'How a gallant should behave himself in a playhouse' is full of vivid and revealing details about theatre practice.[17] This is, it would seem, a composite picture, drawing material both from the public and the private playhouses. Dekker's satirical purposes naturally lead him to exaggeration and caricature, but making all allowances for that, it is possible to reconstruct the way a gallant may have conducted himself on a visit to a theatre. We read of 'the gatherers' – money collectors – 'of the public or private playhouse', who 'stand to receive the afternoon's rent', and of the rushes strewn on the stage 'where the comedy is to dance'. It will be wise of the gallant to arrive by water and to pay three times the normal fare so that the boatmen will praise him even at times when he is not in need of their services. He is advised not to present himself 'on the stage, especially at a new play, until the quaking Prologue hath by rubbing got colour into his cheeks and is ready to give the trumpets their cue that he's upon point to enter'. But if he arrives early, he may 'fall to cards'. Otherwise, as though he 'were one of the properties' or had 'dropped out of the hangings', it is time for him 'to creep from behind the arras' – the curtain at the back of the stage – with his '"three-footed stool" in one hand and a teston [sixpenny piece] mounted between a forefinger and a thumb in the other'. (The very way he holds his coin speaks of affectation.) By advancing 'himself up to the throne of the stage' he may 'with small cost purchase the dear acquaintance of the boys' and reveal 'the best and most essential parts of a gallant – good clothes, a proportionable leg, white hand, the Persian lock [a lovelock], and a tolerable beard'. He is better off there than in the lords' room, which is now 'but the stage's suburbs', 'contemptibly thrust into the rear', where 'much new satin' is 'damned by being smothered to death in darkness'. By sitting on the stage he 'may lawfully presume to be a girder [mocker] and stand at the helm to steer the passage of scenes' – even if in doing so he obtains 'the title of an insolent overweening coxcomb'. And he may learn 'what particular part any of the infants present'. Even if 'the scarecrows in the yard' hoot, hiss or spit at him, he should endure it all and 'laugh at the silly animals'. But if they go so far as to cry, 'with a full throat', 'Away with the fool!', he would be 'worse than a madman' to put up with it. When the play has begun, he will win the highest commendation if he laughs aloud in the most serious part of a tragedy; then 'all the eyes in the galleries will leave walking after the players and only follow' him. If the dramatist has satirized him or flirted with his mistress, the gallant may take his revenge by standing up in the middle of the play 'with a screwed and discontented face', greeting all his friends who are on the stage with him, and persuading as many of them as may be to depart with him. But if he stays, he may choose to 'take up a rush and tickle the earnest ears' of his fellow gallants, 'to make other fools fall a-laughing; mew at passionate speeches, blare at merry, find fault with the music, whew at the children's action, whistle at the songs', and generally make a nuisance of himself. And when all is done, he should feed his lean wit by hoarding up 'the finest play-scraps' before moving from playhouse to tavern.

Dekker's long period of imprisonment for debt left him little opportunity to write anything other than letters begging for help – some of them to the wealthy ex-actor Edward Alleyn – though in 1616 six chapters about prison life were added to his frequently revised pamphlet *Lantern and Candlelight*, first printed in 1608. In this book he writes poignantly of his experiences: 'Remember, O cruel man, the prisoner pines in a gaol, his wife at home, his children beg, servants starve; his goods are seized on, reputation ruined, his name forgotten, health shaken, his wits distracted, his conversation blasted, his life miserable, his death contemptible.'[18] Also in 1616, Mary, his first wife, died and was buried in Clerkenwell. They had three daughters.

After his release from prison Dekker's career dwindled, but he continued to collaborate with, especially, John Ford. With Ford he worked on one of the more remarkable lost plays of the period, which drew raw materials from daily life around them in London. Its title was *Keep the Widow Waking*, and almost everything we know about it comes from legal documents relating to court cases of the 1620s which lay gathering dust until they were brought to light and studied in a book published in 1936.[19] As often, written testimony and, above all, verbatim transcripts of evidence given orally in court bring us closer than anything else to the actual speech of men and women of the time. If the play but not the legal documents had survived we should have been likely to assume that its events were fictional. As it is, we know that it portrayed truths that are stranger than many fictions. It combined two stories linked only, it would seem, by the fact that its two central characters were up for trial on the same day.

On 3 September 1624 Tobias Audley was prosecuted at the Old Bailey for felony, and Nathaniel Tindall for murder. The widow in the case was one Anne Elsdon, a 62-year-old woman of means who had the misfortune to attract the attentions of Tobias Audley 'of Wood Street in your City of London, a keeper of a tobacco shop and a most notorious lewd person and of no worth of [or?] credit'. He was about 25 years old. Audley paid court to the gullible widow, and on the evening of 21 July 1624 they met together in a private room in the Greyhound Tavern on Fleet Street with, among others, a prostitute, her madam and two unscrupulous clergymen. Audley had promised substantial rewards to his cronies for helping him to win the widow and her wealth, by fair means or by foul. They plied her with drink, and she spent the next four days in a state of alcoholic stupor. A witness admitted 'with weeping tears' that Anne 'was very sick and senseless and yet the defendants did pour down such vials of hot waters [spirits] down her throat that she thought was able to kill a horse'. Audley made no attempt to conceal his mercenary motives, saying, when one of the company expressed a fear that Anne would die, 'Let her be hanged, I'll have her goods and let them take her lands'. She was put through a marriage ceremony while too stupefied to know what was happening to her. A male witness, going to congratulate her, 'found her sitting in a chair, leaning her body all on one side, and drivelling'. 'Speaking somewhat loud unto her, and shaking her, and bidding God give her joy, she was unable to speak unto him again.' When Anne came to, her attempts to deny that she was married were met with insults. The prostitute suggested to Audley that he should 'make much of her, and so stop her exclamations', but he replied 'that he had as lief go to bed to an old sow'. She was soon dead drunk again. Revelries continued at great expense, Audley looted his unwitting bride's house, and Anne was heard 'crying out ... "I will go home, I will go home" ... making great moan that she was detained there against her will, diverse persons ... telling her that she should not go'. After a few days, Audley, alarmed by the efforts of Anne's daughter and son-in-law to rescue her, abandoned her, and she lay 'in a manner speechless' for nine or ten days. Violence ensued, Audley was prosecuted and jailed on more than one charge, and the cases dragged on until well after Anne died, on 24 March 1626.

In the meantime both a play and a ballad which summarizes and advertises it, with the refrain 'keep the widow waking', had entertained fellow Londoners. The two-part ballad, in seventeen stanzas, ends:

> Thus sometimes that haps in an hour
>   That comes not in seven year,
> Therefore let young men that are poor
>   Come take example here,
> And you who fain would hear the full
>   Discourse of this match-making,
> The play will teach you at the Bull
>   To keep the widow waking.

Heartlessly, the ballad was sung repeatedly under Anne Elsdon's window.

At the time of the trial the play dramatizing the terrible happenings for which Audley and Tindall were prosecuted had already been set forth on the stage of the Red Bull in Clerkenwell, which had a particular reputation as a playhouse that catered for the lower end of the market. Dekker was one of the play's four authors – the others were John Webster, author already of two great tragedies, *The White Devil* and *The Duchess of Malfi*, the young John Ford, who would go on to write some of the finest tragedies of the reign of King Charles I, and William Rowley, best remembered for his collaboration with Thomas Middleton on *The Changeling*. Dekker refers to the play in a legal statement as *The Late Murder in Whitechapel; or, Keep the Widow Waking*. The play entwined Anne Elsdon's story with that of the unhappy young Nathaniel Tindall's murder of his mother by stabbing her with a knife in the throat and the left breast, which provoked two ballads, one entitled 'The Penitent Son's Tears for his Murdered Mother', the other 'A Most Bloody Unnatural and Unmatchable Murder Committed in Whitechapel by Nathaniel Tindall upon his own Mother'. Tindall confessed to the crime, and was sentenced to be 'hanged near the house where he committed the murder'.

Astonishingly, it was alleged in the court of Star Chamber that Audley and his confederates had compounded their offences by inciting Dekker, Rowley and others to 'make, devise, and contrive one scandalous interlude or play most tauntingly naming the same interlude or play *Keep the Widow Waking*, thereby setting forth and intimating how long . . . Anne Elsdon was kept waking and the manner of . . . Anne Elsdon's distemperature with wine and hot waters and the loss of her estate . . . to the great infamy and scandal of . . . Anne Elsdon'. Dekker gave written evidence testifying that he 'did often see the . . . play or part thereof acted but how often he cannot depose'. Presumably he felt a professional duty to be present in the playhouse where the play he had helped to write was being performed. We do not know exactly how work on this play was divided among its collaborators, but Dekker reveals that he wrote 'two sheets [eight pages] of paper containing the first act' – which was completed within a month – 'and a speech in the last scene of the last act of the boy who had killed his mother' – probably this was Nathaniel's death speech at the point of execution. Dekker's composition of the first act suggests that he laid down the lines of the plot that his collaborators would develop. Shakespeare, in his collaborations with Middleton and Fletcher, seems to have worked in the same way.

Dekker was also able to continue his lifelong celebration of the City of London in pageants and in the annual entertainments offered to the incoming Lord Mayor. Fees for this kind of work could be high: in 1629 the Ironmongers' Company paid him £180 for writing *London's Tempe, or, The Field of Happiness*, as the inaugural pageant for the Lord Mayoralty of Sir James Campbell, an immensely wealthy merchant. (The title was intended as wordplay on the mayor-elect's name of 'Campe-bell or *Le Beau Champe*, or fair and glorious field'.) But mortality was catching up with him. Dedicating his play *Match*

Me in London – which in spite of its title is set in Spain – to the playwright and courtier Lodowick Carlell in 1631 he wrote: 'I have been a priest in Apollo's temple many years, my voice is decaying with my age, yet yours being clear and above mine' – Carlell was around 30 at this time – 'shall much honour me if you but listen to my old tunes.'[20] And he could not keep out of debt. After he died and was buried in Clerkenwell in August of the following year, his widow Elizabeth (he had married again) renounced administration of his estate, indicating that he had nothing to leave to posterity except his writings.

5

Ben Jonson

8. Ben Jonson. This fine oil painting of Jonson was commissioned, probably by George Villiers, 1st Duke of Buckingham, from the Flemish artist Abraham van Blyenberch in or around 1617, the year after Jonson published his Works.

Ben Jonson was the most aggressively self-opinionated, conceited, quarrelsome, vociferous and self-advertising literary and theatrical figure of his time. He was also one of its most powerful satirists, a lyric poet of genius, a playwright of great though uneven achievement, the finest of all creators of court masques, an autodidact who turned himself from a bricklayer's apprentice into a considerable classical scholar, and perhaps the most powerful advocate in his time of the value to society of the artist as critic. His career touched Shakespeare's at various points, posthumously as well as during their lifetimes. He was at different times both a friend and a rival to Shakespeare, appreciative of his personal and professional qualities, ready to find fault with his style, his stagecraft and his taste, but ready also to praise his artistry, to absorb his influence, and to promote his reputation.

There are resemblances in their early lives. Jonson, born in 1572, was eight years younger than Shakespeare and, like him, of relatively humble birth. Some of what we know of him derives from conversations he had with William Drummond, laird of Hawthornden, a Scottish poet and landowner, in whose bachelor household close to Edinburgh Jonson stayed for two weeks while on a lengthy walking tour in 1618. They talked freely – or at least, Jonson talked and Drummond listened – no doubt late into the night and, often, bibulously, of many things – poetry and poets, the English literary scene, their views of Queen Elizabeth and of King James, their own earlier lives, sex and drink. Drummond, hypnotized by his visitor's forceful personality, took notes, recording only Jonson's side of their conversations and grouping them by topics, so the version that survives must have been written after the visit was over.[1]

What little is known of Jonson's origins and early life derives mainly, though not entirely, from these conversations. His father, a northerner and a Protestant, lost all his estate and was imprisoned as a result of religious persecution during the reign of the Catholic Mary Tudor, after which he became a minister, dying a month before Jonson was born, on 11 June 1572. Ben's mother, who lived in Hartshorn Lane outside the City of London walls and close to the royal city of Westminster, went on to marry a bricklayer who became Master of the Tilers' and Bricklayers' Company. Though neither Shakespeare nor Jonson attended university, both (like Marlowe) were fortunate in their education. Shakespeare received a good literary training at the Stratford grammar school, but Jonson was of a more scholarly bent. When he was 7 years old a benefactor, recognizing his talent, secured him a place as a day-boy at Westminster School, one of the finest and most fashionable in the country. He was taught by the great scholar William Camden, under whom Jonson laid the foundations of a classical and grammatical education in which he was to take inordinate though justified pride, and on which he was to build for the rest of his life. He left school when he was around 16 – as Shakespeare had probably done – without taking a scholarship to university, but in 1619 the University of Oxford, at the instigation of its Chancellor, Jonson's patron William Herbert, 3rd Earl of Pembroke, awarded him an honorary MA, noting that he was 'happily versed in all humane literature'.

As a young man, Jonson took time to find his feet. Disliking his apprenticeship to his stepfather's trade, he joined the English army in the Netherlands and, to his great satisfaction, killed a man in single combat, taking 'opima spolia' from him – that is, stripping him of armour and weapons. By his own account Jonson, like Shakespeare, who married at the age of 18, was sexually active early in life – but more promiscuously than we have any reason to believe of Shakespeare. He boasted to Drummond that in youth he was 'given to venery', and that he 'thought the use of a maid nothing in comparison to the wantonness of a wife'. Elaborating upon his exploits, he claimed that one deviant husband 'made his own wife to court him', and 'one day finding them by chance, was passingly delighted with it'. Frustratingly, one woman 'showed him all that he wished except the last act, which she would never agree unto'. He was not above playing tricks on the women he seduced. In an episode that might have come from one of his own plays he, with the connivance of a friend, 'cozened a lady with whom he had made an appointment to meet an old astrologer in the suburbs, which she kept; and it was himself disguised in a long gown and a white beard at the light of a dim-burning candle, up in a little cabinet reached unto by a ladder'.

When Jonson was in his early twenties, in 1594, he married Anne Lewis – 'who was a shrew yet honest' – and their first son, Ben, was born in 1596. The marriage had periods of instability: Ben and Anne lived apart for some years in the early part of the seventeenth century, but came together again around 1605. Like Shakespeare's only son Hamnet, who was born the year before little Ben and lived only to the age of 11, the boy had a tragically short life. During the terrible plague year of 1603, Jonson left his family in London to stay in the Huntingdonshire home of Robert Cotton, also a former pupil of Camden with whom the latter had founded the Society of Antiquaries around 1584. Cotton owned a splendid library which was a great resource for Jonson throughout his life. While there, he told Drummond, he saw his 7-year-old son Ben 'in a vision', as if grown to manhood, 'with the mark of a bloody cross on his forehead ... at which, amazed, he prayed unto God'. On the following morning Camden, who also was staying in the house, reassured him that it was 'but an apprehension of his fantasy', but soon afterwards news arrived from his wife that the boy had died of plague. Jonson's epitaph, 'On my First Son', is among his most touchingly personal writings:

> Farewell, thou child of my right hand, and joy;
> My sin was too much hope of thee, loved boy.
> Seven years thou wert lent to me, and I thee pay,
> Exacted by thy fate, on the just day.
> O, could I lose all father now! For why
> Will man lament the state he should envy?
> To have so soon 'scaped world's and flesh's rage,
> And, if no other misery, yet age?
> Rest in soft peace, and, asked, say 'here doth lie
> Ben Jonson his best piece of poetry,
> For whose sake, henceforth, all his vows be such
> As what he loves may never like too much.'[2]

Jonson's second son, Joseph, was baptized in the last month of the sixteenth century, and his daughter, Mary, arrived a year or so later. She died after a few months, and probably Joseph, like his elder brother, was a victim of the plague of 1603. A second Ben, born early in 1608, lived only four and a half years, and there is reason to believe that Jonson had several other children, some of them illegitimate.

Some of what we know about Jonson comes obliquely, through satirical references in plays by his contemporaries. It is no doubt coloured by art, and sometimes by malice, but may convey truth all the same. Like Shakespeare before him, he appears to have left the marital home as a young man to join a company of players. Thomas Dekker, in his play *Satiromastix*, published in 1602, caricatures him under the name of Horace, implying that he joined a company of strolling players and played the role of Hieronimo in Kyd's *The Spanish Tragedy*: 'Thou hast forgot how thou ambledest in a leather pilch [apron] by a play wagon in the highway, and took'st mad Hieronimo's part.' This was probably with the 2nd Earl of Pembroke's Men, who were on tour with Kyd's play in 1595–6. (Jonson's generous patron, the 3rd Earl of Pembroke, sent him £20 every New Year's Day to buy books.)

Before long, instead of acting Jonson was writing plays; the first appears to have been *The Case is Altered*, written in the early part of 1597 (though possibly later revised). This comedy, based, like Shakespeare's *The Comedy of Errors*, on two plays by the Roman dramatist Plautus (neither of which had been translated into English at the time), contains, more characteristically of Jonson's later work, what has been described as 'the most grossly scatological scene in all of Elizabethan drama',[3] in which an old miser named Jaques (punning on 'jakes', a privy) enters 'with his gold and a scuttle full of horse dung'. Hiding the gold under the dung he crawls around asking 'who will suppose that such a precious nest / Is crowned with such a dunghill excrement?' (3.5.14–15). Like both Marlowe's Barabas and Shakespeare's Shylock, Jaques values his gold no less than his daughter. *The Case is Altered* is full of echoes (or pre-echoes) of Shakespeare, yet its tone is wholly individual – the prose scenes especially crackle with intelligence, the writing is brilliantly theatrical, the plot shifts and turns as the case – the circumstances in which the characters find themselves – alters and alters again in a series of cleverly devised situations (the title phrase constantly recurs as a refrain to the action), and the copiousness and superabundant vitality of language challenge the audience's and the actors' responses in a manner that must command respect for both. Yet Jonson, presumably regarding it as unworthy, chose to exclude it from the 1616 edition (see below) of his works, and it has scarcely ever been performed since his time.

In the summer of the same year, 1597, Jonson completed a play, now lost, started by Thomas Nashe and called *The Isle of Dogs*. It was probably a satire on the court; the Isle of Dogs was a narrow spit of land across the river from Greenwich, where the Queen held court for most of 1597. Its performance caused a major scandal; the authorities described it as 'a lewd play ... containing very seditious and slanderous matter'.[4] Nashe escaped punishment by fleeing to Yarmouth, apparently in terror at the mere thought of the possible consequences of what he had set on foot, but Jonson, along with some of the actors, was imprisoned in the Marshalsea. If the demands of the Privy Council had been effectively carried through, the consequences for the history of the English theatre could have been drastic. They ordered not only that no plays should be performed in London during that summer, but that 'those playhouses that are erected and built only for such purposes shall be plucked down – namely the Curtain and the Theatre near to Shoreditch or any other within that county'.[5] The councillors appear, however, not really to have meant what they said, or to have lacked the power to enforce it; the playhouses survived, and playing resumed after a short hiatus. Jonson spent six weeks in prison, along with two of the actors, one of whom was Gabriel Spencer; within a matter of months Jonson's fiery temperament was to get him into hot water again when Spencer challenged him to a duel. The cause of their enmity is unknown. Jonson was to tell Drummond that Spencer had hurt him in the arm with a sword ten inches longer than his; Jonson killed him, 'for the which he was imprisoned, and almost at the gallows'. Henslowe wrote scornfully to Edward Alleyn, then on a visit to Brill in Sussex: 'I have lost one of my company, which hurteth me greatly; that is Gabriel, for he is slain in Hogsdon Fields by the hands of Benjamin Jonson, bricklayer; therefore I would fain have a little of your counsel if I could.'[6] Jonson claimed benefit of clergy, a loophole in the law which enabled a murderer to escape hanging for a first offence by showing that he could read; nevertheless his goods were confiscated, and he was branded on the thumb with the letter T, standing for Tyburn, the place of execution where his life would end if he offended again. While he was awaiting trial a priestly inmate converted him to Roman Catholicism, and, by his own account, he remained in this religion for the next twelve years. This resulted in charges of recusancy against both him and his wife. When he returned to the Protestant fold he celebrated, 'in token of true reconciliation', by quaffing a full cup of communion wine – as, in *The Taming of the Shrew*, Petruccio does at his own wedding.[7]

In the year of Gabriel Spencer's death the Lord Chamberlain's Men were playing Jonson's comedy *Every Man in His Humour* at the Curtain playhouse. Its title, and its technique, responded to George Chapman's popular *Comedy of Humours*, also known as *A Humorous Day's Mirth*, set in Paris, which the Lord Admiral's Men had put on at the Rose in the previous year.[8] At around this time Shakespeare was writing some of his greatest comedies – *The Merchant of Venice*, *Much Ado About Nothing* and the Falstaff plays – but he was not above taking a leading role in Jonson's play; which one we can only guess. In 1709 Nicholas Rowe, in the first formal biography of Shake-speare, related an anecdote to the effect that the company was about to reject Jonson's play when, happily, Shakespeare 'cast his eye upon it, and found something so well in it as to engage him first to read it through, and afterwards to recommend Mr Jonson and his writings to the public. After this they were professed friends, though I don't know whether the other ever made him an equal return of gentleness and sincerity.'[9] And indeed it does not seem gentle or grateful of Jonson to have added to the revised edition of the play printed in 1616 a Prologue in which he declared his superiority to dramatic conventions that Shakespeare practised. Far more of a theorist than Shakespeare, he scorns the idea that he might

> make a child now swaddled to proceed
> Man, and then shoot up in one beard, and weed
> Past threescore years

(as, Jonson may have thought, Shakespeare had in *Pericles*)

> or, with three rusty swords
> And help of some few foot and half-foot words,
> Fight over York and Lancaster's long jars,
> And in the tiring-house bring wounds to scars –

as in Shakespeare's Henry VI plays. Jonson declares himself to be above all that:

> He rather prays you will be pleas'd to see
> One such today as other plays should be:
> Where neither Chorus wafts you o'er the seas –

as in *Henry V*, and *Pericles*,

> Nor creaking throne comes down, the boys to please

as in *Cymbeline* . . .

> Nor nimble squib is seen to make afear'd
> The gentlewomen, nor roll'd bullet heard
> To say, it thunders, nor tempestuous drum
> Rumbles, to tell you when the storm doth come –

as in *King Lear* . . . No, what Jonson claims to offer is:

> deeds and language such as men do use,
> And persons such as Comedy would choose
> When she would show an image of the times,
> And sport with human follies, not with crimes.

And finally Jonson expresses the hope that under his influence the audience, who 'have so grac'd monsters' – like Caliban – 'may like men'.

Jonson's emphasis on 'the times' has not been entirely to the advantage of his posthumous reputation. The topical aspects of his satire are apt to inhibit understanding by later ages. And his fascination with the spoken language of his day and with technical jargon (such as that of alchemy, as we shall see later) can make for difficulties in reading and, to a lesser extent, in performance.

Most of Jonson's plays are comedies, often with topical settings and relevance. He originally set *Every Man in His Humour* in Italy, like most of Shakespeare's comedies of the 1590s, but his revision, probably made around 1612 as he was preparing his 1616 edition, transfers the action to London and gives the characters English instead of Italian names. This revision, far more deeply rooted in Elizabethan life than any play by Shakespeare, was nevertheless popular in a version prepared by the eighteenth-century actor David Garrick. Later, Charles Dickens enjoyed directing the play and taking the role of Bobadil in amateur performances, perhaps because the play is almost Dickensian in its vivid use of social detail. Judiciously cut, it has had successful later revivals including one by the Royal Shakespeare Company in 1986. At least in its printed form of 1601, it includes allusions to Shakespeare's Justice Silence and to Falstaff, and, in the words 'Not without mustard', what may be a jibe at Shakespeare's recently acquired motto, 'Non sans droit'.

Jonson was the victim of his own theorizing. His third comedy, *Every Man Out of His Humour* (1599), opens with a passage that forms a kind of critical manifesto. After the trumpets summoning playgoers have sounded for the second time, Asper – the name means 'sharp' – enters as presenter with Cordatus, described as 'the author's friend', and Mitis. Asper, inveighing against the evils of the age, declares his intention to 'strip the ragged follies of the time / Naked, as at their birth'. His integrity is not to be impugned:

> I fear no strumpet's drugs, nor ruffian's stab,
> Should I detect their hateful luxuries,
> No broker's usurer's or lawyer's gripe
> Were I disposed to say they're all corrupt.

His companions implore him to moderate his passion, but he cannot restrain himself. Pretending that he 'not observed this throngèd round till now', he welcomes the audience and declares that he has no wish to avoid their criticism. Mitis warns him that 'this humour will come ill to some – / You will be thought to be too peremptory', and this leads neatly in to a discussion of the word 'humour'. Jonson does this not simply to formulate his own theory of comedy. The word 'humour' was in the air as a fashionable term of physiological-psychological jargon. Like many such words, then as now, it could be loosely applied; Asper says he will 'give these ignorant well-spoken days / Some taste of their abuse of this word "humour"', and obliges at some length in a manner which may well have induced yawns in some of the groundlings. Essentially he distinguishes between on the one hand superficial affectations, such as eccentricities of dress, and on the other hand an imbalance of natural qualities, as

> when some one peculiar quality
> Doth so possess a man that it doth draw
> All his affects, his spirits, and his powers
> In their confluctions all to run one way:
> This may be truly said to be a humour.

The purpose of his play will be to reveal the follies of those who glorify their affectations with the name of humours. After much more theorizing the trumpets are at last allowed to sound for the third time, presumably permitting the entry of latecomers who might be relieved if they had known what they had missed, and the play proper starts.

Although Jonson's theorizing has been invaluable to dramatic historians – would that we had anything like it from Shakespeare, whose views can be gleaned only obliquely, from passages such as Hamlet's advice to the players – it was unwise of him to wash so much clean linen in public. *Every Man Out of His Humour* has had little if any theatrical appeal for later ages.[10]

Dramatic activity in Shakespeare's time was by no means confined to professionals, and plays written and acted by amateurs can shed light on the theatrical scene. An uneasy relationship between Jonson and Shakespeare comes to the fore in the first part of *The Return from Parnassus*, the second of three fascinating plays written and performed by undergraduates of St John's College, Cambridge between 1598 and 1602. The writers clearly took a keen interest in contemporary literature and, as we have seen, theatre. In this play a foolish fellow, Gullio, expresses adoration of 'Sweet Master Shakespeare' and swears that he will 'have his picture in my study at the court' and that 'to honour him' he 'will lay his *Venus and Adonis*' under his pillow (lines 1032–3, 1202–3).

Then, as now, many students aspired to careers in the theatre. In the episode in the second part of *The Return from Parnassus* in which Burbage and Kemp audition recent undergraduates, Kemp, ever the professional, fears that as writers for the popular theatre the students will be too keen to show off their classical education: they 'smell too much of that writer Ovid, and that writer *Metamorphoses*, and talk too much of "Proserpina" and "Jupiter"'. They are not a patch on Shakespeare and Jonson: 'Why, here's our fellow Shakespeare puts them all down, ay, and Ben Jonson too. O, that Ben Jonson is a pestilent fellow: he brought up Horace giving the poets a pill, but our fellow Shakespeare hath given him a purge that made him bewray his credit' (lines 1767–73). This alludes obliquely to an episode known to later ages as the War of the Theatres, centring on plays written from 1599 to 1602 by Jonson (*Every Man Out of His Humour*), John Marston (*Histriomastix*, *Jack Drum's Entertainment* and *What You Will*) and Dekker together with Marston (*Satiromastix*), in which they girded satirically at each other. Much of the satire has lost its edge, and it is not easy to be sure which characters in the plays would have been understood to satirize living people, but the cruel imitation in *Satiromastix* of Jonson's constipated efforts to compose a wedding ode must sound chords in anyone who has tried to write rhyming verse:

O me, thy priest inspire!
For I to thee and thine immortal name,
In – in – in golden tunes . . .
For I to thee and thine immortal name –
In – sacred raptures flowing – flowing – – swimming, swimming:
In sacred raptures swimming,
Immortal name – game, dame, tame – lame, lame, lame –
Pox ha't, shame, proclaim, – O –
In sacred raptures flowing, will proclaim, not:
O me thy priest inspire!
For I to thee and thine immortal name
In flowing numbers filled with sprite and flame –
Good! Good! – in flowing numbers filled with sprite and flame.

(1.2.8–20)

The quarrel lying behind the War of the Theatres appears to have been started by Marston, who ridicules Jonson in *What You Will*. Jonson retaliated in *Poetaster*, ostensibly set in ancient Rome, in which he depicts himself as Horace, giving a pill to Crispinus, representing Marston, causing him to vomit into a basin all the hard words he had used in his satires. This is the 'pill' that Jonson gave 'the poets'; we do not know for certain what is the 'purge' Shakespeare gave Jonson that made him 'bewray his credit', but possibly Jonson was thought to be satirized in the bragging and doltish figure of Ajax in Shakespeare's *Troilus and Cressida*, written probably in 1602.

Jonson's ambitions as a classicist seem to be reflected in the amount of interest he shows in Shakespeare's *Julius Caesar*, of 1599. In the third act of *Every Man Out of His Humour*, which must have appeared very soon after Shakespeare's play, Clove says 'reason long since is fled to animals, you know' (3.4.33), clearly echoing Mark Antony's words over Caesar's corpse: 'O judgement, thou art fled to brutish beasts, / And men have lost their reason!' (*Julius Caesar*, 3.2.105–6), and in the last act Caesar's 'Et tu Brute?' – not, of course, original to Shakespeare – is quoted (5.6.79). But being Jonson, he was nothing if not critical, and Shakespeare appears to have accepted at least one of his criticisms. In the notebooks published posthumously in 1640 as *Timber, or Discoveries made upon men and matter, as they have flowed out of his daily readings, or had their reflux to his peculiar notion of the times*, Jonson wrote: 'Many times he fell into those things could not escape laughter, as when he said in the person of Caesar, one speaking to him, "Caesar, thou never didst wrong", he replied "Caesar never did wrong without just cause", and such like, which were ridiculous.' This may have been true of the play as first acted, but in the published text of 1623 the illogicality of the notion that doing wrong could be justifiable is ironed out: Caesar says 'Caesar doth not wrong, nor without cause / Will he be satisfied' (3.1.47–8, where, however, the Oxford edition reverts to the original as reported by Jonson).

However Jonson may have carped about details of the text, it may have been in emulation of *Julius Caesar* that he turned, in 1603, to write his first surviving classical tragedy, *Sejanus, His Fall*. Indeed there is even a sense in which Jonson's play, which explicitly evokes memories of Brutus and Cassius, could be regarded as a distant sequel to Shakespeare's. It may be no accident, too, that Shakespeare's most heavily classical play, *Troilus and Cressida*, preceded this by only one year. But *Sejanus* far outgoes both *Julius Caesar* and *Troilus and Cressida* in the thoroughness and the ostentation of its classicism, at least in the form in which it was printed in 1605. The tragedy portrays events of Roman history with great moral earnestness. In his youth the low-born central character, Sejanus, had 'prostituted his abused body / To that great gourmand, fat Apicius, / And was the noted pathic [passive homosexual partner] of the time' (1.1.214–16). Now a sycophantic follower of the decadent Emperor Tiberius, he seeks to undermine the Emperor's power by encouraging him to indulge his 'unnatural pleasures' on the Isle of Capri where he 'hath his slaughter-house', 'doth study murder as an art', and 'hath his boys and beauteous girls ta'en up / Out of our noblest houses, the best formed, / Best nurtured, and most modest; what's their good / Serves to provoke his bad' (4.5.130–37). But Sejanus overreaches himself and, in a grand climax, a ceremony held in the Senate apparently designed to do him unprecedented honour turns into a public indictment engineered by Tiberius, as a result of which Sejanus is 'accused, condemned, and torn in pieces by the rage of the people', as Jonson writes in the Argument to the play. In keeping with the tenets of classical tragedy the horrific deaths of Sejanus and his son and daughter are narrated rather than shown – which in any case would scarcely have been possible.

The text of the play as acted is lost. But in the printed version of 1605 Jonson presents it with all the apparatus of a work of scholarly literature – just the sort of thing that is lacking from any early edition of a Shakespeare play. This ostentatious piece of one-upmanship is clearly designed to show Jonson's university-educated colleagues that the grammar school boy was no whit inferior to them in the range and depth of his reading. The Epistle to the Readers admits that this 'is not the same with that which was acted on the public stage, wherein a second pen had good share'. If, as seems likely, this is true, the identity of the collaborator can only be guessed at. With what sounds suspiciously like ironically mock modesty, Jonson says he has replaced his collaborator's contributions with 'weaker – and no doubt less pleasing' – matter of his own rather 'than to defraud so happy a genius of his right by my loathed usurpation'. The usual guess is that Chapman worked with Jonson on the original text. But Anne Barton, noting that 'Chapman never wrote for the King's Men, and has no known connection with them', intriguingly speculates that the company may have

felt sufficiently nervous about so intransigently learned a tragedy as to insist upon a certain amount of re-writing, extending to the provision of entire, substitute scenes, before putting the play into rehearsal. If they did, Shakespeare, who in any case was going to act in *Sejanus*, would seem a logical choice as someone who could alter the text, with Jonson's cooperation, for performance.[11]

If this is indeed what happened, Shakespeare's rewritings of *Sejanus* must be counted among his lost works; but there is no proof that they ever existed.

Jonson confesses that his play does not adhere strictly to the conventions of classical tragedy, while claiming nevertheless that it observes 'truth of argument, dignity of persons, gravity and height of elocution, fullness and frequency of sentence' – that is, a wealth of quotable remarks, or 'wise saws and modern instances', as Jaques calls them in Shakespeare's *As You Like It* (2.7.156). Most remarkably, Jonson refers to the fact that the printed text is surrounded by a multitude of notes referring the reader to the classical texts to which he is indebted. His principal source is Tacitus' *Annals*. As he puts it, with pedantic particularity and cryptic abbreviation, 'I have quoted the page, to name what editions I followed: *Tacit. Lips.* in 4°. *Antuerp. Edit. Dio. Folio. Hen. Step.* 92. For the rest, as *Sueton. Seneca.* etc, the chapter doth sufficiently direct . . .' (What all this means is that he has used Justus Lipsius's Antwerp edition of Tacitus' *Annals*, Dio Cassius' *Roman History* published by Henry Estienne in 1592, Gaius Suetonius' *Lives of the Caesars*, and the works of Seneca.) Modern editions tend to remove the notes, or relegate them to the back of the book, presupposing readers who will be more interested in the text as drama than as scholarly reconstruction.

Jonson's Epistle to the Readers is followed by seven commendatory poems, the first of them, 188 lines long, a typically cloudy effusion by Chapman. Another of the eulogists, surprisingly, is John Marston, with whom Jonson often crossed swords; and the final poem, a sonnet ascribed cryptically to 'Ev. B', berates the spectators in 'the Globe's fair ring, our world's best stage', who received the play with 'beastly rage, / Bent to confound thy grave and learned toil / That cost thee so much sweat and so much oil'. No doubt Jonson personally orchestrated this unusually elaborate chorus of commendation. A note added to the reprint of the play in Jonson's 1616 edition lists Shakespeare among the 'principal tragedians' of the first performance; it has been conjectured that he played the Emperor Tiberius, perhaps because of John Davies's remark that he had 'played some kingly parts in sport' (p. 29).

A modern reader may be astonished, not that the play failed with its early audience, but that Shakespeare and his fellow actors had the courage to offer it to them in the first place and that they felt sufficient loyalty to its young author to commit to memory lines whose weightiness may well have daunted them. Indeed it is a tribute to the players and to their confidence (even if ultimately misplaced) in their audience that they accepted the play for performance. At times they may have felt like echoing one of the characters, Arruntius, when he says: 'By Jove, I am not Oedipus enough / To understand this Sphinx' (3.1.64–5). Still, the fact that the play exists only in a rewritten form means that judgements on the stageworthiness of the original text can only be provisional. And it must be recorded that Gregory Doran's production for the Royal Shakespeare Company in 2005 was a resounding success – though admittedly it cut at least 800 lines (about as many as are lost in most productions of *Hamlet*).

At around 3,250 lines, Jonson's revised play is long, though not as long as some of Shakespeare's tragedies and a few other plays of the period. A deeply serious study of courtly corruption, *Sejanus* is full of extended speeches, many of them designed to direct the audience's moral judgement in choric fashion and written entirely in verse, except for the 'huge, long, worded letter' (5.10.312) indicting Sejanus which Tiberius sends from Capri. One of the longest speeches in the play (3.1.407–60) versifies a direct translation of a passage from Tacitus. In it Cordus defends himself for having praised Brutus and Cassius, 'slain / Seventy years since'. Shakespeare too had praised them, in *Julius Caesar*, written only a few years earlier. It is understandable that when William Poel produced the play in 1928 he had Cordus made up as Shakespeare; Jonson was the cynical commentator Arruntius.

This may all sound forbidding, but the dialogue displays Jonson's usual trenchant energy, and includes passages of scurrilous satire which he might have expected to exert popular appeal. Sejanus's questioning of a physician about the personal habits of court ladies would be at home in one of Jonson's London comedies:

> Why sir, I do not ask you of their urines,
> Whose smells most violet [used as a cure for constipation]
>   or whose siege [excrement] is best?
> Or who makes hardest face [faeces?] on the stool?
> Which lady sleeps with her own face a-nights?
> Which puts her teeth off, with her clothes, in court?
> Or which her hair? Which her complexion,
> And in which box she puts it?
>
>   (1.1.304–10)

The writing can rise above exposition and argument to heights of subtle irony, as in the passage at the end of the second act, after Sejanus has engineered the murder of Drusus Senior:

DRUSUS JUNIOR Hear you the rumour?

AGRIPPINA   What?

DRUSUS JUNIOR   Drusus is dying.

AGRIPPINA Dying?

NERO   That's strange!

AGRIPPINA   You were with him yesternight.

DRUSUS JUNIOR One met Eudemus the physician,
   Sent for but now, who thinks he cannot live.

SILIUS Thinks? If't be arrived at that, he knows,
   Or none.

AGRIPPINA That's quick! What should be his disease?

SILIUS Poison, poison.

AGRIPPINA   How, Silius!

NERO   What's that?

SILIUS Nay, nothing. There was – late – a certain blow
   Given o' the face.

NERO   Ay, to Sejanus?

SILIUS   True.

DRUSUS JUNIOR And what of that?

SILIUS   I am glad I gave it not.

                                   (2.4.52–61)

Like many other plays of its period, including Shakespeare's Roman
tragedies, *Sejanus* presupposes in its audience an interest in and knowledge of the events of Roman history, with which all those who had
attended a grammar school would have been familiar. Nevertheless,
its treatment of court politics was clearly capable of topical application
since Jonson told Drummond that he 'was called before the [Privy]
Council for his *Sejanus*'.[12] What precise allegations were made is not
known, but Sejanus is aware that writings about the past may make
oblique criticisms of the present:

> Then is there one Cremutius
> Cordus, a writing fellow they have got
> To gather notes of the precedent times
> And make them into annals; a most tart
> And bitter spirit, I hear, who under colour
> Of praising those, doth tax the present state,

Censures the men, the actions, leaves no trick,
No practice unexamined, parallels
The times, the governments; a professed champion
For the old liberty . . .

(2.2.165–74)

It is possible that Jonson designed the parade of learning in the side notes of the printed edition to draw attention away from the play's topical resonances by presenting it as a close dramatization of events of the past.[13]

Jonson was soon in trouble again over the comedy *Eastward Ho*, which he wrote in collaboration with two of those who had commended *Sejanus*, George Chapman and John Marston, and which was acted by the Children of the Queen's Revels at the Blackfriars in summer 1605. This delightful satirical comedy, performed with great success by the Royal Shakespeare Company in 2002, bears incidental witness to the contemporary popularity of *Hamlet*, first performed about five years previously, in the presence of a distracted footman of the same name whose entry '*in haste*' provokes the question ''Sfoot, Hamlet, are you mad? Whither run you now?' The tininess of his role is no doubt part of the joke. (It means that there is now a bit-part player who can justly claim to have acted Hamlet at Stratford.) It is interesting too that one of the more entertaining female characters has the same name as Hamlet's mother, Gertrude. For some unknown reason the authors failed to submit the play to the Lord Chamberlain (perhaps taking advantage of the fact that he was away from London for most of the summer), which was particularly unwise since the text includes both general mockery of the Scots and specific satire on King James's practice of raising funds by selling knighthoods: 'Farewell, farewell, we will not know you for shaming of you. I ken the man weel, he's one of my thirty pound-knights,' says a gentleman, adopting a Scottish accent for the purpose, of the debauched knight Sir Petronel Flash (4.1.177–8). Some gibes against the Scots were edited out of the printed text, but others got through. Whether or not Jonson was directly responsible for them, he had to accept a share of the blame when (as he told Drummond) a Scottish courtier, Sir James Murray, complained to the King that Jonson had written 'something against

the Scots' as a consequence of which he 'voluntarily imprisoned himself with Chapman and Marston, who had written it amongst them'.[14]
The three men were threatened with having their ears and noses slit,
but Jonson wrote distressed letters from prison appealing to, among
others, his patrons the Earl of Pembroke and the King's cousin Lord
D'Aubigny, and eventually he and his collaborators received a pardon
from the Lord Chamberlain. Always ready for a party, Jonson celebrated by giving a banquet for all his friends, including his former headmaster William Camden and the fledgling antiquarian John Selden.
Among the guests was his mother, whose action during the meal suggests that he inherited his strength of character from her: 'At the midst
of the feast his old mother drank to him, and showed him a paper which
she had, if the sentence had taken execution, to have mixed in the prison
among his drink, which was full of lusty strong poison. And that she
was no churl, she told she minded first to have drunk of it herself.'
Whether her son would have preferred death by poison administered
by his mother to the slitting of his ears and nose is not recorded.

Jonson's attitude to royalty is characteristically ambivalent, at once
high-minded and self-serving. Though he was willing to endorse satire
of the King, he cultivated an association with the court which was
profitable both financially and artistically. In this he differed conspicuously from Shakespeare. In 1603 Henry Chettle had mourned Queen
Elizabeth's death, in a work named *England's Mourning Garment*, in
the course of which he notes that neither Shakespeare, Chapman nor
Jonson has composed an elegy for her. Equally, Shakespeare is not
known to have made any public acknowledgement of James's
accession even though the King soon became patron of the acting
company to which he belonged, or of the death of the King's
immensely talented elder son, Henry Prince of Wales, at the tragically
early age of 17 in 1612. But Chettle implies that Jonson may have
kept silence about Elizabeth because he knew which side his bread
was buttered: 'His Muse another path desires to tread.'[15] Sure enough,
before long Jonson was energetically engaged in celebrating James's
accession to the throne, writing speeches for the royal entry into the
City (postponed because of plague) on 15 March 1604, as well as a
sycophantic panegyric to James on opening his first Parliament four
days later, and a series of flattering epigrams.

Still more significantly for the future, Jonson had already devised an entertainment for the Queen and Prince Henry, to be performed at Althorp on their journey from Scotland to London, a gesture which, as we shall see, preluded a quarter of a century and more of participation in entertainments devised for the courts of James and, after his death, Charles I.

For a while, however, Jonson was to continue to channel his most strongly creative energies into the series of comedies – *Eastward Ho* (1605), *Volpone* (1606), *The Alchemist* (1612) and *Bartholomew Fair* (1614) – for which he is best remembered. Except for Shakespeare's, no other comedies from the period have been so admired in later times; and Jonson's comedies of the first decade or so of the seventeenth century are even more different from the tragicomedies, such as *All's Well That Ends Well* and *Measure for Measure*, that Shakespeare was writing during this period than they are from Shakespeare's generally romantic comedies of the previous decade. Jonson's are harder edged, more topical, but more classical in origin and dramatic style, more obviously intellectual while also more robust and farcical, and far more satirical of the age. Jonson recognized Shakespeare's greatness, but clearly found his romances, with their defiance of classical concepts of decorum, difficult to take. Notoriously, he wrote (in 1629, when disillusioned with 'the loathèd stage' after the failure of his play *The New Inn*) of 'some mouldy tale / Like *Pericles*'.[16] It was 'mouldy' because out-of-date. Jonson, who took pride in his active engagement with current affairs, must have found Shakespeare hopelessly romantic in his obsession with the past and with shadowily distant landscapes.

For all his astonishing productivity, Jonson could be a laboured writer; he told Drummond that 'he wrote all' his verses 'first in prose, for so his master Camden had learned him',[17] and he appears to have toiled for a year on *Sejanus*; but he took pride in having written the first of the great comedies, *Volpone*, in five weeks, single-handed. It was given at the Globe early in 1606, with Richard Burbage, who was also playing Hamlet, Othello and Lear, in the cast, doubtless as Volpone. The play's plot is encapsulated in the Argument which Jonson casts as an acrostic:

V olpone, childless, rich, feigns sick, despairs,
O ffers his state to hopes of several heirs,
L ies languishing; his parasite receives
P resents of all, assures, deludes; then weaves
O ther cross-plots, which ope themselves, are told.
N ew tricks for safety are sought; they thrive; when, bold,
E ach tempts th' other again, and all are sold.

Jonson draws on his classical learning for the basic situation; Volpone is what the Romans called a captator, a legacy-hunter. But a thoroughly classical setting would have reduced his opportunities for topical satire, so he compromises by placing the action in contemporary Venice, which enables him to introduce English figures. Characteristically, the play is full of rogues to whom Jonson gives names from the bestiary – Volpone, the fox, his parasite Mosca, the house-fly, and the schemers Voltore, the vulture, Corbaccio, the raven, and Corvino, also like a raven. Volpone pretends to be mortally sick in the hope of extracting wealth from his supposed friends on the expectation of legacies; the legacy-hunters deceive each other; and the go-between, Mosca, turns out to be deceptive of both his master and those whose interests he pretends to serve. The play is heavy with irony. Practically everyone in it is acting a part, consciously and with intent to deceive. Volpone acts to his 'suitors'; they act to him. Mosca – the parasite who, like an actor, gains his living by abnegating personality – acts a different part both to the suitors and to Volpone. Like Robin Goodfellow in *A Midsummer Night's Dream*, he boasts of his shape-changing talents, likening himself to a

> fine, elegant rascal, that can rise
> And stoop (almost together) like an arrow;
> Shoot through the air, as nimbly as a star;
> Turn short, as doth a swallow; and be here,
> And there, and here, and yonder, all at once;
> Present to any humour, all occasion;
> And change a visor swifter than a thought!
>
> (3.1.23–9)

This is virtuosic writing in the rhythmic impetus of the verse as it moves with the thought, in the unimpeded diction, using scarcely any adjectives, and in the vividly appropriate imagery.

In his manipulation of dramatic situation Jonson brilliantly exploits the possibilities of multi-layered irony: an extra dimension is given to the scenes in which Mosca intrigues with the suitors by the fact that Volpone himself is on stage, apparently incapable of knowing what is going on, but actually – as both we and Mosca know – perfectly aware of it all. And the main plot is masterly in its construction, moving dextrously towards the climax in which Volpone overreaches himself, thinking to delude the tricksters by pretending to be dead and that Mosca is his heir.

At the opening of the second act Jonson introduces the principal English character, Sir Politic Would-be, a more typical inhabitant of Jonson's satiric world, as his fellow traveller, Peregrine, tells the audience:

> Oh, this knight
> (Were he well known) would be a precious thing
> To fit our English stage; he that should write
> But such a fellow, should be thought to feign
> Extremely, if not maliciously.
>
> (2.1.56–60)

The theatrical self-awareness of these lines is closely akin to Fabian's remark in Shakespeare's *Twelfth Night*, written some four years previously: 'If this were played upon a stage, now, I could condemn it as an improbable fiction' (3.4.125–6). It is through Sir Politic and his absurdly affected wife, Fine Lady Would-Be, that Jonson can introduce topical allusion – absent from the whole of the first act – and give the audience the masochistic pleasure of enjoying satire on the common theme of the Englishman abroad. But Jonson takes the risk of diluting the mastery with which he shapes his main plot in the digressive satire on Lady Would-be's vulgarity and garrulity, and the farcicality of the episodes in which her husband hides under a tortoise shell.

Jonson's superabundant inventiveness can lead him into redundancy, but the vigour of his comic writing in both prose and verse can still speak to us loud and clear. Volpone's patter in his disguise as a mountebank is of a kind that has echoes in the marketplaces and fairgrounds of today: 'Wherefore, now mark; I asked you six crowns; and six crowns, at other times, you have paid me; you shall not give me six crowns, nor five, nor four, nor three, nor two, nor one; nor half a ducat; no, nor a *mocenigo* [a Venetian coin]; six – pence it will cost you, or six hundred pound . . .' (2.2.197–201). The play's ending is harsh, reflecting Jonson's belief in the moral purpose of comedy: Mosca, who has turned against his master, is sentenced to be whipped and to serve as a galley slave; and Volpone's possessions are confiscated and given to the poor:

> And since the most was gotten by imposture,
> By feigning lame, gout, palsy, and such diseases,
> Thou art to lie in prison cramped with irons,
> Till thou be'st sick and lame indeed.
>
> (5.12.121–4)

But in the Epilogue Volpone recovers himself in his request for applause:

> Now, though the Fox be punished by the laws,
> He yet doth hope there is no suffering due
> For any fact which he hath done 'gainst you;
> If there be, censure him – here he doubtful stands.
> If not, fare jovially, and clap your hands.

For all the play's ostensibly stern morality, the fact that Jonson can finally give Volpone – or the actor playing the role – a plea for sympathy points to a certain moral ambiguity. The audience may sympathize so much with the energy of Volpone's plotting that, as with Shakespeare's Richard III and even Iago in *Othello*, it may suspend judgement in its enjoyment of the gusto with which Jonson presents the character.

Volpone was revived after the Restoration and bowdlerized in the late eighteenth century; it did not appeal to the Victorians, but since the 1920s has been the most frequently revived of Jonson's plays, largely because of the towering central role which has great appeal for flamboyant and extrovert actors. Sir Donald Wolfit, who gave the play successfully in the 1940s and 1950s on tour in England, in London during the war, on Broadway and on British television, wrote how, after appearing in Tyrone Guthrie's 1938 production, which stressed the play's 'bitter savagery', he later 'discovered the great gusty laughter of Jonson which disarmed the nastiness of the theme'.[18]

After his Venetian excursion, Jonson's playwriting career slowed down, but he returned decisively to London for the setting of his next three comedies. *Epicene, or The Silent Woman* – the subtitle is intended as a contradiction in terms – was given by a boys' company, the Children of the Queen's Revels, late in 1609 or early the following year. After this it continued to be played by adult companies, and was among the very first plays to be performed after the Restoration in 1660. When Samuel Pepys saw it for the first time in 1661 he thought it 'an excellent play',[19] and several years later he was to write that he 'never was more taken with a play than I am with this *Silent Woman*, as old as it is – and as often as I have seen it. There is more wit in it than goes into ten new plays.'[20] It has been less successful in later times, perhaps because of its self-conscious artificiality. Though the plot is characteristically complicated, it relies on the basically simple device of a central character, a man named Morose who has an obsessive aversion to noise, and is in search of a wife who will speak as little as possible. He thinks he has found one in the person of Epicene, who however turns out after marriage to be in every way the exact opposite of what he wanted. The twist in the tail of the plot comes at the end when Epicene is revealed to have been a boy in disguise – as of course would have been literally true in the original performances. Pepys saw Edward Kynaston (1643–?1712), then aged 17, in the role, noting that he had the good fortune 'to appear in three shapes: 1, as a poor woman in ordinary clothes to please Morose; then in fine clothes as a gallant, and in them was clearly the prettiest woman in the whole house – and lastly, as a man; and then likewise did appear the handsomest man in the house'.[21] In modern performance the play offers opportunities for complex juggling of sexual identities. A rare professional production by the Royal Shakespeare Company in 1989 cast a man, John Hannah, as Epicene but listed him in the programme as Hannah John so that the climactic revelation of his true identity came as no less of a surprise to the audience than to Morose.

Jonson's career was not without its diversions: in 1612 he had even acted as tutor to Sir Walter Ralegh's 'lavishly inclined' 19-year-old son, also named Walter, on a kind of grand tour which took them to France, where his pupil 'caused him to be drunken and dead drunk, so that he knew not where he was; thereafter laid him on a car [some sort of cart] which he made to be drawn by pioneers through the streets, at every corner showing his governor stretched out, and telling them that was a more lively [lifelike] image of the crucifix than any they had'.[22] This kind of robust commitment to the life around him no doubt fed Jonson's creative capacities.

It is a paradox that whereas Shakespeare seems to have had no interest in the printing of his plays, he offers easier pleasures to the reader than Jonson, whereas Jonson, whose writing in his next play, *The Alchemist*, is supremely theatrical and consequently more demanding of the reader, nevertheless presented his plays with great care for a reading public. There are many anthologies of set pieces from Shakespeare, none that I know of for Jonson. Indeed part of the point of some of Jonson's comic writing is its unintelligibility. His rogues blind their dupes with scientific jargon, rattling off impressive but totally mystifying technical terms which they know will delude their hearers into the illusion that they are immensely learned. So Subtle asks Ananias:

> Can you sublime and dulcify? Calcine?
> Know you the sapor pontic? Sapor stiptic?
> Or what is homogene, or heterogene?
> ANANIAS I understand no heathen language, truly.
> SUBTLE Heathen, you Knipperdollink? Is *ars sacra*,
> Or *chrysopoeia*, or *spagyrica*,
> Or the pamphysic, or panarchic knowledge,
> A heathen language?
>
> (2.5.9–16)

And the scene continues with much more 'heathen language' which makes for excellent theatre but hard reading. The great director Tyrone Guthrie, who directed the play several times, acknowledged this when he said that Jonson never wrote anything to compare with Shakespeare's romances and tragedies, but his farces are better than Shakespeare's. They're a chore to read because their plots are so complex, and the words are difficult to learn although they have to come sizzling from the actors. When they are known and the actors are rushing round firing off those lines, you find that even sentences which seem syntactically difficult sound quite natural and easy to comprehend.[23]

Paradoxically *The Alchemist*, which, more than any other play of the period, observes the neo-classical unities of time, place and action, and which draws on conventions of Roman comedy, is at the same time one of those most firmly anchored in the society in which it is set. Jonson has calculated the action so that it takes place at the exact time in 1610 at which he expected the play to be first performed, and at the very same place in London, the Blackfriars, where it was to be played. Plague was raging in London, and is responsible for the central plot device, the idea that Lovewit, the owner of the house where the action takes place, has left London for fear of it. (In actuality the plague became so severe that Jonson's plans were thwarted and his play had to be given in Oxford before it could be staged in London.) It opens with a verbal – and, if the actor playing Subtle can manage it, a physical – explosion:

> FACE Believe't, I will.
> SUBTLE   Thy worst. I fart at thee.

From that moment onwards the play charges forward with a verbal energy that is surely unparalleled in any other English comedy. This is a play in a hurry, peopled by characters who cannot wait to satisfy their greed and gratify their lusts. The dialogue draws on an amazingly wide range of verbal registers – colloquial, formal, scientific, alchemical, culinary, legal, theological, medical, classical – in portraying a gallery of characters that is Dickensian in its range. Dramatic decorum might seem to demand that the dialogue of a play that includes so many low-life figures should be written in prose, and indeed a listener who had not read it might well be surprised to learn that it is in verse, but, in spite of what Jonson said about his methods of composition, this is not just versified prose but genuine poetry in its complexity of allusion and depth of resonance. A few speeches are quotable out of context, such as Sir Epicure Mammon's visions of the pleasures he will enjoy if he can indeed possess the philosopher's stone that was the aim of the alchemists:

> I will have all my beds blown up, not stuffed;
> Down is too hard. And then mine oval room
> Filled with such pictures as Tiberius took
> From Elephantis, and dull Aretine
> But coldly imitated. Then, my glasses
> Cut in more subtle angles, to disperse
> And multiply the figures as I walk
> Naked between my *succubae*. My mists
> I'll have of perfume, vapoured 'bout the room,
> To loose ourselves in; and my baths like pits
> To fall into, from whence we will come forth
> And roll us dry in gossamer and roses . . .
>
> (2.2.41–52)

But even here the verse is fully integrated into the action. For all the frequent lowness of his diction, Jonson creates in this play a poetry of resonance, irony and multiple associations with enormous linguistic vitality.

Over the centuries *The Alchemist* has been Jonson's most popular play. David Garrick had such a success in the comparatively minor role of Abel Drugger, the tobacconist, that an adaptation of 1770 was called *The Tobacconist*. His performance provoked an enchanting description from the biographer James Boaden:

Abel Drugger's first appearance would disconcert the muscular economy of the wisest. His attitude, his dread of offending the doctor [Subtle], his saying nothing, his gradual stealing in farther and farther, his impatience to be introduced, his joy to his friend Face, are imitable by none. Mr Garrick has taken that walk to himself, and is the *ridiculous* above all conception. When he first opens his mouth, the features of his face seem, as it were, to drop upon his tongue; it is all caution; it is timorous, stammering, and inexpressible. When he stands under the conjurer to have his features examined, his teeth, his beard, his little finger, his awkward simplicity, and his concern, mixed with hope and fear, and joy and avarice, and good-nature, are above painting.[24]

Clearly this was creative acting, yet it was interpretative too, building upon hints in the text, especially the eager yet hesitant manner of Drugger's first extended speech:

> I am a young beginner, and am building
> Of a new shop, an't like your worship; just
> At corner of a street – here's the plot on't –
> And I would know by art, sir, of your worship,
> Which way I should make my door, by necromancy.
> And where my shelves. And which should be for boxes.
> And which for pots. I would be glad to thrive, sir.
> And I was wished to your worship by a gentleman,
> One Captain Face, that says you know men's planets,
> And their good angels, and their bad.
>
> (1.3.7–16)

Only in the Victorian period did *The Alchemist* fall out of favour; a play opening with a fart would have been unlikely to appeal to the decorous audiences of that era.

Jonson followed *The Alchemist* with his second surviving classical tragedy, *Catiline, His Conspiracy*, also acted by the King's Men, a play that demands even more of its audiences than *Sejanus* – it includes a virtually uninterrupted speech by Cicero which is over 300 lines long – and which spectacularly failed to please.

Whereas *The Alchemist* is so tightly constructed that Coleridge classed it with Sophocles' tragedy *Oedipus the King* and Henry Fielding's novel *Tom Jones* as one of the three best plots of literature (not perhaps a very intelligent remark), the last of Jonson's great comedies, *Bartholomew Fair*, is more of a pageant than a plot, a sprawling, episodic masterpiece of social and linguistic observation, unusual for its time in being written almost entirely in prose. Ursula the pig-woman is Falstaffian in both dimensions and verbal imagination: 'I am all fire and fat,[25] Nightingale; I shall e'en melt away to the first woman, a rib again, I am afraid. I do water the ground in knots as I go, like a great garden-pot; you may follow me by the S's I make' (2.2.49–52). The idea that she may 'water the ground' as she walks may recall Prince Harry's idea that Falstaff 'lards the lean earth as he walks along' (*1 Henry IV*, 2.3.17). As often in plays of this period, the text looks back in a self-referential manner to plays written when the drama was beginning to establish itself. In *The Alchemist*, Abel Drugger, looking for a disguise, had been told that he can borrow from the players: 'Hieronimo's old cloak, ruff, and hat will serve' (4.7.71), an allusion to Kyd's *The Spanish Tragedy* of 1587, in which Jonson had acted as a young man and for which Henslowe had commissioned him to write additional scenes in 1601. Now in the Induction to *Bartholomew Fair* Jonson writes disparagingly of both this and one of Shakespeare's earliest successes, sneering, as we have seen, at them in a manner that may evoke the flavour of sour grapes: 'He that will swear, *Jeronimo* or *Andronicus* are the best plays, yet shall pass unexcepted at, here, as a man whose judgement shows it is constant, and hath stood still these five and twenty or thirty years' (Induction, 94–7). And the play reaches its climax in a puppet play which parodies a poem written twenty years earlier, Marlowe's *Hero and Leander*.

As Jonson wrote *Bartholomew Fair* in 1614 Shakespeare's career was virtually at its end. Jonson must have observed that the older writer's output, which had been steady for close on a quarter of a century, had dwindled, first from around 1608 into collaborations with George Wilkins (*Pericles*), Thomas Middleton (*Timon of Athens*) and John Fletcher (*All is True*, or *Henry VIII*, *The Two Noble Kinsmen* and the lost *Cardenio*), then, since around 1613, into silence. It may be mere coincidence that Shakespeare stopped writing within months of the destruction by fire of the Globe theatre – or could this disaster have broken his spirit? A few years later Jonson too was to suffer from fire: in 1623 many of his books and substantial unpublished manuscripts were destroyed in a fire in his study, which he commemorated in the commendably good-humoured poem 'An Execration upon Vulcan'. In this he mentions being present at the burning of the Globe:

> the glory of the Bank
> Which, though it were the fort of the whole parish,
> Flanked with a ditch and forced out of a marish [swamp],
> I saw with two poor chambers taken in,
> And razed . . . nothing but the piles
> Left! and wit since to cover it with tiles.[26]

The second Globe, operative within a year, was indeed tiled, not thatched.

Maybe Shakespeare's withdrawal from the dramatic scene created in Jonson too a sense of an ending, or at least a desire to look back, to assess his achievement, and to raise his own monument to posterity in the Folio collection of his writings, *The Works of Ben Jonson*, that he brought to publication in 1616. In this unique volume Jonson, as in previous publications, presented his own works as if they were ancient classics. It was the first collection of the plays and other works of any English dramatic author that did not appear posthumously. And Jonson did not simply take to a publisher his previously printed works along with a selection of unpublished manuscripts, but, acting as his own editor, decided to exclude some that he preferred to forget, even some that had already appeared in print, and to revise and re-present others, almost as if his career was at an end and he was drawing up an inventory of his legacies to posterity.

The 1616 Folio is a handsome volume of more than a thousand pages, printed in double columns, with an elaborately designed, emblematic title page bearing a defiant motto characteristically adapted from Horace:

> *neque me ut miretur turba, laboro;*
> *Contentus paucis lectoribus –*

'I don't work to be gaped at by the mob, but am happy with a few readers.' (His publishers may not have concurred.) There are commendatory verses, some of them reprinted from earlier quartos; each of the nine plays has a separate title page, and they are given with information about the date, company and actors in their first performances. The volume also includes two collections of Jonson's poems, a heavily annotated script of the entertainment for the King's entry into London in 1604, and a number of other royal entertainments and masques. Many of the texts are corrected, some are extensively revised, and passages omitted for topical reasons when the plays were first given are restored. The plays are presented according to the conventions adopted in reprints of Roman drama – for example, names of characters are listed at the head of the scene in which they appear, not at points of individual entry. The sheets were heavily corrected as they went through the press: probably Jonson worked regularly at the printing house while the volume was being prepared.

In some quarters Jonson's pretensions aroused derision. Two epigrams are preserved, the first addressed 'To Mr Ben Jonson, demanding the reason why he called his plays works':

> Pray tell me, Ben, where doth the mystery lurk:
> What others call a play you call a work.

The second is headed:

> *Thus answered by a friend in Mr Jonson's defence:*
> Ben's plays are works, when others' works are plays.

Sir John Suckling was later to write, more charitably,

> The first that broke silence was good old Ben,
> Prepared before with canary wine,
> And he told them plainly he deserved the bays,
> For his were called works, where others' were but plays.

The tenor of these comments suggests that Jonson was regarded primarily as a playwright, but it would have been fair to note that the book actually included more than plays.

Jonson may have seen his walking tour to Scotland in 1618 as a well-deserved, if long delayed, holiday after the labours of publishing his Folio. In any case his visit to William Drummond gave him plenty of opportunity to pontificate about literary matters. Considering Drummond's verses pedantic and old-fashioned – they 'smelled too much of the schools, and were not after the fancy of the time'[27] – he advised his host how to improve his poetic skills, while sweetening his criticism with flattery appropriate from a guest. Revelling in the chance to show off before one whom he thought he could patronize as a provincial second-rater, he indulged himself in outrageous generalizations, pontificating about his contemporaries and rivals and bragging of his own exploits. The poet John Donne, 'for not keeping of accent' – for writing irregular verse – 'deserved hanging'; nevertheless Jonson esteemed him 'the first poet in the world in some things'. Samuel Daniel 'was a good honest man, had no children, but no poet'. 'That next himself only Fletcher and Chapman could write a masque'.

And (whether or not as a consequence) 'That Chapman and Fletcher were loved of him'. 'He beat Marston, and took his pistol from him.' Most notoriously, 'Shakespeare wanted art' and (of *The Winter's Tale*) 'Shakespeare in a play brought in a number of men saying they had suffered shipwreck in Bohemia, where there is no sea by some 100 miles'. More than one of Jonson's comments might be disconcerting to current students of authorship: he reported that Sidney 'had translated some of the psalms which went abroad under the name of the Countess of Pembroke' (Sidney's sister), and that 'Marston wrote his father-in-law's preachings, and his father-in-law his comedies'. (The satirical, often obscene, poet and playwright John Marston, who collaborated with Jonson but had a stormy relationship with him, gave up literature in favour of a career in the church in 1609, to the astonishment of many of his contemporaries. His father-in-law, William Wilkes, was one of the King's chaplains.)

In spite of Jonson's protestations that he would have been content with few readers, the 1616 Folio was not a commercial failure. It went into a second edition in 1640, but well before then another volume which drew together his greatest rival's collected plays was on the market. Probably the Shakespeare First Folio of 1623 would not have appeared without Jonson's as a precedent, in which case we should have been without some of the greatest and most popular plays ever written – the sixteen, including *Twelfth Night*, *Macbeth*, *Antony and Cleopatra*, *The Winter's Tale* and *The Tempest* that had not previously appeared in print. The title page, we cannot help noticing, avoids describing the contents as works: these are 'Mr William Shakespeare's Comedies, Histories, and Tragedies, published according to the true original copies'. It is appropriate – but is it also self-advertising? – that the first words printed in the volume, the address 'To the reader', should have been written by Jonson, who also contributes the substantial and deeply considered poem headed 'To the memory of my beloved, the author, Master William Shakespeare, and what he hath left us'. Whatever Jonson's underlying motives may have been, these lines counterbalance his more unbuttoned, and sometimes less complimentary, comments on Shakespeare's art found elsewhere.

The first, short poem claims, with rather clumsy play on the use of brass for engravings and for memorial plates, that if the engraver of the portrait of 'gentle Shakespeare' had 'drawn his wit / As well in brass as he hath hit / His face, the print would then surpass / All that was ever writ in brass'. The longer poem represents the most serious and the finest appraisal of Shakespeare's art before the writings of John Dryden much later in the century. Part of it is straightforward eulogy:

> Soul of the age!
> The applause, delight, the wonder of our stage!

Shakespeare is a 'monument without a tomb' (and indeed there is a monument but no tomb (only a grave) in Holy Trinity Church, Stratford). His merits outshine those of Lyly, 'sporting Kyd' – the adjective plays facetiously and inappropriately on Kyd's name – and 'Marlowe's mighty line'; and – the dig that Jonson the classicist could not resist – though Shakespeare had 'small Latin, and less Greek', he rivals the greatest dramatists of antiquity. Britain should take pride in him:

> Triumph, my Britain! thou hast one to show
> To whom all scenes of Europe homage owe.
> He was not of an age, but for all time . . .

Shakespeare was indebted not only to Nature but also to Art, which impelled him often to revise what he wrote – to 'strike the second heat / Upon the muses' anvil' – because 'a good poet's made as well as born'. And Jonson suggests that Shakespeare's imagination and demeanour are reflected in his writings: 'the race / Of Shakespeare's mind and manners brightly shines / In his well-turnèd and true-filèd lines'. It is to be wished that we could still see this 'Sweet swan of Avon' 'upon the banks of Thames' – where the theatres were – but now that he has been metamorphosed into a constellation, Jonson prays that the 'drooping stage', which grieves over his loss, may nevertheless be illumined by the light cast by this volume of his plays.[28]

This poem represents Jonson the formal eulogist; elsewhere, and less publicly, he expressed more uneasily qualified admiration for Shakespeare. In his notebooks published posthumously as *Timber, or Discoveries*, he opined that Shakespeare had not struck 'the second heat' – that is, had not thoroughly refined his meaning on the anvil of his mind – often enough: 'I remember the players have often mentioned it as an honour to Shakespeare that in his writing he never blotted a line. My answer hath been, "Would he had blotted a thousand."' Perhaps here he was echoing what Heminges and Condell wrote in their introduction to the First Folio: 'His mind and hand went together, and what he thought he uttered with that easiness that we have scarce received from him a blot in his papers.' Apparently they considered this 'a malevolent speech', but Jonson defended his candour with a tribute that seems all the more heartfelt for not being effusive: 'I loved the man, and do honour his memory – on this side idolatry – as much as any. He was, indeed, of an open and free nature; had an excellent fantasy [imagination], brave notions [admirable ideas], and gentle expressions [a noble way of expressing them], wherein he flowed with that facility that sometimes it was necessary he should be stopped.' The gist of Jonson's criticism is that Shakespeare lacked discipline: 'His wit was in his own power; would the rule of it had been so too. Many times he fell into those things could not escape laughter' – and he continues with the criticism of a passage in *Julius Caesar* quoted on p. 139 which, as we have seen, Shakespeare appears to have accepted and acted upon. Although Jonson had reservations about Shakespeare as an artist, and had stormy relations even with many of his own friends, he expresses nothing but admiration for Shakespeare as a man.

Jonson's Folio represents a major punctuation mark in his career, but he continued to write prolifically after it appeared. A new play, *The Devil is an Ass*, was acted by the King's Men while the Folio was in the final stages of preparation. And Jonson allowed himself interludes in which writing was not his main preoccupation. Already in summer 1617 he was planning the walking tour to and from Scotland on which he embarked a year later, intending to capitalize on his travels by writing a versified account of his adventures, and also perhaps in the hope of losing weight – at this time he turned the scales at almost twenty stone, and had 'a mountain belly'. He was becoming a national institution.

In 1616, a few months before the publication of his Folio, he had been granted a royal pension of 100 marks – £66. 13s. 4d. – which effectively made him Britain's first poet laureate.[29] When he got to Edinburgh in August 1618 the Town Council made him an Honorary

Burgess and entertained him at great expense. Other marks of royal favour were to follow. In 1621 he appears to have turned down a knighthood, perhaps because he would have been expected to pay for it, and soon after that he was nominated to the succession of the Mastership of the Revels, which, however, did not fall vacant during his lifetime. A poem of March 1628 thanks King Charles for 'A Hundred Pounds he Sent me in my Sickness', and in 1630 the annual royal pension was increased to £100, along with an undoubtedly welcome grant of 42 gallons of Spanish wine from the King's own cellars.

Jonson's playwriting career went into abeyance between 1616 and 1626, but throughout this period he maintained his output of court masques, many of them devised in collaboration with the great artist and architect Inigo Jones. The masque is a form of entertainment that had a relatively brief period of glory from 1605, when Jonson and Jones first worked together, on *The Masque of Blackness*, to the early 1630s, when Jonson's always troubled relationship with Jones finally collapsed in acrimony. Even more collaborative in nature than the drama, masque called upon the combined talents of poets, designers, composers, musicians, actors (both professional and amateur, often aristocratic and even royal) and choreographers in the devising of complex and wildly expensive entertainments that were given only once and were often designed as political gestures, intended to impress overseas visitors with the wealth and influence of the court. Though Jonson was the greatest of the Jacobean and Caroline masque writers, he had to struggle to subdue himself to the occasion and to work harmoniously with his collaborators. He believed passionately that his should be the controlling mind, devising the main concept of the masque, to which all else should be subordinate, and writing the words in which the ideas found part – but only part – of their expression.

An example is one of his early masques, *Hymenaei* (1606). It was written for the ill-fated marriage of the 3rd Earl of Essex to Lady Frances Howard (they were later divorced in messy circumstances), and its central theme is union. Jonson ingeniously makes many aspects of the entertainment illustrative of the theme. The seriousness with which he approached his task is clear from his introductory remarks, where he says that things which are 'subjected to understanding' –

that is, which make demands upon the intellect – have an advantage over 'those which are objected to sense' – that is, appeal only to the senses. The advantage is that 'the one sort are but momentary, and merely taking; the other impressing, and lasting: else the glory of all these solemnities had perished like a blaze, and gone out in the beholders' eyes, so short-lived are the bodies of all things, in comparison of their souls'.[30] He goes on to explain that when he designs a masque there is something for the mind to grapple with as well as more transitory attractions. On this occasion all came together to his total satisfaction. The performance was so exquisite as to 'surprise with delight, and steal away the spectators from themselves'. Everything was perfect – the sumptuousness and originality of the costumes, the dances, the 'magnificence of the scene', and the 'divine rapture of music'. The only cause for regret was 'that it lasted not still, or, now it is past, cannot by imagination, much less description, be recovered to a part of that spirit it had in the gliding by'.[31] The printed text, Jonson knew, was inadequate to re-create the occasion, whether for those who were present or those who were not.

As time went by Jonson found the collaborative demands of the form increasingly irksome. Much of the success of the masques had been due to Inigo Jones's genius as a designer of costumes, scenes, and the often elaborate machines which carried the spectacle. Happily many of Jones's designs survive. Jonson, coming to feel that Jones was too prominent, complained that the masques were valued rather for their spectacle than for their intellectual and moral content and their poetic appeal. A split came when Jones felt himself inadequately acknowledged in the printed text of the masque *Chloridia* (1631), and found expression in Jonson's bitter poem of 1631, 'An Expostulation with Inigo Jones'.

> O shows! shows! Mighty shows!
> The eloquence of masques! What need of prose,
> Or verse, or sense, to express immortal you?
> You are the spectacles of state! 'Tis true
> Court hieroglyphics, and all arts afford
> In the mere perspective of an inch-board!
> . . .

> Oh, to make boards to speak! There is a task!
> Painting and carpentry are the soul of masque.
> Pack with your peddling poetry to the stage:
> This is the money-get, mechanic age![32]

After this Jonson wrote no more masques, and Jones worked with other collaborators.

Jonson was by no means the only poet and dramatist of the early seventeenth century to compose court masques. Others were Samuel Daniel, Thomas Middleton, Francis Beaumont, James Shirley and, at the end of the period, William Davenant, but Shakespeare was not among them. His plays were often presented at court, from 1603 he was officially a servant of the King, entitled, indeed on occasion required, to wear the royal livery, and he must often have been in the royal presence, but there is no sign that he employed his talents in works written specifically for either Queen Elizabeth or King James. He may (or may not) allude to Elizabeth as 'the imperial vot'ress' in *A Midsummer Night's Dream* (2.1.163), but his only blatant flattery of either monarch comes in allusions to James in a scene (4.3) in *Macbeth* which may in any case have been written by Middleton and, oleaginously, at the end of *All is True* (*Henry VIII*), in lines which any admirer of Shakespeare must hope – fortunately with good reason – were written by his collaborator John Fletcher. There is no reason to suppose that Shakespeare refused to work for the court; more probably he simply felt that his genius was more suited to the drama.

The last decade or so of Jonson's life was a period of physical decline and of financial difficulty, but he continued to write energetically and inventively. In a final burst of playwriting he produced *The Staple of News* (1626), *The New Inn* (1629), and finally *A Tale of a Tub* (1633). Dryden was to characterize these late works as 'dotages'; late-twentieth-century attempts at a more favourable reassessment of them have not succeeded in demonstrating their theatrical as opposed to their literary merits, though in John Caird's brave revival of *The New Inn* for the RSC in 1987 the rapt attention paid by the audience to John Carlisle's delivery of Lovel's great lines on love challenged views that Jonson's longer poetical speeches cannot work in the theatre.

Grossly overweight, Jonson seems to have suffered a paralytic stroke around 1627 or 1628, but he went on creating masques and royal entertainments. Hospitable and self-indulgent, he constantly lived above his income. His appointment in 1628 to the post of City Chronologer would have given him 100 nobles a year if he had carried out his duties with more efficiency than he did. Izaak Walton (1593–1683), author of *The Compleat Angler*, in a letter written late in his long life was to record that, in Jonson's final years, when he was lodging near Westminster Abbey, he was looked after by 'a woman that governed him . . . and that neither he nor she took much care for next week, and would be sure not to want wine, of which he usually took too much before he went to bed, if not oftener and sooner'. No wonder Drummond had said that drink 'was one of the elements in which he lived'. He died in August 1637, aged 65, and was buried in Westminster Abbey, where his memorial stone bears the inscription: 'O rare Ben Jonson'. His status as the most distinguished and productive literary figure of the previous forty years was recognized by many printed tributes – far more than had marked Shakespeare's passing – including the publication of a collection of memorial poems; and a second, much enlarged, three-volume edition of his Folio appeared in 1640.

For the remainder of the seventeenth century Jonson's reputation and influence equalled and possibly exceeded Shakespeare's, but in the eighteenth century the balance shifted, above all with the virtual deification of Shakespeare from the time of the Garrick Jubilee, in 1769, onwards. Some of Jonson's best work, especially the masques, had a built-in obsolescence. A few lyrics, such as the exquisite 'Drink to me only with thine eyes' and 'Have you seen but a white lily grow?', are timeless in their appeal, and other poems are highly regarded. But his reputation survives mainly through the best of his comedies, in their way no less fine than Shakespeare's. To see Shakespeare's overall output in relation to Jonson's is to realize that, although Shakespeare's range within his plays exceeds that of any of his contemporaries, he is far less versatile than some of them, including Jonson, in the overall scope of his output. Shakespeare wrote only plays, narrative poems, sonnets and a few lyrics; Jonson, by contrast, wrote plays, masques, miscellaneous entertainments and hundreds of poems, both secular and religious, in many different forms, along with translations of Latin literature and works of historical scholarship and other prose. He is both one of the most fascinatingly complex characters and the most complete man of letters in the whole of British literature.

6

Thomas Middleton and Shakespeare

9. Thomas Middleton. This posthumously published engraving showing Middleton wearing the writer's crown of bays probably derives from a painted miniature.

In my opening chapter I quoted Ben Jonson's boast, in his Prologue to *Volpone*, about how he had written the play all on his own, and in record time:

> five weeks fully penned it –
> From his own hand, without a co-adjutor,
> Novice, journeyman or tutor.

These four terms, I suggested, define the different functions of a collaborator. As we shall see in this chapter, all four could be applied to the relationship, at various points of their careers, between Shakespeare and his younger contemporary Thomas Middleton. There is a sense in which Shakespeare acted as tutor to Middleton, and to Shakespeare Middleton served at different times as an apprentice, as a journeyman and as an equal collaborator.

Born in 1580, sixteen years after Shakespeare, Middleton was the son of a member of the Tilers' and Bricklayers' Company of which Ben Jonson's stepfather was to become Master. Middleton's father died when the boy was no more than 6 years old, leaving an estate valued at the substantial though not enormous sum of around £335.[1] His widow, Anne, soon took as her second husband a gentleman grocer named Thomas Harvey who had spent a year as a member of the unsuccessful colony established by Sir Walter Ralegh at Roanoke, Virginia. It was an unhappy experience, from which Harvey had recently returned, destitute and dispirited, in a ship commanded by Sir Francis Drake which was sent to rescue the colonists.[2] Anne had created a trust to protect her children's inheritance, and within weeks of their marriage the couple had embarked upon a series of mutually recriminative legal wrangles that were to continue over the next fifteen years, much of which time Harvey spent either dodging his creditors overseas or in a debtors' prison. It is unsurprising that the wiles of lawyers are frequently satirized in his stepson's plays. In spite of the family's problems Thomas went up to Queen's College, Oxford in 1598, but, as was not uncommon, he left after a couple of years without taking a degree.

Even before going to university Thomas, at the age of 17, had demonstrated poetic ambition along with an interest in religion in an interminable poem (at 4,166 lines it is longer than the longest text of *Hamlet*), *The Wisdom of Solomon Paraphrased*, obsequiously dedicated to the Earl of Essex (who can hardly be expected to have read it). If he obtains the Earl's 'cheerful countenance', the youth declares, his 'harvest of joy will soon be ripened'. The poem was not a success. One of Middleton's early editors, A. H. Bullen, wrote: 'I have read at various times much indifferent verse and much execrable verse, but I can conscientiously say that *The Wisdom of Solomon Paraphrased* is the most damnable piece of flatness that has ever fallen in my way.'[3] Whatever the poem's faults, it shows that Middleton had already acquired great technical facility. It uses the seven-line stanza form known as rhyme royal which Shakespeare employed in his immensely popular *The Rape of Lucrece*, first published in 1594, and before long

Middleton became a kind of 'novice' to Shakespeare in an imitative poem called *The Ghost of Lucrece*.[4]

This mercifully shorter poem of 539 lines was printed as an independent pamphlet in 1600, ascribed only to 'T. M. Gent.'[5] There is no doubt that 'T. M.' is Thomas Middleton, and the poem probably dates from his Oxford days. It is a fluent rhetorical exercise in the popular genre of the literary complaint which Shakespeare employs in 'A Lover's Complaint', published along with his sonnets in 1609 but possibly written years before. Like both *The Wisdom of Solomon* and *The Rape of Lucrece*, Middleton's *The Ghost of Lucrece* is composed in rhyme royal, and in subject matter it is a sequel to Shakespeare's narrative poem, from which, too, it derives much of its imagery. Middleton also draws heavily on a euphuistic prose romance, *Ciceronis Amor* (1589), by Robert Greene, whose accounts of the seamier side of London life known as the coney-catching pamphlets were to form part of the background to Middleton's city comedies.

The Ghost of Lucrece is theatrical in some of its form and imagery, even to the extent of beginning with a Prologue and concluding with an Epilogue, bearing witness to an interest in the theatre which appears to have drawn Middleton away from Oxford before he was due to take a degree. In February 1601 a witness in one of his family's innumerable and acrimonious lawsuits said that he was 'in London daily accompanying the players', which may imply that he had entered on some kind of unofficial apprenticeship as a writer. A couple of months later, on coming of age, he was able to take possession of the £25 which was all that remained to him from his father's estate. Seeking to live by his pen, he published satirical pamphlets, and soon tried his hand at playwriting for Henslowe. For most of the next twenty-five years, until he died in 1627, the theatre was to provide his main source of income, though like Dekker he maintained a prolific output of pamphlets, pageants, Lord Mayors' shows, and other entertainments.

Immensely industrious, versatile, a brilliant writer whose work developed in power and profundity as his experience grew, Middleton led a quiet life in comparison with, for instance, Marlowe and Jonson – though his career was to end in a blaze of publicity. Regrettably, partly perhaps because so much of his work was done in collaboration with others, there is for him no equivalent of the Jonson and

Shakespeare Folios of 1616 and 1623 respectively. This helps to explain why the canon of his plays has been a source of much scholarly debate. Some of them were published anonymously, some attributed to other writers, including Shakespeare. A major redefinition has been undertaken in recent years in the preparation of the Oxford edition of Middleton's *Complete Works*, and in this chapter I shall accept its attributions, concentrating on those of the many plays with which he was involved that have the strongest links with Shakespeare.

Middleton started his playwriting career in May 1602 as 'co-adjutor' with no fewer than four other writers – Thomas Dekker, Michael Drayton, Anthony Munday and John Webster – on a play, now lost, with the weird title of *Caesar's Fall, or Two Shapes*, for which they received £8. 'Shapes' could mean actors, but even so the title is odd. In subject matter the play sounds as if it was a competitor on behalf of the Lord Admiral's Men for Shakespeare's *Julius Caesar*, written two or three years previously for the rival company, the Lord Chamberlain's Men. Middleton and Webster, both in their early twenties, were 'novices', working with more experienced partners. A few months later Middleton wrote 'without co-adjutor' *Randulf, Earl of Chester, or The Chester Tragedy*, which made him £7. This too is lost, as are the Prologue and Epilogue that he contributed as a 'journeyman' in December 1602 for a court performance of Robert Greene's *Friar Bacon and Friar Bungay*, for which he was rewarded with five shillings.

It was probably soon after this, in early 1603, that Middleton married. His bride, Magdalen (or Mary) Marbeck (1575–1628), came from a distinguished family; she was a granddaughter of the writer and composer John Marbeck (?1505–?1585), who compiled the first concordance in English to cover the whole Bible, and who also, in *The Book of Common Prayer Noted* (1550), composed the first musical settings of services prescribed by the 1549 Prayer Book. And Magdalen was also the niece of Roger Marbeck, Queen Elizabeth's chief physician. Middleton may have met her through her brother Thomas, who was an actor with the Lord Admiral's Men. Their only child, Edward, was born between November 1603 and November 1604. For most of their married life they lived in Newington Butts, close to modern London's Elephant and Castle and not far from the south-bank playhouses.

It was also in 1603 that the Queen died and was succeeded by King James I. Over the next few years Middleton, obviously having gained in confidence, wrote, mostly without co-adjutor, a brilliant series of comedies centred, whether explicitly or not, on London life of the day, and intended mainly for the boys' companies, then in their heyday. These boys were all the rage. We have seen from *Hamlet* that they provoked envy among the adult companies (p. 53), and in Middleton's pamphlet *Father Hubburd's Tales, or The Ant and the Nightingale* (1604) a foolish young gentleman is advised to 'call in at the Blackfriars, where he should see a nest of boys able to ravish a man'.[6] It is difficult for us to imagine the effect produced by these young actors when they were performing the highly sophisticated, often bawdy, plays written specifically for them. Boys played women in the adult companies, but in the all-boy companies they were required to personate not only women young and old, maidens and whores, charmers and termagants, but also an equally wide range of male roles, attractive young men and villainous rogues, aged cuckolds and grasping schemers. Jonson's tribute to Samuel Pavy (p. 56), who acted 'Old men so duly' that the Fates 'thought him one, / He played so truly', suggests that it was possible for boys to identify themselves totally with their roles; on the other hand the idea that they could 'ravish a man' may indicate that audiences were no less conscious of the physical charm of the performers themselves than of their acting abilities. Their performances may have had the appeal of miniaturization, an effect not unlike that produced by seeing a Mozart opera performed by puppets. There must surely have been an element of burlesque in their need to wear false beards and artificial bosoms, to pad themselves into portliness, to deepen their voices into martial gruffness or raise them into the squeakiness of senility, and to assume other physical characteristics of adulthood. And there may even have been a touch of ambivalent sexuality in audiences' reactions to the adolescent, or pre-adolescent, boys' impersonation of nubile young women and of sexually mature, sometimes corrupt adults.

It is hard to tell exactly the order in which Middleton wrote his plays, but it seems clear that the first to survive is *The Phoenix*, acted by Paul's Boys probably in 1603 and performed before the new King during his first court season, on 24 February 1604. Middleton was beginning to make his mark: three weeks later he was one of those who contributed speeches for the *Magnificent Entertainment Given to King James* produced for the King's ceremonial entry into the City of London – others were Dekker and Jonson. *The Phoenix* is one of a small group of early Jacobean plays which adopt the motif of a ruler or his deputy who disguises himself as a way of looking into the abuses of his kingdom. They were all written within two or three years of each other – probably from mid- to late 1603 to 1605 – but it is impossible to say exactly when and in what order. Best known is Shakespeare's *Measure for Measure*. Others are two plays by John Marston: *The Malcontent* and *Parasitaster: or The Fawn*. Middleton's dukedom is ostensibly Ferrara, but the conventionally Italian setting only thinly disguises his concern with abuses practised in England, and most specifically in London. Though Middleton writes with moral purpose, he does not forget that he has an audience to entertain. In tone his play, written in a mixture of verse and prose, the one often shading into the other, fluctuates between morality drama, melodrama, social satire and genial comedy.

Whereas Shakespeare's Duke of Vienna, apparently in the prime of life, pretends to leave the city and disguises himself with the intention of looking into the abuses that are practised there, Middleton's Duke is an old man who, having reigned for forty-five years, sends his son, Phoenix, out into the world to gain experience that will make him a better ruler when he succeeds his father. But just as Shakespeare's Duke Vincentio only pretends to leave his dukedom, while actually remaining on home territory disguised as a friar, so Phoenix decides that instead of travelling overseas he will, attended by only one servant, Fidelio, 'look into the heart and bowels of this dukedom, and, in disguise, mark all abuses ready for reformation or punishment' (1.1.100–102). Certain that 'there are infectious dealings in most offices, and foul mysteries throughout all professions', he is willing to 'fit' his 'body to the humblest form and bearing, so the labour may be fruitful' (1.1.108–13). This enterprise of Phoenix may recall the tavern exploits of Prince Harry in Shakespeare's *Henry IV*, Part One, written some six or seven years previously, but Harry's quest is more self-centred than Phoenix's.

There are four main threads to the action. One concerns a villainous former Sea Captain – surely a reflection of Middleton's stepfather – who, apparently in a fit of amnesia, has married Fidelio's mother, Castiza. 'What lustful passion came aboard of me, that I should marry? was I drunk?' he asks himself (1.2.43–4). He puts her up for sale, receives a bid of five hundred crowns – £125 – from the villainous and hypocritical courtier Proditor, and receives the cash in a brilliantly written scene in which Fidelio, disguised as a scrivener, reads out the terms of the agreement in counterpoint with, on the one hand, moralizing speeches from Phoenix, including a long and solemn verse disquisition on 'Reverend and honourable Matrimony', and on the other hand the rapacious gloating of the Captain as he counts out his coins, one by one. Another thread portrays a cheerfully amoral relationship between a Jeweller's Wife in search of a friend at court and an impecunious Knight in search of money. The Knight is there partly as an opportunity for Middleton (like Jonson in *Eastward Ho*) to satirize King James's indiscriminate creation and sale of knighthoods, a practice which he often used as a way of replenishing the royal coffers. On a single day, 23 July 1603, for instance, the King created 300 knighthoods in the gardens at Whitehall, and a courtier named Philip Gawdy described recently dubbed knights as 'a scum of such as it would make a man sick to think of them'.[7] So in Middleton's comedy the Jeweller's Wife's father, a former highwayman turned corrupt Justice of the Peace named Falso, asks: 'Daughter, what gentleman might this be?' To which she replies with pride: 'No gentleman, sir; he's a knight.' But her father puts her down with: 'Is he but a knight? troth, I would 'a sworn had been a gentleman; to see, to see, to see' (1.6.148–51). And later he rubs home the mockery to the Knight himself with 'I cry ye mercy, sir; I call you gentleman still; I forget you're but a knight' (2.3.3–4). In a third thread we witness Falso's would-be incestuous attempts to seduce his niece, Fidelio's wife, who indignantly rejects him. Middleton makes capital out of his own unhappy experiences with the legal profession in his portrayal of the litigious Tangle, who constantly (and, at least for a modern reader, tediously) lards his speeches, and attempts to impress his clients, with Latin law tags: 'For the first party after the *procedendo* you'll get costs; the cause being found, you'll have a judgment; *nunc pro tunc*, you'll get a *venire facias* to warn your jury, a *decem tales* to fill up the number, and a *capias utlagatum* for your execution' (1.4.95–101). The fourth thread is provided by Proditor's efforts to usurp the dukedom. The play's series of comic scenes is interspersed with moralizing soliloquies from Phoenix, an authorial voice commenting on the wickedness he witnesses, and tying up the action by doling out punishments at its conclusion.

Middleton's productivity was great. Like Dekker, and indeed in collaboration with him, he turned his hand to pamphlets during the plague years of 1603 and 1604 – Dekker's *News from Gravesend* incorporates about 100 lines written by Middleton, and Middleton's *The Meeting of Gallants at an Ordinary* has a contribution of similar length by Dekker. In 1604 Middleton published two pamphlets of his own, *Father Hubburd's Tales* and *The Black Book*, which is a sequel to *Pierce Penniless* by Thomas Nashe, who had died some three years earlier. And in February 1604 Middleton and Dekker received an advance of £5 for, as Henslowe put it, 'their play called the patient man and the honest whore', now known as *The Honest Whore*, Part One. It was a big hit, and a sequel written by Dekker alone soon followed.

Brilliant comedies continued to flow from Middleton's pen – *Michaelmas Term* (1604), *A Trick to Catch the Old One* and *A Mad World, My Masters* (1605), *The Puritan Widow* (1606) and *Your Five Gallants* (1607), all of them written for boys' companies. In general these satirical city comedies are a far cry from the Shakespearian style, though there are affinities in the pungency of the dialogue with, for example, the tavern scenes of *Henry IV* and with some of the more robust passages in plays such as *The Merry Wives of Windsor* and *Twelfth Night*. There are even, in *A Mad World, My Masters*, direct echoes. In the opening scene of that play young Follywit laments that he has been 'bewitched' by the 'company of villains' whom he nevertheless loves:

I was as well given till I fell to be wicked, my grand-sire had hope of me; I went all in black, swore but o' Sundays, never came home drunk but upon fasting nights to cleanse my stomach; 'slid, now I'm quite altered, blown into light colours, let out oaths by th'minute, sit up late till it be early, drink drunk

till I am sober, sink down dead in a tavern, and rise in a tobacco shop.
(1.1.11–17)

Surely Middleton's audience were conscious as they heard these words
from the mouth of a boy actor that they had heard similar phrases
spoken by a fat old knight: 'I was as virtuously given as a gentleman
need to be; virtuous enough; swore little; diced not – above seven
times a week; went to a bawdy-house not – above once in a quarter –
of an hour . . .' (1 Henry IV, 3.3.13–16). And maybe they also heard
echoes of another reprobate, Sir Toby Belch in Twelfth Night: 'Not
to be abed after midnight is to be up betimes' (2.3.1–2).

The admiration for Shakespeare's poems that Middleton had displayed as a novice may have made him particularly keen to learn
personally from his senior and to work with him in the theatre. In
any case, the opportunity to write for the most prestigious of the
London companies, the King's Men, must have been welcome. It came
in rather curious circumstances. On 23 April 1605 a young Yorkshire
man of good family, Walter Calverley, murdered two of his three little
boys – one aged around eighteen months, the other no more than five
years – and grievously wounded their mother, his wife. Admitting the
crimes, he claimed that his wife had provoked him into the belief that
he was not the children's father, and also that he had lived in fear that
she would murder him. Put formally on trial he bravely refused to
plead – which meant that his estate, instead of being confiscated,
would remain in the family – and consequently brought upon himself
the horrific punishment of la peine forte et dure, pressing to death, in
which stones or weights were piled upon him until the breath was
literally crushed out of his body.

The case caused a national stir. Before Calverley died his story was
told in a pamphlet called Two Most Unnatural and Bloody Murders,
and this was followed by a ballad and another account, neither of
which has survived, both registered for publication in 1605, one
shortly before, the other soon after Calverley's death. In addition, two
plays, both apparently performed by the King's Men, took the events
as starting points for their action. One is a full-length tragicomedy,
The Miseries of Enforced Marriage, which treats the facts of the
case inventively to create a social drama portraying many fictional

characters and often adopting a comic perspective. Published in 1607, it was written by George Wilkins, who, it is now generally believed, collaborated with Shakespeare in the composition of *Pericles*.

Of more relevance here is *A Yorkshire Tragedy*. This exceptionally short play – it is only 700 lines long, considerably less than one-third the length of Shakespeare's shortest tragedy, *Macbeth* – was registered for publication on 2 May 1608 as having been written by 'William Shakespeare'. As the Wife, in her last speech, says she intends to sue for her husband's pardon, implying that he is still alive, it appears to have been written in 1605, before Calverley's death. It appeared soon after registration with a title page stating that it was 'acted by his majesty's players at the Globe', describing it as 'not so new as lament-able and true', and repeating the ascription to Shakespeare. More information, along with an alternative title, is given in the head title to the play itself, which reads 'All's One, or one of the four plays in one, called "A Yorkshire Tragedy", as it was played by the King's majesty's players'.

The twice-repeated ascription to Shakespeare seems like excellent evidence that he wrote it. Thomas Pavier, who published the first edition, reprinted it in a collection of Shakespearian and pseudo-Shakespearian quartos which he issued in 1619, but it was not in-cluded in the First Folio of 1623. It was however one of the seven plays added to the third Folio of 1664, only one of which – *Pericles* – is now accepted as being at least partly by Shakespeare. Throughout the nineteenth and twentieth centuries most commentators were unable to believe that Shakespeare wrote *A Yorkshire Tragedy*, rather because of its individual, non-Shakespearian dramatic style than because they thought it unworthy of him. In the later part of the twentieth century sophisticated studies of the play's linguistic features and of its dramatic style have created strong reasons for believing that it was actually written by Middleton; it has to be admitted, however, that nothing in Middleton's output up to this date would have pre-pared one for the possibility that he could have written so powerful a tragedy at this stage of his career.

Though all but its first scene is based closely not only on the events of the case but also on the very wording of the pamphlet, *A Yorkshire Tragedy* is no mere piece of reportage. In an introductory scene a group of servants gossip about their mistress's love for a wastrel who is already married, beats his wife, has run through all his wealth, and has made his brother, a university student, stand security for his debts. The tone is relaxed, but after this the drama makes a fresh start, unfolding in what Hamlet calls a 'torrent, tempest, and . . . whirlwind' of passion (*Hamlet*, 3.2.6–7), and giving the impression of having been written at white heat. Characteristically of Middleton, none of the characters in the body of the play has a personal name. The long-suffering Wife laments her 'half mad' husband's prodigality and cruelty, and the Husband, brutalized into hatred of his Wife and children by his passion for gambling and for women, curses both her and his fate, demands yet more money from her, declares that his three sons are 'Bastard, bastards, / Bastards begot in tricks', and says he has never loved her. But he is a victim as well as an oppressor, expressing anguished consciousness of sin in both prose and verse speeches of rare psychological complexity. Though there are no direct verbal links, it is difficult not to think of Macbeth as one hears the Husband's guilt-ridden soliloquies. And the portrayal of the crazed man's murder of his sons has a pathos that recalls the slaughter of Lady Macduff and her family:

SON What ails you, father, are you not well? I cannot scourge my top as long as you stand so. You take up all the room with your wide legs. Puh, you cannot make me afeard with this. I fear no vizards nor bugbears.

Husband takes up the child by the skirts of his long coat in one hand and draws his dagger with th'other.

HUSBAND Up, sir, for here thou hast no inheritance left.

SON O, what will you do father? – I am your white boy [favourite].

HUSBAND (*strikes him*) Thou shalt be my red boy. Take that!

SON O, you hurt me, father!

HUSBAND My eldest beggar. Thou shalt not live to ask an usurer bread, to cry at a great man's gate, or follow 'good your honour' by a crouch, no, nor your brother. 'Tis a charity to brain you.

SON How shall I learn now my head's broke?

HUSBAND Bleed, bleed, rather than beg, beg.

The Son's innocent prattle here is not a world away from that of Macduff's son (who also – like Lady Macbeth – has no personal name):

MACDUFF'S SON Was my father a traitor, mother?

LADY MACDUFF Ay, that he was.

MACDUFF'S SON What is a traitor?

LADY MACDUFF Why, one that swears and lies.

MACDUFF'S SON And be all traitors that do so?

LADY MACDUFF Everyone that does so is a traitor, and must be hanged.

  (*Macbeth*, 4.2.45–51)

The situation in *A Yorkshire Tragedy* is if anything even more horrific than in *Macbeth* in that here the killer is not an impersonal murderer but the child's father. If the play was indeed written before Calverley's execution, and if there is any influence from one dramatist to the other, then Shakespeare is likely to be indebted to Middleton rather than vice versa.

As the play develops, Middleton introduces the idea that the Husband's actions result from demoniac possession (one may think of Lady Macbeth's 'Come, you spirits / That tend on mortal thoughts . . .'; *Macbeth*, 1.5.39–40). He sees his condition as that of a man who has sold his soul to the devil:

> Divines and dying men may talk of hell,
> But in my heart her several torments dwell,
> Slavery and misery. Who in this case
> Would not take up money upon his soul,
> Pawn his salvation, live at interest?[8]

And in the final scene, moved to penitence by his Wife's forgiveness, he feels the devil losing possession of his body in lines that, in their raw physicality, their self-conscious rhetoric and their appeal to a spiritual world, bear comparison with Faustus's great final speech in Marlowe's play:

>   now glides the devil from me,
> Departs at every joint, heaves up my nails.
> O, catch him new torments that were ne'er invented,
> Bind him one thousand more, you blessed angels,
> In that pit bottomless, let him not rise
> To make men act unnatural tragedies,
> To spread into a father and, in fury,

> Make him his children's executioners,
> Murder his wife, his servants and who not?
> For that man's dark where heaven is quite forgot.

There are echoes here too of Othello:

> Whip me, ye devils,
> From the possession of this heavenly sight.
> Blow me about in winds, roast me in sulphur,
> Wash me in steep-down gulfs of liquid fire!
>
> (5.2.284–7)

A Yorkshire Tragedy is among the finest one-act plays in English.

The question of authorship is not the only puzzle about it. If the statement that it is by Shakespeare is untrue, can we trust the other claims that are made for it? It is said to have been 'one of . . . four plays in one'. Such entertainments existed: a work of uncertain date (?1613), possibly written for a boys' company, with this title – to be exact, Four Plays, or Moral Representations in One – was printed in the Beaumont and Fletcher Folio of 1647, but this is not it. There is no record of a four-part entertainment having been acted by the King's Men or any other company around the time when A Yorkshire Tragedy was written, and no other short plays that might have been acted along with it survive.

As I have said, the opening scene is written in so different a style from the rest of the play as to seem detached from it. The servants who appear there have no other function. It could easily have been written after the body of the play had been composed. What might we deduce from this about the manuscript from which the printers worked? There are many signs that it represented the author very much in the process of hasty composition, writing with the source pamphlet before him, not stopping to polish his verse, and leaving decisions crucial to the play's staging to be sorted out later. I have a hunch that Middleton, working with frenzied inspiration, sketched the play from the opening of what is now the second scene, found that it came out far too short for independent performance, embarked upon a process of expansion by writing an introductory scene in a more relaxed manner, decided that this didn't work, and as a way of cutting his losses turned the whole play over to a printer who agreed to publish it provided he could say it was by Shakespeare. I cannot prove this; but equally, so far as I know, no one can disprove it.

Middleton probably wrote *A Yorkshire Tragedy* 'without co-adjutor', to use Jonson's phrase. If we can believe what the printed text tells us, this play was written for the King's Men performing at the Globe, and with Shakespeare as their principal playwright. So was *The Revenger's Tragedy*, which appeared in print anonymously for the first time in 1607 (some copies are dated 1608) as having been 'sundry times acted by the King's majesty's servants'. In a play list printed in 1656 the author is said to be Cyril Tourneur (died 1626), a professional soldier and writer who published a satirical poem, *The Transformed Metamorphosis*, in 1600, and who seems to have had a brief period of success as a dramatist a few years after that. A play called *The Atheist's Tragedy, or The Honest Man's Revenge*, acted by an unidentified company, was printed as his in 1611, and his lost tragicomedy *The Nobleman* was registered for publication and acted by the King's Men in 1612. *The Atheist's Tragedy* is a remarkable work which climaxes in a death that is bizarre even by the standards of Jacobean drama. The revenger, D'Amville, raises the axe to execute his victim, Charlemont, but topples over and 'strikes out his own brains'; as he 'staggers off the scaffold', the professional Executioner, whose task he has usurped, remarks: 'In lifting up of the axe, I think h'as knocked/His brains out.' The mid-seventeenth-century attribution of *The Revenger's Tragedy* to the writer of *The Atheist's Tragedy* may be the consequence simply of the resemblance between the plays' titles. At any rate, the long-held suspicion that Middleton wrote the earlier play has hardened into conviction in many scholars' minds as the result of intensive authorship studies conducted during the later part of the twentieth century.

Though *The Revenger's Tragedy*, written around five years later than *Hamlet*, resembles Shakespeare's play in some ways, it is a brilliantly funny, primarily ironic, and fundamentally moralistic work which in its sardonic humour comes closer to Marlowe's *The Jew of Malta* but which also, in its portrayal of abstract vices, stretches back to the medieval morality tradition. Characteristically of Middleton – but not of Shakespeare – some characters, most conspicuously Vindice (the revenger) but also including Lussurioso (most luxurious, or lech-erous, one), Spurio (the false one, a bastard), Castiza (a chaste woman – the name also of Fidelio's mother in *The Phoenix*) and Ambitioso (the ambitious one) have allegorical names; others, such as the Duke and Duchess, are known only by their rank.

Typically, revenge tragedies centre on a wronged man who under-takes a bad deed for a good motive. He is likely to be bitter because of the wrong done him by the deed he is required to avenge, and his bitterness is likely to issue in satirical utterances. He is likely, too, to be working secretly for his revenge, unsuspected by the society in which he finds himself, and this will create a strong disparity between the appearance he presents to the world and the reality he acknowl-edges to himself. This may result in implicit irony, understood by the audience but not by the other characters of the play, and also in direct satirical attacks made either in soliloquy or to a confidant – such as Horatio in *Hamlet*.

Hamlet is – except for *Timon of Athens*, which as we shall see is a special case – the most satirically ironical of Shakespeare's tragedies. Its hero indulges in both general and particular satire. He is the wittiest of tragic heroes, and his wit is one of the means by which he pierces through the false appearances that surround him. His satirical treat-ment of Polonius and of Rosencrantz and Guildenstern, for example, creates ironies that are apprehended by the audience and that may even be at least suspected by the victims themselves. Sometimes his satire broadens and becomes more general, as in the 'nunnery' scene (3.1), when he expands from criticism of Ophelia to generalized remarks on womankind, and in the graveyard scene (5.1), with its satire of lawyers. Yet ultimately Hamlet is not satirically presented, nor does he himself adopt a consistently ironic attitude.

Hamlet may then be thought of as a romantic rather than, like *The Revenger's Tragedy*, an ironic tragedy, but its influence on the later play is apparent. As *The Revenger's Tragedy* opens we see Vindice in the attitude most closely associated with Hamlet: he is holding a skull and gazing into its eye sockets. But this is the skull, not of a long-dead jester, but of Vindice's murdered mistress, Gloriana, whose face, he says, had been

> far beyond the artificial shine
> Of any woman's bought complexion –
>
> (1.1.21–2)

words which must recall those spoken by Hamlet as he contemplates Yorick's skull: 'Let her paint an inch thick, to this favour she must come.' Like Hamlet, Vindice is determined to revenge his lover's death on the Duke, who has poisoned her because she refused to become his mistress, and also like Hamlet he sees the skull as an emblem of man's mortality and as a mockery of pretensions to greatness:

> Advance thee, O thou terror to fat folks,
> To have their costly three-piled flesh worn off
> As bare as this – for banquets, ease and laughter
> Can make great men, as greatness goes by clay,
> But wise men little are more great than they.
>
> (1.1.45–9)

The sententiousness of these lines is characteristic of Vindice, but the vitality that informs even his choric generalizations results from his personal involvement – this is not just a skull that he is contemplating, but the skull of the woman he loved. Interaction such as this between the general and the particular gives the play's brilliantly contrived fable much of its impetus. The action proceeds through a complex and ingeniously plotted series of ironies that reveal the corruption of the court, and that climax – though not conclude – in a scene in which Vindice, required to act as a pimp for the Duke, arranges for him to meet a woman for sex in a place where his Duchess, who 'will do with the devil', already has a rendezvous with his no less lecherous illegitimate son, Spurio. Vindice produces, not a live paramour, but a woman's skeleton – and, with added ironical intent, the skeleton of his own murdered mistress. The 'bony lady', as he calls her, is the final reality behind all disguises, the last truth beneath all pretence. Before presenting it to the Duke, Vindice meditates in terms which again recall *Hamlet*, terms which reach out from the immediate theatrical situation to become a meditation on the human condition:

> Does the silkworm expend her yellow labours
> For thee? for thee does she undo herself?

Are lordships sold to maintain ladyships
For the poor benefit of a bewitching minute?
Why does yon fellow falsify highways,
And put his life between the judge's lips,
To refine such a thing, keeps horse and men
To beat their valours for her?
Surely we are all mad people, and they
Whom we think are, are not; we mistake those:
'Tis we are mad in sense, they but in clothes.

(3.5.71–81)

The Duke, tricked into kissing the poisoned skull, is killed by the lady he had himself poisoned years before. And before he dies Vindice torments him with the sight of his bastard and his Duchess making love, mocking him, Spurio expressing hatred for him:

So deadly do I loathe him for my birth,
That if he took me hasped within his bed,
I would add murder to adultery,
And with my sword give up his years to death.

(3.5.210–13)

Much though Middleton learnt from Shakespeare in *The Revenger's Tragedy*, he created a very different play, and one which, along with other non-Shakespearian tragedies, has suffered in reputation because of its differences. Shakespeare's tragedies have dominated the English theatrical tradition, creating expectations which lessen the chances of success of others which, though they may be no less brilliant in themselves, are written in a different mode. *The Revenger's Tragedy* does not purge us, in a neo-Aristotelian manner, with pity and horror. It is less of a psychological study than a dramatized argument. As a result it is easily misunderstood and under-appreciated by audiences brought up on Shakespeare. On its first major revival, by the Royal Shakespeare Company in 1966, the critic of the *Sunday Times*, Harold Hobson, described it as 'an encyclopaedia of moral obscenities, an incursion into the filthy recesses of the Jacobean mind'.[9] But any implication that this is an immoral play, presenting with approval a degenerate society, would be totally mistaken. Vindice's reactions to the sexual immorality that he sees around him are devastating in their implicit condemnation of what they describe:

> Now 'tis full sea abed over the world,
> There's juggling of all sides; some that were maids
> E'en at sunset are now perhaps i' th' toll-book.
> This woman in immodest thin apparel
> Lets in her friend [lover] by water; here a dame,
> Cunning, nails leather hinges to a door
> To avoid proclamation. Now cuckolds are
> A-coining, apace, apace, apace, apace!
> And careful sisters spin that thread i' th' night
> That does maintain them and their bawds i' th' day.
>
> (2.2.134–43)

In this play Middleton not merely displays a strict concern for Christian morality but constructs the action with rigorous and totally unsentimental intellectuality, and also with brilliant theatricality and verbal skill, to display and exercise this concern.

Different though Shakespeare was from his younger colleague in his approach to tragedy, he appears all the same to have been willing to work with him, and even perhaps to attempt to extend his own range in the process, by accepting him as a coadjutor on *Timon of Athens*. It was a significant change in direction for a playwright who had worked entirely on his own since the founding of the Lord Chamberlain's Men some eleven or twelve years previously, but we can only speculate what brought it about. Conceivably Shakespeare was ill and needed help. Or he may simply have wished to encourage a younger colleague. *Timon of Athens* did not appear in print until 1623; it is exceptionally difficult to know when it was written, but resemblances to *King Lear* suggest that it may date from around the same period as that play, that is, 1605 or 1606 – not far in time from *The Revenger's Tragedy*. Maybe that play's success when performed by the King's Men – quite possibly with Shakespeare in the cast[10] – encouraged him to accept Middleton, sixteen years his junior, as a kind of senior apprentice.

The untypical quality of *Timon of Athens* by comparison with Shakespeare's other tragedies is self-evident. Although tragic in form, it is bitterly and satirically comic in its presentation of the sycophantic friends who sponge on Timon in his affluence but reject him when he loses his wealth, and even in its presentation of Timon's later misogyny. The possibility that Shakespeare was not its sole author was mooted as early as the 1830s, but the identification of Middleton as co-author, first made explicit in 1920, gained in strength during the later part of the twentieth century and is now strongly supported.

Like *The Revenger's Tragedy*, *Timon of Athens* is exceptionally schematic in construction, a parable in which elements of the design lie close to the surface, and in which characters are more important to the play's pattern of ideas than as individuals. As in the Middleton play, and untypically of Shakespeare, a high proportion of the characters, such as the Poet, the Painter, the Jeweller, the Merchant, the Fool, and a number of Senators and Servants who figure prominently in the action, have no personal names. Much of the verse, too, is irregular in a manner that is more typical of Middleton than of Shakespeare. The plausibility of the notion that the play is a collaborative work was enhanced by the discovery that the compilers of the First Folio, who excluded *Pericles*, in which Shakespeare collaborated with Wilkins, and two Fletcher collaborations, *The Two Noble Kinsmen* and the lost *Cardenio*, appear originally not to have intended to include *Timon of Athens*: study of the way that volume was put together has shown that this play occupies space originally intended for *Troilus and Cressida*. And intensive analysis of the play's structure and language has revealed many indications that two different authors worked on the text, and that these are very likely to have been Shakespeare and Middleton. Shakespeare seems to have 'concentrated on the opening, the scenes dealing most fully with Timon himself, and the conclusion'.[11]

The opening scene is an emblematic episode in which a Poet describes an allegorical poem showing how,

> When Fortune in her shift and change of mood
> Spurns down her late belovèd, all his dependants,
> Which laboured after him to the mountain's top
> Even on their knees and hands, let him fall down,
> Not one accompanying his declining foot.
>
> (1.1.85–9)

These lines, succinctly sketching Timon's progress through the play, summarize its design in a manner entirely untypical of Shakespeare's work to date. And in the action that follows, the play's scenario sticks through its sometimes inadequate flesh and blood like the skeleton of an emaciated body. It falls very clearly into two parts, the second a kind of mirror image of the first.

In the earlier part a sequence of episodes illustrate Timon's prodigal generosity, the fidelity of his Steward, Flavius, and the hypocrisy and greed of his fellow Senators. Middleton's experience as a writer of city comedies was invaluable in the composition of the satirically entertaining scenes in which Timon's friends show themselves in their true colours. Athens here stands in for London just as Ferrara had in *The Phoenix*. Middleton almost certainly composed the delightful coda to the climactic scene in which Timon reveals his disillusionment with his supposed friends by entertaining them to a banquet at which '*The dishes are uncovered, and seen to be full of steaming water* [*and stones*].' They leave in disarray after Timon throws water and stones at them and himself storms off, then return ignominiously to collect the belongings they have left behind them in their haste:

> THIRD LORD Push! Did you see my cap?
> FOURTH LORD   I have lost my gown.
> FIRST LORD He's but a mad lord, and naught but humours
>   sways him. He gave me a jewel th'other day, and now he has
>   beat it out of my hat.
>   Did you see my jewel?
> THIRD LORD   Did you see my cap?
> SECOND LORD Here 'tis.
> FOURTH LORD   Here lies my gown.
> FIRST LORD   Let's make no stay.
> SECOND LORD Lord Timon's mad.
> THIRD LORD   I feel't upon my bones.
> FOURTH LORD One day he gives us diamonds, next day stones.
>   *Exeunt* (3.7.107–end)

Timon's slow disillusionment with Athenian society reaches a climax as he banishes himself:

> Nothing I'll bear from thee
> But nakedness, thou detestable town.
>
> (4.1.32–3)

The play's second part, cast virtually in the form of an interrupted soliloquy, shows Timon living as a hermit in a cave where he receives a sequence of visitors whom he treats to diatribes on the corruptive power of gold.

The collaboration on this play between Shakespeare and his younger colleague may not have been entirely happy; indeed it is quite likely that they gave it up as a bad job before the play was complete. So far as we know it was not acted in its own time, and the manuscript from which it was printed in the First Folio clearly needed a lot of work before it could be put into production. Stage directions give information that is at odds with what happens in the text. Characters are inexactly identified, so that it is often unclear exactly who should say what. The play is much concerned with money and the most commonly used sum of money is the talent, but its value seems to veer drastically from one speech to another. Timon dies of no apparent cause, and his grave bears two contradictory epitaphs.

The most conspicuous evidence that the play as we have it is unfinished relates to the character of Alcibiades. He takes part in the early scenes as a warrior on whom Timon bestows bounty. After Timon has invited his false friends to a mock banquet, we suddenly have a scene with Alcibiades at the centre in which he pleads passionately before the Athenian Senate for the life of an unidentified and unseen friend who has apparently killed a man in unexplained circumstances. His petition is refused, and he himself is banished in spite of his great services to the state. It is easy to guess how Middleton and Shakespeare planned to bind the scene into the rest of the play: it adds to our sense of the corruption in Athens, helps to justify Timon by replicating the hypocrisy and ingratitude of his supposed friends on the highest and most official level, and provides an opening for a counter-action in which Alcibiades, rather than retreating into bitter misanthropy like Timon, will lead his forces against his own city. Probably it was intended to bear the same relationship to the main plot as that of Gloucester's blinding in *King Lear*, but it is inadequately worked out and imperfectly integrated into the story.

Editors quite properly tidy up many of the play's anomalies – if you want to get a full sense of them you have to read it as it was originally printed, in the First Folio – and theatre directors need to go further, even to the extent of doing a bit – or a lot – of rewriting if the play is to come across in performance as a coherent whole. For all this, it is a fascinating play with many outstanding passages that show the genius of both its authors.

Middleton was only in his mid-twenties at the time he appears to have been working directly with Shakespeare. After that his career developed in various directions, some of them different from those he had already followed. He continued for a while to write London comedies, including *The Puritan Widow* (1606) and *Your Five Gallants* (1607), for the boys' companies. During the plague years of 1608 to 1610 he became seriously short of cash – he was arrested for a debt of £5 in December 1608, someone sued him for the sum of £16 early in the following year, and in July 1609 he still owed £7. 9s. to a publican in Westminster. Poverty forced him to diversify, even to cheat. In spring 1609 he had published a translation and adaptation of a Latin text that had originally appeared in Poland advocating an alliance between Europe and the Turks, under the title of *Sir Robert Shirley his Entertainment in Cracovia*, and he followed this later in the same year with *The Two Gates of Salvation, or The Marriage of the Old and New Testament*, which offers a Calvinistic reading of scripture. The cheating lies in the fact that both works appeared with dedications to different patrons in different copies, no doubt in the hope of multiple reward for the same work. He returned to the adult theatre with all his old energy in 1611 with three plays centring on women characters: he wrote again with his old friend Thomas Dekker in *The Roaring Girl* (see pp. 121–2) and worked independently on *No Wit, No Help Like a Woman's* for the Fortune theatre and on a bizarre tragedy of horror based on *Don Quixote* that has come down to us in manuscript without a title, but has been known as *The Second Maiden's Tragedy* and, more recently, as *The Lady's* (or *Ladies'*) *Tragedy*. Because his masterly comedy *A Chaste Maid in Cheapside* of 1613 was written for an amalgamated company which could muster more than the usual complement of boy actors, he was able to put as many as eleven speaking female characters on stage at once. In the same year he started what was to become a fruitful collaboration with William Rowley, a comic actor-writer famous for his girth, in the comedy *Wit at Several Weapons*, and also branched out into the first of his series of Lord Mayor's pageants and other commissioned entertainments which were to help to maintain him and his family for the rest of his life.

More independent and collaborative plays followed – too many even to name in a chapter which centres on his relations with Shakespeare – but one that needs to be mentioned is a tragicomedy called *The Witch*. It survives only in a manuscript, in which it is said to have been acted by the King's Men at the Blackfriars, and there is reason to suspect that its publication may have been blocked by the authorities because it concealed allusions to a contemporary scandal in high life.[12] It is relevant here because it shows Middleton in the capacity, as envisaged by Jonson, of a 'journeyman' commissioned, probably, by the King's Men, to adapt plays previously written for the company in order to fit them to new circumstances of representation. It is the same kind of task that we have seen Shakespeare undertaking in *Sir Thomas More*, Jonson in his provision of new mad scenes for *The Spanish Tragedy*, and Middleton himself, in a small way, in writing a new prologue for *Friar Bacon and Friar Bungay*. Middleton appears to have undertaken this role for two plays, probably after Shakespeare had retired, or after he had died.

There is a firm point of contact – indeed, of identity – between *The Witch* and *Macbeth*. In Shakespeare's play, as originally printed in the First Folio, there are cues for two songs: '*Sing within. Come away, come away, &c.*' (3.5.34), and '*Musicke and a Song. Blacke spirits, &c.*' (4.1.44). The cue lines quote the opening words of songs found in *The Witch* (3.3.39 and 5.2.60). In both plays they occur in scenes centring on Hecate, the chief witch. In *Macbeth* these scenes stick out from the rest of the play in several ways. Hecate appears in them only. The episodes in which she features are composed largely in octosyllabic couplets in a style conspicuously different from the rest of the play. It has long been suspected that a writer other than Shakespeare interpolated these episodes, indeed Middleton himself was mentioned as early as 1869. And there are other reasons to suppose that the text as we have it may be an adaptation. It is exceptionally brief – at around 2,350 lines, some 750 lines shorter than, for instance, *Romeo and Juliet*, and well over 1,400 lines fewer than *Coriolanus*.[13] Moreover, the account of the play given by Simon Forman (mentioned earlier in relation to the acting style of Richard Burbage and reproduced in Documents, pp. 240–41 below) of a performance that he saw on 20 April 1611 differs in some ways from the text as we have it: for instance, although Forman, an astrologer and magician, had a keen interest in the supernatural, he makes no mention of Hecate, or of the cauldron scene in which she figures, and he describes the weird sisters as 'Nimphes' who are encountered in a wood, rather than upon the heath. These various pieces of admittedly circumstantial evidence conspire together to suggest that Middleton, who had learnt from Shakespeare in his earliest writings, who had written several plays for the company to which Shakespeare belonged during his lifetime, and who, we believe, collaborated closely with him in the composition of *Timon of Athens*, was entrusted by the company with the task of revising *Macbeth*, for reasons that we can only guess at, as a late service to the master he had followed.

The other Shakespeare play which, modern scholarship indicates, Middleton may have adapted is *Measure for Measure*.[14] There are good reasons to believe that the play started life as one of the disguised Duke plays – which as we have seen include Middleton's *The Phoenix* – written soon after King James I came to the throne in March 1603. But the only text that has come down to us – the one printed in the First Folio – shows signs of having been altered at a later date. For one thing, there is a curious absence of profanity, which suggests that it had been tampered with after May 1606, which saw the passing of the 'Act to Restrain Abuses of Players' (reprinted in Documents, pp. 238–9 below). This law instituted a fine of £10 for each time an actor 'jestingly or profanely' spoke the name of God or Jesus Christ. The provision that half of the fine should be paid to any member of the public who informed on the players no doubt helped to ensure that the law was enforced. Furthermore, the First Folio text includes one stanza of a song, 'Take, O take those lips away', which is found in a two-stanza version in a much later play, *Rollo, Duke of Normandy* (also known as *The Bloody Brother*), written by John Fletcher and others probably around 1617–19; it was set to music by the composer and lutenist John Wilson (1595–1674), who was only 9 years old in 1604 when *Measure for Measure* was probably first acted. So it may well be that the one-stanza version is a late addition to *Measure for Measure*.

On top of all this, a passage at the opening of the second scene gives every indication of alluding to events that happened a good many years after the play was first written. At its start Lucio says: 'If the Duke with the other dukes come not to composition with the King of Hungary, why then, all the dukes fall upon the King.' To which a Gentleman replies: 'Heaven grant us its peace, but not the King of Hungary's!' (1.2.1–5). This sounds like a topical allusion, but attempts to link the lines with events of the early years of James's reign have been unconvincing. Recently, however, they have been shown to make excellent sense in relation to the political situation in Hungary in 1620–21, and to events which were widely reported in England since they involved James's Protestant son-in-law, Frederick of Bohemia, deposed by the Catholic Emperor Ferdinand II. Cumulatively, all these circumstances considered together point convincingly to the belief that the text as we have it is an adaptation made around 1621, and a number of Middleton's linguistic fingerprints in lines that appear to have been added in this process suggest that he was the adapter.

The adaptation theory also helps to explain another oddity about the play. It has always seemed puzzling that though the action is set in Vienna, most of the characters have Italian names – Isabella, Lucio, Claudio, Angelo and so on. A strong case has been made for the belief that in the process of adaptation the action was moved from Italy to Austria as a means of increasing its topicality at a time when the King of Hungary was making war against Austria and attacking Vienna. Specifically, it is suggested, the play may originally, like Middleton's *The Phoenix*, have been set in Ferrara.[15]

Although Middleton was willing to undertake journeyman tasks, he remained an original creative force to the end of his career, both in single-authored works and in collaboration with a range of partners old and new, including Webster, Dekker and Ford. *Women Beware Women* (1621) and *The Changeling* (1622), in which his partnership with William Rowley climaxed, are two of the most powerful Jacobean tragedies. And his bold and daring commitment to topicality was vividly demonstrated in *A Game at Chess* (1624), with which he resumed his links with the King's Men. In this allegorical anti-Spanish and anti-Catholic drama, all the characters, represented as chessmen, stand for contemporary political figures. White pieces represent the English court and church, and the black pieces are Spaniards. The Black Knight is a recent Spanish Ambassador, Count Gondomar; he suffered from an anal fistula, and was scurrilously represented on stage in a litter and seated on his special chair with a hole in it. In the final scene, the current Ambassador reported, 'he who acted the Prince of Wales heartily beat and kicked the "Count of Gondomar" into Hell, which consisted of a great hole and hideous figures; and the White King drove the Black King and even his Queen into Hell almost as offensively'.

Few plays ever written have caused such a scandal.[16] As a result it survives in six different manuscript copies, more than for almost any other play of the period. Gleeful audiences flocked in their thousands to the unprecedented number of nine consecutive performances given at the Globe from 5 August 1624. The Spanish Ambassador reported home that 'there were more than 3,000 persons there on the day that the audience was smallest. There was such merriment, hubbub and applause that even if I had been many leagues away it would not have been possible for me not to have taken notice of it.'[17] He complained to the English King and threatened to withdraw from the country if the perpetrators were not severely punished. James was out of town, 'feasting and fawning upon the French ambassador', and the King's Men are said to have been able to rake in the astonishing sum of at least £100 a day until further performances were banned.[18] Officially, James was horrified, but the Spaniards expressed understandable scepticism about the genuineness of his disapproval. The Privy Council summoned the actors to appear before them, reprimanded them, and forbade them to play until further notice – the ban lasted for only a couple of months – but Middleton went into hiding and was represented at the official hearing by his son. He may have been imprisoned, and released on condition that he give up playwriting: this is his last known work for the stage. He continued to devise pageants and other entertainments for the City of London, but did not always satisfy his employers, who withheld payments due to him. He was buried on 4 July 1627, and his widow survived him for only a year.

Both the trajectory of Middleton's career and his strengths as a dramatist were different from Shakespeare's. He was more of an independent spirit, with no long-lasting allegiance to a single company of players. The canon of his works, some of which – like *The Revenger's Tragedy* – appeared anonymously or even (like *A Yorkshire Tragedy*) with false attributions, is still being redefined. No collected edition of his writings appeared until the nineteenth century. He engaged far more closely with the life of his times than Shakespeare, and did so largely from a satirical point of view. The varied styles and dramatic modes that he adopted make him an exceptionally protean figure, but he is gradually coming into focus as a playwright of astonishing versatility and power.

7

The Move to Tragicomedy: John Fletcher and Others

10. John Fletcher. The only known life-time portrait of Fletcher, by an unknown artist, shows him expensively dressed as befits a man of his social origins.

The only dramatist with whom, on the basis of evidence likely to be accepted in a court of law, it can confidently be said that Shakespeare collaborated is, as we shall see, John Fletcher (1579–1625). His name is indelibly associated with that of Francis Beaumont. Indeed the earliest biographical account of Fletcher comes in the entry for Beaumont in the scrappy and often unreliable but nevertheless continuously entertaining and informative notebooks of John Aubrey (1626–97) known as his *Brief Lives*, which he wrote mostly around 1679–80 but which were not published until after he died. His gossipy few sentences suggest that Beaumont and Fletcher were the closest of friends, soulmates as well as professional colleagues. The 'dearness of friendship between them' arose, writes Aubrey, from 'a wonderful consimility[1] of fancy'. He continues: 'I think they were both of Queens' College in Cambridge.'[2] On this point Aubrey, who had not known the men personally and was writing several decades after they had died, was probably wrong. A youth called John Fletcher who went to Corpus Christi, Cambridge at the surprisingly but not impossibly early age of 11 in 1591 is likely to be the dramatist. Beaumont, younger by some five years, began his university career when he was only one year older, at Broadgates Hall – later Pembroke College – Oxford, in 1597. He left in the following year, after his father died, and continued his education at the Inner Temple in London.

Aubrey's demonstrable errors and his reliance on gossip do not inspire confidence, but at least he seems to have spoken to someone who actually knew the men. 'I have heard Dr John Earles, since Bishop of Sarum, who knew them, say that Mr Beaumont's main business was to lop the overflowings of Mr Fletcher's luxuriant fancy and flowing wit.' 'Earles' (John Earle, 1598–1665) knew Beaumont well enough to write a poem on his death in 1616. Aubrey goes on with more intimate information which is irresistible in the plausibility of its picture of a bohemian bachelor household: 'They lived together on the Bankside, not far from the playhouse, both bachelors; lay together; had one wench in the house between them, which they did so admire [probably meaning that each of them admired her as much as the other did]; the same clothes and cloak etc. between them.'[3] What exact living arrangements Aubrey was hinting at – and what happened if they both wanted to go out when it was raining – is impossible to determine. The friends may not have been able to afford extensive wardrobes, but Beaumont, to judge by his engraved portrait, managed to employ an excellent barber and hairdresser. So far as we know, Fletcher never married, but the bachelor household cannot have survived after 1613, when Fletcher was 34, since in that year Beaumont took a wife who was to bear him two daughters.

Fletcher, who belonged to a distinguished ecclesiastic and literary family, would have been aware of national politics from an early age. His father, Richard, was a clergyman who, with the backing of the Earl of Essex, became Bishop of London in 1595. Previously, as Dean of Peterborough, he had been deeply involved in the trial and

11. Francis Beaumont. This handsome engraving of Beaumont is based on a portrait by an unknown artist.

execution of Mary, Queen of Scots, exhorting her on the scaffold to return to the Protestant fold and praying for her soul before she was beheaded. This was in 1587, when the future playwright was 8 years old. Richard was a tough-minded preacher, militant in his faith, and not afraid of rebuking even his Queen from the pulpit. Preaching before Elizabeth only a few days after the execution, he sternly rebuked her for indulging in remorse and called for even more rigorous persecution of her Catholic enemies. In spite of this his life came to a peaceful if abrupt end. Smoking a pipe of tobacco in his house in Chelsea on the evening of 15 June 1596 he said to his servant, 'Boy, I die', and expired on the spot. His brother Giles, a poet and diplomat who travelled to Moscow on a special mission in 1588 and wrote a book about his experiences – many of them extremely trying – on his return, took over the upbringing of the Bishop's eight children, including the future playwright. Giles's son Phineas (1582–1650) was also a clergyman and poet. So John Fletcher had every encouragement to embark upon a literary career.

The first play in which he is known to have been involved is *The Woman Hater, or the Hungry Courtier*, written for Paul's Boys around

1606 and published in 1607. This was a collaboration with Beaumont who had already, at the age of 22, written single-handed what is now his best-known work, *The Knight of the Burning Pestle* – a failure in its own time, perhaps because of its structural originality. Both plays quote from Shakespeare to comic effect. *The Knight of the Burning Pestle*, written for a boys' company, opens with an Induction in which a Grocer, soon followed by his wife and his apprentice, Rafe (or Ralph), leaps upon the stage to hijack the play that the boys have been intending to give, demanding instead one that will glorify his trade. Offering her son as a substitute actor, the grocer's wife boasts that the lad

will act you sometimes at our house that all the neighbours cry out on him. He will fetch you up a couraging part so in the garret that we are all as feared, I warrant you, that we quake again. We'll fear our children with him if they be never so unruly. Do but cry 'Rafe comes, Rafe comes!' to them and they'll be as quiet as lambs. (lines 66–72)

This may only subliminally recall Bottom in *A Midsummer Night's Dream* – 'I will roar that I will do any man's heart good to hear me. I will roar that I will make the Duke say "Let him roar again; let him roar again!"'(1.2.66–9). Immediately after it, however, there is an undeniable Shakespeare quotation as the Wife, abetted by the Grocer, instructs her son to demonstrate his mettle by speaking 'a huffing part', whereupon Ralph launches into five lines only slightly misquoted from a speech of Hotspur in one of Shakespeare's most popular plays, *Henry IV*, Part One:

> By heaven, methinks it were an easy leap
> To pluck bright honour from the pale-faced moon,
> Or dive into the bottom of the sea,
> Where never fathom-line touched any ground,
> And pluck up drowned honour from the lake of hell.[4]

The misquotation may imply that Beaumont thought he knew the lines well enough to quote them from memory. Later in the comedy comes a burlesque episode which must recall the dead Banquo's appearance to Macbeth in the banquet scene. The apprentice Jasper, who has pretended to be dead, disguises himself as his own ghost in the attempt to frighten his master Venturewell into allowing him to marry his daughter, Luce. Entering 'with his face mealed', Jasper threatens Venturewell:

> When thou art at thy table with thy friends,
> Merry in heart and filled with swelling wine,
> I'll come in midst of all thy pride and mirth,
> Invisible to all men but thyself,
> And whisper such a sad tale in thine ear
> Shall make thee let the cup fall from thy hand,
> And stand as mute and pale as Death itself.
>
> (Scene 5, lines 22–8)

Shakespeare's most popular play, *Hamlet*, provides the basis for a jest in *The Woman Hater, or the Hungry Courtier*, a delightful comedy well worthy of revival.[5] An unusual fish has been caught and, as 'a rare novelty', the head has been 'appointed by special commandment for the Duke's own table this dinner'. Lazarello, known as 'the hungry courtier', goes to great lengths to manoeuvre an invitation to taste 'this sacred dish'. But disaster strikes, and Count Valore breaks the news to him and comments on it with lines borrowed from the Ghost in *Hamlet*:

> VALORE ... hear me with patience.
> LAZARELLO Let me not fall from myself!
>   *Speak! I am bound to hear!*
> VALORE *So art thou to revenge, when thou shalt hear.*
>   The fish head is gone, and we know not whither.
>
> (2.1.343–8)

The transference of the lines in which the Ghost of Hamlet's father prepares Hamlet for the information that he was murdered (*Hamlet*, 1.5.5–6) to the trivial situation of the theft of a fish head is parodic, but the joke is on Lazarello rather than on Shakespeare.

There are hints of Shakespeare too in Fletcher's first solo-authored play, *The Faithful Shepherdess*, a pastoral fantasy written in a mixture of blank and rhymed verse, probably in 1607 or 1608. Here the echoes are subliminal, suggesting that Fletcher has absorbed both the spirit and the letter of Shakespearian comedy so fully that phrases from plays float to the surface of his mind as he writes. In the opening scene, for instance, the Satyr's exit couplet, 'I must go, I must run, / Swifter than the fiery sun', recalls Robin Goodfellow's 'I go, I go – look how I go, / Swifter than arrow from the Tartar's bow' (*A Midsummer Night's Dream*, 3.2.100–101). And only a few lines later the faithful shepherdess, Clorin, grieving over the grave of her dead lover, speaks of herself in lines that faintly recall Titania's memories of the Indian boy's mother who 'being mortal, of that boy did die' (2.1.135) while also trembling with echoes of Shylock in *The Merchant of Venice*, as well as recalling, at least to a modern reader, Poor Tom in *King Lear*:

> He was mortal,
> And she that bore me mortal: prick my hand,
> And it will bleed; a fever shakes me,
> And the self-same wind that makes the young lambs shrink
> Makes me a-cold.[6]

In his address 'To the Reader' of the published text[7] Fletcher describes this play as 'a pastoral tragi-comedy' and says that it had angered its first audiences when it was performed by the Children of the Queen's Revels in the Blackfriars because they had expected something more robust – 'a play of country hired shepherds in grey cloaks, with cur-tailed dogs in strings, sometimes laughing together, and sometimes killing one another'. The misfortune that both Beaumont and Fletcher started their careers with solo-authored plays that failed to please theatre audiences may have helped them to realize that their gifts were to some extent complementary, and that they were more likely to succeed if they worked in tandem, or with other writers, than on their own. Indeed, this theory fits well enough with Aubrey's statement that Mr Beaumont's main business was 'to lop the overflowings of Mr Fletcher's luxuriant fancy and flowing wit'.

Fletcher's address to the reader continues with what has become the classic definition of a tragicomedy:

A tragi-comedy is not called so in respect of mirth and killing, but in respect it wants deaths, which is enough to make it no tragedy, yet brings some near it, which is enough to make it no comedy, which must be a representation of familiar people, with such kind of trouble as no life be questioned [that is, with problems that are not life-threatening].

It would be easy enough to apply this definition to previously written plays that we are happy enough to call comedies without qualification. In *The Comedy of Errors*, for example, Egeon comes close to death, as does Antonio in *The Merchant of Venice*, both plays of the 1590s; and in Shakespeare's early seventeenth-century play *Measure for Measure*, classed in the First Folio as a comedy, death looms even larger in the threatened executions of Claudio and Barnardine and the onstage presence of not only the executioner Abhorson but the severed head of the 'most notorious pirate Ragusine' (4.3.68). And although some of the low-life characters in *Measure for Measure*, especially, have links with the society of Shakespeare's day, these plays do not exactly offer a 'representation' of people who would have been 'familiar' to the audience such as is found in the city comedies of Dekker, Middleton and Jonson. But while there is nothing revolutionary in the genre of tragicomedy as newly defined by Fletcher, his preface and the play that it accompanies signify a shift in dramaturgy that finds different but related expression in the subsequent tragicomedies that he wrote with Beaumont and in the tragicomic plays that have come to be known as romances composed by Shakespeare, working in at least one of them along with Fletcher.

The first of Shakespeare's full-blown romances, *Pericles*, written in or around 1607, was ascribed only to him on its publication in 1609, in a raggedly corrupt text, but its omission from the First Folio encourages doubt about his sole authorship. So does the highly uneven quality of the writing; one of the commonest clichés of Shakespeare criticism is that his authentic voice is not heard until the start of the third act (Scene 11 in the Oxford edition), with Pericles's lines beginning:

> The god of this great vast rebuke these surges
> Which wash both heav'n and hell; and thou that hast
> Upon the winds command, bind them in brass,
> Having called them from the deep.

Everything points to this having been a collaborative play, and modern scholarship has established fairly conclusively that Shakespeare's partner in its composition was the shadowy figure of George Wilkins, whom we have encountered as the author of *The Miseries of Enforced*

Marriage, successfully performed by the King's Men probably in 1607, and as part-author, with John Day and William Rowley, of *The Travels of the Three English Brothers*.[8] Little is known of Wilkins's early life, and all his known writings belong to the period 1606–8, after which he kept a London inn which doubled as a brothel. He died in 1618.

Wilkins was a violent character, frequently in court for a variety of offences, but, in 1612, as a witness in a lawsuit in which Shakespeare also testified. Eight years previously, Stephen Belott, apprentice to a Huguenot refugee named Christopher Mountjoy, who made ladies' wigs and headdresses, had married his master's daughter Marie, and Shakespeare, who at the time was a lodger in the household, had good-naturedly acted as a go-between in the marriage negotiations. Relations between the couple and their in-laws deteriorated soon after the marriage, and the newly-weds went to lodge with Wilkins. Eventually Belott sued his father-in-law, alleging broken promises over money matters. Both Shakespeare and Wilkins were called as witnesses; Wilkins deposed that he would not have given more than £5 for the goods they brought with them. Nothing emerges to his discredit from this case, but on 3 March 1611 he had been accused of 'kicking a woman on the belly which was then great with child', and a year later, three months before the Mountjoy hearing, he was stated to have 'outrageously beaten one Judith Walton and stamped upon her so that she was carried home in a chair'.[9]

This disreputable figure may seem an unlikely collaborator for respectable Master Shakespeare, but there is little doubt that, although Wilkins was principally responsible for the composition of the first two acts (or ten scenes in the Oxford edition) of *Pericles*, and Shakespeare for the rest of the play, they worked closely on it together; Wilkins's first-hand experience may have come in handy in the composition of the scenes set in a brothel.[10] He went on to exploit the collaboration by slinging together a prose romance called *The Painful Adventures of Pericles Prince of Tyre* (1608), described as 'the true history of the play of *Pericles*', which takes over speeches of the play word for word.[11]

Pericles is a play of extremes. It subjects its central characters to intensely 'painful adventures' such as imprisonment in a brothel, narrow escape from assassination, threats of rape, burial alive at sea, and prolonged coma, while finally granting them miraculous restorations to happiness effected in part by supernatural agency. This is the first of Shakespeare's plays to include a theophany – the appearance of a god – except for the underdeveloped figure of Hymen who brings about the resolution of *As You Like It*. *Pericles* was immensely popular, and its success must have encouraged both Shakespeare and the Beaumont and Fletcher team to continue to write plays that similarly draw together greater extremes of emotional experience than are associated with the conventional genres of comedy and tragedy.[12] At the same time, however, the dramatists continued to work within more traditional genres. There is no doubt that they interacted with each other, but absence of information about when plays were first performed, compounded with the fact that throughout the period many of them did not appear in print until long after they were written, means that it is impossible to tell a straightforward story, and therefore that we are often unsure whether one came before another. Nevertheless, it seems clear that within a year or two after the King's Men performed *Pericles* Fletcher came into the company's orbit, and thus also into Shakespeare's, by working for it with Beaumont on what became a series of successful plays. They had one of their earliest hits with *The Maid's Tragedy*, a sensational, highly wrought story of revenge and courtly corruption which has affinities with *Hamlet* and which, though its ostensible setting is Rhodes, might well have caused members of the Jacobean court to look over their shoulders. This play has a tragic conclusion, and after *Pericles* Shakespeare too returned to tragedy with *Antony and Cleopatra* and *Coriolanus*, but two other Beaumont and Fletcher collaborations of the period, *Philaster* and *A King and No King* (which can be pretty precisely dated to 1611), are tragicomedies that may easily be seen as forerunners of Shakespeare's later romances and of his collaborations with Fletcher.

In the meantime (probably around 1610) Fletcher, apparently unaided, engaged directly with Shakespeare, and with the Shakespeare of some twenty years previously, in the only dramatic sequel to any of his plays written before the Restoration. It was bold of the young dramatist to take on his senior in this way, especially because *The Woman's Prize, or The Tamer Tamed* adopts a very different attitude

JOHN FLETCHER AND OTHERS

to the place of women in society from that offered in *The Taming of the Shrew*.

At the end of Shakespeare's play the shrew, Kate, has, it appears, been thoroughly tamed and expresses her sense of wifely duty in a long speech of joyful submission which has stuck in the gullets of readers and spectators to such an extent that a century and more ago Bernard Shaw declared: 'No man with any decency of feeling can sit it out in the company of a woman without being extremely ashamed of the lord-of-creation moral implied in the wager and the speech put into the woman's own mouth.'[13] Some modern interpreters evade the implications of this speech by causing Kate to deliver it tongue in cheek. Fletcher anticipated them. We gather from the opening scene of his play that Kate's submission had been far from total, or at least that it had not lasted long. Now she is dead and Petruccio has remarried even though, his friends say,

> . . . the bare remembrance of his first wife –
> I tell ye on my knowledge, and a truth too –
> Will make him start in's sleep, and very often
> Cry out for cudgels, colestaves, anything,
> And hide his breeches out of fear her ghost
> Should walk and wear 'em yet.
>
> (1.1.31–6)

Some of them fear that he will make his new wife, Maria, suffer because of what he had to put up with from Kate. But as soon as Maria appears she makes it clear that she can hold her own:

> I am no more the gentle tame Maria.
> Mistake me not; I have a new soul in me
> Made of a north wind, nothing but tempest,
> And like a tempest shall it make all ruins
> Till I have run my will out.
>
> (1.2.70–74)

She immediately asserts her independence by refusing to sleep with her husband and barricading herself into her bedroom with her comrade, 'Colonel Bianca', arming all the windows with fully charged chamber pots ready to resist attack until Petruccio, who has 'been famous for a woman-tamer', and who bears 'the feared name of a brave wife-breaker', will show that he is himself tamed. Friends bring supplies of food and wine to help the women to withstand a siege. Other wives join them, led by a tanner's wife who 'flayed her husband in her youth, and made / Reins of his hide to ride the parish'. Gaining strength through numbers, they have a high old time in their fortress, singing a song dedicated 'To the woman that bears the sway / And wears the breeches', and dancing 'with their coats tucked up to their bare breeches'. A truce is called, subject to a string of conditions: Maria must have freedom to do as she pleases, fine clothes of her own choice, control over the family finances, power to entertain as she wishes, new coaches and buildings, tapestries and horses, along with agreement that her younger sister shall not be forced to marry against her will. Petruccio signs the agreement, but his troubles are not over. Though he rejoins Maria, whom he still loves, in a series of episodes recalling those in Shakespeare's play in which Petruccio tames Kate, she does not let him 'touch her all this night'; she orders expensive clothes, horses and falcons, complains that their house 'stands in an ill air' and is 'nothing / But a tiled fog', and rebukes him for the way he treated his first wife. Left alone, he expresses amazement that after all he suffered from Kate he was so foolish as to marry again, and decides to pretend to be dying in the attempt to tame Maria. She joins gleefully in the game, clearing the house in the pretence that he is suffering from the plague and having him sealed within it in spite of all his protestations that he is in perfectly good health. Claiming that she has been a 'little peevish' to him 'only to try [his] temper', she pretends distress that he will not accept her comfort and love. All this provokes him into paroxysms of abuse issuing in the threat that he will travel overseas, a plan of which she thoroughly approves; as a climactic trick he pretends to be dead and has himself brought before her in a coffin. Now at last she considers that the tamer is tamed:

> I have done my worst, and have my end:
> . . . I have tamed ye,
> And now am vowed your servant.
>
> (5.4.45–7)

The epilogue written anonymously for the 1633 revival points the moral of what has gone before: the play is 'meant / To teach both sexes due equality / And, as they stand bound, to love mutually'.

The Woman's Prize, or The Tamer Tamed is an intriguing intervention in the sexual politics of the age. There is no sign that in writing it Fletcher stood in the relation of pupil or apprentice to Shakespeare. Indeed it is fascinating that, only about twenty years after Shakespeare had given expression in *The Taming of the Shrew* to the orthodox patriarchal view of the place of women in marriage, Fletcher should produce so powerful and so independently plotted a counterblast to it, and especially that he should do so for Shakespeare's company and, it would seem, with his approval. It has been well said that 'If we ever needed proof (if his plays are somehow not enough) that Shakespeare had a sense of humour, then this is surely it'.[14] When the King's Men planned a revival at the Blackfriars in 1633 it was suppressed by the Master of the Revels, Sir Henry Herbert, on the grounds that he had received 'complaints of foul and offensive matters contained therein'. Rapidly purging it of 'oaths, profaneness, and ribaldry' he returned it to the players, and a few weeks later they performed it back to back with *The Taming of the Shrew* at court before Charles I and his queen, Henrietta Maria.[15] No such purgations were thought necessary when the play was given what may well have been its next performances, also along with Shakespeare's comedy, by the Royal Shakespeare Company in 2003.

There is something symbolic about Fletcher's successful composition of a Shakespeare sequel for the King's Men. It marks a point of transition. Shakespeare was in his mid-forties and his output was beginning to dwindle. With or without his approval, the other members of his company may have begun to look to a future when he would no longer be their principal dramatist. He had collaborated with – should we even say, received help from? – Middleton on *Timon of Athens*, perhaps in 1606 (this is one of the most difficult of his plays to date), and with Wilkins on *Pericles* a year or so later. Fletcher and his regular partner Francis Beaumont were newly established, extremely hard-working young dramatists who already had a string of successes to their names, both individually and in collaboration. The genre of romantic tragicomedy which seems especially to have appealed to Fletcher is one that Shakespeare too found congenial in what turned out to be his last years. From about 1602 onwards he had been tentatively approaching it with his darker comedies, *Measure for Measure* and *All's Well That Ends Well*, and then fully committed himself to it in *Pericles*. After that all his plays with a comic structure – *The Winter's Tale, Cymbeline, The Tempest, The Two Noble Kinsmen*, even the historical romance of *All is True (Henry VIII)*, and presumably the lost *Cardenio* – whether or not they were written with Fletcher, have clear affinities or direct connections with the younger dramatist's work.

Among the hallmarks of Beaumont and Fletcher's plays of this period is a dependence for theatrical effectiveness on sudden reversals and unexpected revelations of the kind that, centuries later, W. S. Gilbert was to parody in the Savoy operas. In *A King and No King*, for example, King Arbaces of Iberia falls passionately in love with Panthea, whom he believes to be his sister; and she returns his passion. Tormented with apparently incestuous desire, he resolves to rape her and then kill himself; but the necessity for so extreme a course of action is happily averted when we – and, more importantly, he – learn that Panthea is not his sister after all, so they are free to marry. Rather similarly, the climax of *Philaster* comes when the hero's page, Bellario, reveals 'him'-self to be in reality a woman, Euphrasia, and so opens the way to Philaster's marriage.

Or take *The Maid's Tragedy*. In order to conceal his affair with Evadne, the King has forced his friend Amintor to marry her and to break off his engagement to Aspatia. She falls into a decline, and Evadne, overcome with remorse, kills the King in a sensational bedroom scene – she ties his arms to the bed, and he thinks she's offering him kinky sex until she disillusions him and stabs him to death. Later Aspatia disguises herself as a soldier and, in a final if misjudged effort to demonstrate her devotion to Amintor, fights a duel with him in the hope that she will die on his sword, a martyr to love. She falls wounded, Evadne kills herself, Aspatia drops her disguise, and Amintor too commits suicide.

Plot devices such as these find parallels in Shakespeare's late plays. Earlier in his career he had avoided surprising us. His dramaturgy relied rather on the creation and fulfilment of expectation than on unexpected revelation. Although in many of his Elizabethan comedies characters disguised themselves, the audience was always let into the secret. The only sudden revelation in any of these plays comes at the climax of *The Comedy of Errors*, written by 1594, when the Abbess turns out to be the long-lost wife of Egeon and the mother of the twin Antipholuses. This finds no parallel in Shakespeare's comedies until the revelation in the last scene of *The Winter's Tale* that Hermione, supposed dead, has been concealed for sixteen years and now poses as her own statue before being revealed to her husband, Leontes, and her daughter, Perdita. In Shakespeare's tragedies, too, sudden revelations are rare. Though there are surprises such as Othello's suicide and Lear's devastating entry carrying Cordelia's corpse, they strike us rather as inevitable plot developments than as authorial manipulations. The most Fletcherian of Shakespeare's solo-authored plays, in style as well as in plotting, is *Cymbeline*, written probably just before or just after *The Winter's Tale*. The improbabilities of its plot had Dr Johnson thundering in derision: 'To remark the folly of the fiction, the absurdity of the conduct, the confusion of the names and manners of different times and the improbability of the events in any system of life, were to waste criticism upon unresisting imbecility, upon faults too evident for detection, and too gross for aggravation.'[16]

Strictly, the death of one of the central characters, Cloten, disqualifies *Cymbeline* as a tragicomedy, but this is more than amply compensated for by the multiple resolutions of its final scene, in which happy endings pile upon one another in miraculous multiplicity. The play was probably first performed only a few months after *Philaster*, and some of the 'absurdity' of the 'conduct' finds parallels in that play.[17] Its heroine, Arethusa, loves Philaster but her father has betrothed her to the lecherous 'Prince of Popinjays' Pharamond, rather as in *Cymbeline* Innogen loves Posthumus but her father and mother wish her to marry the vicious dolt Cloten. Arethusa sends to Philaster a pageboy, Bellario, who is actually a girl in disguise, rather as Innogen disguises herself as a boy after being expelled from the court. (Shakespeare had already used the name Bellario in *The Merchant of Venice* for the imaginary lawyer who sends Portia, disguised as Balthasar, to the Duke's court, and the name also resembles that of Belarius in *Cymbeline*.) Arethusa is accused of fornicating with her page, rather as Giacomo claims to have seduced Innogen; and Philaster believes the accusations, rather as Posthumus believes Giacomo's. Bellario falls asleep in a forest and is found by Philaster, as Innogen does in the Welsh hills and is found by her long-lost brothers, Guiderius and Arviragus. The later stages of both plays include prison scenes, and a marriage masque in *Philaster* has something of a counterpart in the appearance of Jupiter and the dream vision of *Cymbeline*. Both plays end in ingeniously contrived resolutions for the virtuous characters.

It is characteristic of Shakespeare's search for diversity that the last of his solo-authored plays, *The Tempest*, while adopting many of the narrative conventions of dramatic romance, totally rejects its typical structure. Reverting to the neo-classical form of *The Comedy of Errors*, the action of which takes place on a single day, possibly in the same town square, he allows the story of events that took place over a period of sixteen years to unfold in retrospect, initially through Prospero's long narrative in which he tells his daughter, Miranda, of what had happened in 'the dark backward and abyss of time' since they were shipwrecked on the island where the action takes place. The play portrays only the last three hours of the story. But if the story is laid out from start to finish its concerns with courtly corruption, with the dramatic opposition of innocence with evil, its privileging of symbolical fantasy over psychological plausibility, and its inherent pastoralism, all of which link it with plays of this period written by Beaumont and Fletcher, become apparent. So it is natural that, as the younger men grew in maturity and in experience as house dramatists for the King's Men, Shakespeare should have found Fletcher, at least, a particularly congenial colleague.

As we have seen, collaboration was not a new activity for Shakespeare. In his earliest years as a playwright he – like most of his fellows, though to a lesser extent than most – had, it seems, occasionally worked in tandem, most probably with George Peele on *Titus Andronicus*, with Thomas Nashe on *Henry VI, Part One*, and with someone unknown on *Edward III* (see p. 26). He had already written the first two of these plays, and quite possibly the third, by the time he became a founder member of the Lord Chamberlain's Men, in 1594. From then onwards, perhaps with a sigh of relief, he became his own master. There is no reason to believe that he collaborated with any other writer from 1594 till the composition of *Timon of Athens*, maybe in 1606.[18] A year or so later he worked with Wilkins on *Pericles*. For several years after this he returned to solo-authored plays – *Antony and Cleopatra, Coriolanus, The Winter's Tale, Cymbeline* and *The Tempest* – but then, in the last active year of his career, worked only in collaboration.

First, it would seem, came *Cardenio*, which exists only in a thoroughly rewritten version dating from 1728, well over a century after the original came into being. There are two pieces of evidence that a play of this name was in existence by 1613. On 20 May of that year the Privy Council authorized payment to John Heminges, acting as payee of the King's Men, for presentation at court of six plays, one of them listed as *Cardenno*. Less than two months later, on 9 July, Heminges received £6. 13s. 4d. for his company's performance before the ambassador of the Duke of Savoy of a play 'called Cardenna'. The name of the play derives from the character Cardenio in the first part of Cervantes' *Don Quixote*, which had appeared in English translation in the previous year. Fletcher was to draw extensively on *Don Quixote* and on Cervantes' *Exemplary Tales* in later plays. No author is named in these entries, but forty years later, on 9 September 1653, a London bookseller, Humphrey Moseley, who in 1647 had published the first Folio edition of previously unpublished plays by Beaumont and Fletcher, entered for publication on the Stationers' Register a batch of plays which included 'The History of Cardenio, by Mr Fletcher and Shakespeare'. As Heminges and Condell had omitted several plays in which Shakespeare is now believed to have had a hand – *Edward III, Pericles, Sir Thomas More* and *The Two Noble Kinsmen*[19] – from the First Folio, the fact that they also omitted *Cardenio* cannot be held as evidence against Moseley's attribution. It is more surprising that Moseley did not include it in the Beaumont and Fletcher volume, which includes much work by other dramatists, including Philip Massinger, Nathan Field and William Rowley. But there are many mysteries about the publication – or in this case the non-publication – of plays in this period, and there is no good reason to doubt that Fletcher and Shakespeare did indeed collaborate on a play called *Cardenio*, especially since in 1728 Lewis Theobald, whose edition of Shakespeare's complete plays was to appear five years later, put into print a play certainly based on the story of Cardenio and called *Double Falsehood, or the Distrest Lovers*, which he said he had 'revised and adapted' from one 'written originally by W. Shakespeare'. Although the language does not seem particularly Shakespearian, it is a tragicomedy which, like *Cymbeline*, has a disguised heroine wronged by her lover, and in which, as in all Shakespeare's romances, parents are reunited and reconciled with their children. Theobald himself said that some of his contemporaries thought the dialogue of the original play sounded more like Fletcher than Shakespeare. It is perfectly possible that he somehow acquired a manuscript of the play performed by the King's Men in 1613 and ascribed in 1653 to Fletcher and Shakespeare and rewrote it to suit the taste of his own times. He claimed to own several manuscripts of a play by Shakespeare, but when he came to edit the *Complete Plays* he included only those of the First Folio, not even adding *Pericles* and *The Two Noble Kinsmen* even though he believed both of them to be partly by Shakespeare. If he was telling the truth, what happened to the original manuscript? In 1770 a newspaper reported that it was 'treasured up in the Museum of Covent Garden Playhouse'. Fire destroyed the theatre and its library in 1808, so probably it went up in smoke.[20] Theobald's play is a performable if undistinguished tragicomedy which had a successful production at Drury Lane before its publication and subsequently.[21]

Only a few weeks after Heminges was paid for the court performance of *Cardenio* the King's Men gave for the first time a play based on the reign of Queen Elizabeth's father, Henry VIII, which, unlike *Cardenio*, was to be included in the First Folio. One of its earliest performances, given on the sunny afternoon of 29 June 1613, is more circumstantially recorded than that of any other Shakespeare play because it literally brought the house down. The fullest account of the disaster is given in a letter written three days later by Sir Henry Wotton, traveller, linguist, diplomat and poet, to his nephew Sir Edmund Bacon:

Now, to let matters of state sleep, I will entertain you at the present with what has happened this week at the Bankside. The King's players had a new play, called *All is True*, representing some principal pieces of the reign of Henry VIII, which was set forth with many extraordinary circumstances of pomp and majesty, even to the matting of the stage; the Knights of the Order

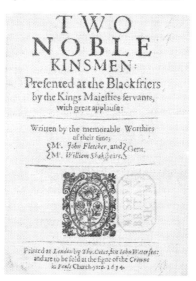

12. The Two Noble Kinsmen. *The title page of the first edition is unequivocal about who wrote the play.*

with their Georges and Garter, the Guards with their embroidered coats, and the like: sufficient in truth within a while to make greatness very familiar, if not ridiculous. Now, King Henry making a masque at the Cardinal Wolsey's house, and certain chambers being shot off at his entry, some of the paper or other stuff wherewith one of them was stopped did light on the thatch, where being thought at first but an idle smoke, and their eyes more attentive to the show, it kindled inwardly and ran round like a train, consuming within less than an hour the whole house to the very grounds. This was the fatal period of that virtuous fabric, wherein yet nothing did perish but wood and straw and a few forsaken cloaks; only one man had his breeches set on fire, that would perhaps have broiled him if he had not by the benefit of a provident wit put it out with bottle ale.[22]

If Wotton was not himself present at the event it is clear that he had talked to someone who was, and luckily several other documents confirm what he wrote and provide additional details, such as the information that 'the people escaped all without hurt except one man who was scalded with the fire by adventuring in to save a child which otherwise had been burnt'. This comes in a letter from a young London merchant, Henry Bluett, which both tells us that this was one of the play's earliest performances and confirms the title under which it was originally acted: 'On Tuesday last there was acted at the Globe a new play called *All is True* which had been acted not passing two or three times before.' This title is clear too from an eight-stanza ballad which is probably one of two entered for publication the day after the fire. Neither survives in print, but one of them exists in an early manuscript. It is printed in full (see Documents below, pp. 242–3) as it is a document of exceptional interest which is not easily available (and which is some-times given in bowdlerized form, omitting the stanza that refers to piss-ing wives). Ballads such as these, which circulated news while at the same time turning it into entertainment, were sung in the streets and in ale-houses, as we have seen with *Keep the Widow Waking* (p. 126), as well as being plastered all over the city in the same manner as playbills.[23] The obvious explanation for the play's being called *Henry VIII* in the First Folio is to bring its title in line with those of all the other English history plays, which are named after the kings whose reigns they dramatize. The original title is restored in the Oxford edition of the *Complete Works*, and was emblazoned on great gates at the back of the stage in Gregory Doran's 1996 RSC production.

None of the contemporary accounts of the fire at the Globe says who wrote the play that caused it. It is obviously the play printed in the First Folio as *Henry VIII*. There is no external evidence to call Shakespeare's sole authorship into question, but as early as 1758 a Cambridge poet and don, Richard Roderick, in what has been described as 'the first serious discussion of Shakespeare's verse style',[24] drew attention to ways in which the versification in it differs from Shakespeare's usual practice, noting particularly the frequency with which blank verse lines end with a redundant syllable. He quotes the following lines:

> Healthful, | and e | ver since | a fresh | admir | er
> Of what | I saw | there. An | untimely a | gue.
>
> (1.1.3–4)

> I was | then pres | ent, saw 'em | salute | on horse | back
>
> (1.1.8)

In their | embrace | ment as | they grew | togeth | er

(1.1.10)

Nearly a century later, in 1849, another scholar, Charles Knight, observed 'repeated instances in which the lines are so constructed that it is impossible to read them with the slightest pause at the end of each line'. Neither Roderick nor Knight connected their observations to doubts about Shakespeare's sole authorship, but only a year after Knight wrote, James Spedding, editor and biographer of Francis Bacon, followed up their remarks in an article called 'Who Wrote Shakspere's *Henry VIII*?'[25] in which he expressed his conviction that the play had at least two different authors, and that 'they had worked, not together, but alternately upon distinct portions of it'.[26] His arguments were both impressionistic and analytical, drawing on statistics concerning the play's versification.

As time passed scholars applied more complex and sophisticated tests both to Shakespeare's and Fletcher's plays and, for the sake of comparison, to those of other dramatists. It emerged, for instance, that Fletcher is more likely to use ' 'em' than 'them', 'has' than 'hath' and 'ye' than 'you', and that Shakespeare in his late work is more likely to use colloquial contractions than Fletcher.[27] These are only selected markers, and signs of authorship can be confused or obliterated by, for instance, the personal habits of scribes who may have copied the play before it was printed, or of the printers themselves. Moreover, the very essence of the dramatist's art, as of the actor's, lies in overlaying personal characteristics with those of the persona adopted. Nevertheless no Jekyll totally transforms himself into Hyde, and although other candidatures have been advanced, and some scholars continued to maintain that Shakespeare wrote the play alone, the overwhelming current consensus, based on a massive accumulation of evidence, is that Shakespeare and Fletcher – possibly with Beaumont – collaborated on its composition. And although it takes its subject matter from English history, this play relates far more closely to Fletcherian tragicomedy than to Shakespeare's history plays of the 1590s, working up after a series of crises to an implausibly romantic happy ending.

In poetic as well as verbal style, too, *All is True* has Fletcherian characteristics. Early in the nineteenth century, Charles Lamb, writing independently of the arguments about this play, produced a classic description of the difference between Fletcher's and Shakespeare's characteristic styles which relates especially to Shakespeare's late plays. Fletcher, he wrote, 'lays line upon line, making up one after another, adding image to image so deliberately that we see where they join. Shakespeare mingles everything, embarrasses sentences and metaphors; before one idea has burst its shell, another is hatched and clamours for disclosure.'[28] It happens that Lamb's observation can be put to the test in two passages of *All is True* which have the same subject matter, the desire of the king to divorce his Queen, Katherine. In Act 2, Scene 2, the Duke of Norfolk speaks of Cardinal Wolsey's influence on the King:

> He counsels a divorce – a loss of her
> That like a jewel has hung twenty years
> About his neck, yet never lost her lustre;
> Of her that loves him with that excellence
> That angels love good men with; even of her
> That, when the greatest stroke of fortune falls,
> Will bless the King – and is not this course pious?
>
> (2.2.30–36)

In the following scene Anne Boleyn speaks on the same subject:

> Not for that neither. Here's the pang that pinches –
> His highness having lived so long with her, and she
> So good a lady that no tongue could ever
> Pronounce dishonour of her – by my life,
> She never knew harm-doing – O now, after
> So many courses of the sun enthronèd,
> Still growing in a majesty and pomp the which
> To leave a thousandfold more bitter than
> 'Tis sweet at first t'acquire – after this process,
> To give her the avaunt, it is a pity
> Would move a monster.
>
> (2.3.1–11)

The first passage, with its orderly movement and consecutive development of three separate images – jewels, angels and stroke of fortune, each dependent on 'loss of her that' – exemplifies what Lamb says of Fletcher. The second, with its multiple imagery, its self-interruptions, elliptical constructions – 'a pity [that] / Would' – run-over lines and complex sentence structure, is far more characteristic of Shakespeare's late style. Yet in the first – of seven lines – there is only one of the redundant syllables at the ends of lines that are seen as signs of Fletcher's presence, whereas in the second – of eleven lines – there are six. Collaboration is not necessarily clear-cut. One writer may revise the other's work, and the habits of one may permeate the other.

Arguments about different shares of authorship are liable to be muddied by value judgements. It is too easy to assume that what one thinks of as the best bits must be by Shakespeare, and the rest by some inferior writer. But it would not be unreasonable to suggest that the orderliness of Fletcher, especially in verse intended to be spoken and to be instantly comprehended by a theatre audience, might be preferable to Shakespearian tumultuousness. In the opening scene, for instance, the description of the Field of the Cloth of Gold is richly characteristic of Shakespeare's late style, a densely complex, idiosyncratic, elliptical piece of verse that could only have been written by a master – but might it not be too introverted for the theatre? Might we not even suspect that Shakespeare is writing here for himself as much as for a listener (or even a reader, because this is no easier to read than to hear):

> The two kings
> Equal in lustre, were now best, now worst,
> As presence did present them. Him in eye
> Still him in praise, and being present both,
> 'Twas said they saw but one, and no discerner
> Durst wag his tongue in censure. When these suns –
> For so they phrase 'em – by their heralds challenged
> The noble spirits to arms, they did perform
> Beyond thought's compass, that former fabulous story
> Being now seen possible enough, got credit
> That *Bevis* was believed.

> (1.1.28–38)

It is not only the passage of time that makes this hard to follow.

Understandably, some of the passages from this play that have become best-known in their own right – the Duke of Buckingham's speeches as he goes to execution (2.1.56–136), the song 'Orpheus with his lute' (3.1.3–14), Cardinal Wolsey's lines beginning 'Farewell, a long farewell to all my greatness' (3.2.352–73), and Queen Katherine's vision and death (4.2) – are among those most confidently ascribed to Fletcher. So too in the final scene is Archbishop Cranmer's tribute to Queen Elizabeth spoken at her baptism – 'In her days every man shall eat in safety / Under his own vine what he plants' – as well as the egregious and sycophantic flattery of King James, patron of the King's Men:

> So shall she leave her blessèdness to one,
> When heaven shall call her from this cloud of darkness,
> Who from the sacred ashes of her honour
> Shall star-like rise as great in fame as she was,
> And so stand fixed. Peace, plenty, love, truth, terror,
> That were the servants to this chosen infant,
> Shall then be his, and, like a vine, grow to him.
> Wherever the bright sun of heaven shall shine,
> His honour and the greatness of his name
> Shall be, and make new nations. He shall flourish,
> And like a mountain cedar reach his branches
> To all the plains about him. Our children's children
> Shall see this, and bless heaven.
>
> (5.4.43–55)

That is, as Celia says in *As You Like It*, 'laid on with a trowel'. It is a relief to think that Shakespeare did not stoop so low as to write it.

Finally we arrive at the one and only surviving play which was clearly stated on its first, posthumous publication to have been written by Shakespeare as a co-adjutor with someone else: *The Two Noble Kinsmen*. Curiously, the evidence that it dates from no earlier than the same year as *All is True* relates not to Fletcher but to Beaumont. One of the pastoral scenes includes a morris dance performed by, among others, 'the Lord of May and Lady bright; / The Chambermaid and Servingman … mine Host / And his fat spouse … the beest-eating Clown; and next, the Fool; / The babion [baboon] with long tail and eke long tool . . .' (3.5.127–34). The same characters figure in an episode of Beaumont's *Masque of the Inner Temple and Gray's Inn* which had been performed before James I at Whitehall Palace on 20 February 1613. On that occasion the dance went down so well with the aristocratic and royal spectators, and even with the King himself, that 'It pleased his Majesty to call for it again at the end'.[29] Very likely the King's Men – some of whom may have taken part – decided to exploit its success and make it available to the general public by recycling it in the play written soon afterwards. Mention in the Prologue to *The Two Noble Kinsmen* of 'our losses' seems to refer to the burning of the Globe in June 1613, so this is probably the last play in which Shakespeare had a hand. Both the entry of the play on the Stationers' Register of 8 April 1634 and the title page of the first edition in the same year unequivocally attribute it to Fletcher and Shakespeare (giving them equal billing in alphabetical order).

Like *Pericles*, also of mixed authorship (though not avowedly so on its first publication), *The Two Noble Kinsmen* had not been printed in the First Folio. But while *Pericles*, with five others, was added to the third Folio of 1663 when it was reissued the following year, and was soon accepted into the Shakespeare canon, *The Two Noble Kinsmen*'s first reprint was in the 1679 second edition of the Beaumont and Fletcher Folio, and it long continued to be regarded more readily as part of the Beaumont and Fletcher than of the Shakespeare canon.

As the Prologue admits, 'Chaucer, of all admired, the story gives'. *The Two Noble Kinsmen* is based on one of the *Canterbury Tales*, the Knight's Tale, which Shakespeare had already drawn on in *A Midsummer Night's Dream*. In fact it begins where that play ends, with Theseus's wedding. The main story concerns the rivalry of the kinsmen, Palamon and Arcite, for the hand of Hippolyta's sister, the fair Emilia. There are two comic subplots, both invented, one of which centres on a Jailer's Daughter (otherwise unnamed) who is comically if touchingly in love with Palamon, the other on a group of rustics who, like Bottom and his fellows in *A Midsummer Night's Dream*, present an entertainment – the morris dance – before Theseus. But so far from being a romantic fantasy, like the earlier play, *The Two*

Noble Kinsmen in its overall design exceeds even the bounds of tragi-comedy as defined by Fletcher, in that the resolution of the principal love plot is achieved only at the expense of the death of one of the central characters, Arcite.

Shakespeare and Fletcher must have talked together to decide both how to treat the story and how to share the labour. As I said in the opening chapter, it seems clear that while Shakespeare agreed to write the first and last acts, which by and large include the most serious and rhetorically ambitious episodes, and Fletcher the lighter, more sentimental and humorous middle parts of the play, nevertheless each contributed scenes to the other's allocations. In verbal style the divisions of labour are more obvious than in *All is True*, but all the same it is perfectly possible that each writer touched up the other's work here and there. Structurally, the playwrights' dovetailing of episodes is skilful, but at a few points they seem not to have fully co-ordinated their thinking – for instance, at the opening of Shakespeare's Act 1, Scene 2, the kinsmen deplore the moral laxity of Thebes whereas in Fletcher's Act 2, Scene 1, they talk of the city they have left with a nostalgia that seems at odds with their former condemnation of its corruption.

The story provides ample scope for the skills characteristic of both writers at this stage in their careers. Like *Pericles*, it is medieval in origin but set in ancient Greece. As in all Shakespeare's late plays, the supernatural looms large in both action and language, and is associated with spectacular stage effects. The appearance of gods in *Pericles* and *Cymbeline*, the supposed statue in *The Winter's Tale*, the trick table and the masque in *The Tempest*, and the dream vision in the joint-authored *All is True* have their principal counterparts in *The Two Noble Kinsmen* in the emblematic signs at the altars of Mars, Venus and Diana in the last act. These too require trick properties, indicated by directions such as '*Here music is heard, doves are seen to flutter*', '*Here the hind vanishes under the altar and in the place ascends a rose tree having one rose upon. it*', and '*Here is heard a sudden twang of instruments and the rose falls from the tree*'. Effects like these are especially associated with plays presented at indoor theatres such as the Blackfriars, where this play was acted.

More characteristic of Fletcher than of Shakespeare are the tender if sentimental exploitation of nostalgia and pathos, tinged at times with hints of sexual ambivalence, as when Palamon and Arcite exchange reminiscences of previous love affairs in Act 3, Scene 3, and the theatrically effective, if psychologically implausible, reversals of behaviour resulting from the conflicting demands made on the kinsmen by love and friendship. These create a high degree of erotic tension, nowhere more apparent than in the imprisoned kinsmen's escalating expressions of love for one another over a long passage at the opening of Act 2, Scene 2, which climax in Arcite's assertion that the two men 'are one another's wife' (line 80) and in Palamon's rhetorical question 'Is there record of any two that loved / Better than we do, Arcite?' (lines 112–13). Then suddenly Emilia appears, and within minutes the cousins are quarrelling over the right to woo her.

Joint authorship is more evident in verbal style than in plotting. The distinction drawn by Charles Lamb between the respective authors' styles which I quoted in writing about *All is True* is no less applicable to this play. The Shakespearian complexity is evident in, to give only one example, a passage often quoted in its own right, Emilia's description of her childhood friendship with Flavina, who died – or, as Shakespeare/Emilia puts it, 'took leave o'th'moon' – when they were both only 11 years old:

> What she liked
> Was then of me approved; what not, condemned –
> No more arraignment. The flower that I would pluck
> And put between my breasts – O then but beginning
> To swell about the blossom – she would long
> Till she had such another, and commit it
> To the like innocent cradle, where, phoenix-like,
> They died in perfume. On my head no toy
> But was her pattern. Her affections – pretty,
> Though happily her careless wear[30] – I followed
> For my most serious decking. Had mine ear
> Stol'n some new air, or at advantage hummed one,[31]
> From musical[32] coinage, why, it was a note
> Whereon her spirits would sojourn – rather dwell on –
> And sing it in her slumbers. This rehearsal –

Which, seely innocence wots well, comes in
Like old emportment's bastard – has this end:
That the true love 'tween maid and maid may be
More than in sex dividual.

(1.3.64–82)

This is Shakespeare at his most complex and convoluted, wresting vocabulary and syntax to new linguistic ends.

One reason why Fletcher was available to collaborate with Shakespeare in 1613 may be that his partnership with Beaumont had broken up. This was the year of Beaumont's marriage and of his retirement from the theatre. Although he went on to father two daughters he seems to have suffered a stroke around this time. He died three years later, on 6 March 1616, and was buried in Westminster Abbey. When Shakespeare also died, less than two months later, a poet named William Basse (c. 1583–1653?) wrote a memorial sonnet inviting the present incumbents of Poets' Corner, including Beaumont, to make room for him:

Renownèd Spenser, lie a thought more nigh
To learnèd Chaucer; and rare Beaumont, lie
A little nearer Spenser, to make room
For Shakespeare in your threefold, fourfold tomb.[33]

But Shakespeare was buried in Stratford. By then Fletcher had taken over as chief dramatist for the King's Men, and was to write a long stream of successful plays, almost always in tandem with another writer – first with the former boy actor Nathan Field and then, after Field died in 1619 or 1620, with Philip Massinger with whom he composed some seventeen plays. Aubrey is again the source of our knowledge of Fletcher's death, writing slightly hazily that 'Fletcher, invited to go with a knight into Norfolk or Suffolk in the plague-time 1625, stayed [in London] but to make himself a suit of clothes, and while it was making, fell sick of the plague and died. This I had (1668) from his tailor, who is now a very old man, and clerk of St Mary Overy's in Southwark.'[34] Apparently Fletcher had some sort of abscess on his arm, which his tailor dressed with ivy leaves. Coming to do this, he found the fatal plague sores on Fletcher. Then, writes Aubrey,

'Death stopped his journey and laid him low here'.[35] He was buried in St Mary's (now Southwark Cathedral). Massinger succeeded him as chief dramatist to the King's Men, and on his death in March 1640 he joined his old friend in the church, reputedly in the same grave. A single memorial stone now commemorates them there.

Shakespeare was to collaborate once more in 1613, this time on a tiny scale, and with an actor, not a writer. Ever since the reign of King Henry VIII annual tournaments had been held before the monarch on special occasions such as anniversaries of the accession, royal birthdays and visits by foreign dignitaries.[36] The aristocratic participants, mounted on elaborately caparisoned steeds, carried, or had pageboys carry for them, pasteboard shields on which cryptic mottoes, usually in Latin or Italian, were inscribed within decorative borders. Commonly the inscriptions encoded a message of homage, or of contrition for offences committed, or hope for favours to be conferred, addressed to the sovereign. Each impresa, as they were known, was presented to the monarch at the start of the tournament, and at the end they were gathered together and taken away to be stored and displayed in a long gallery in Whitehall Palace.[37]

This Shields Gallery was an attraction greatly admired on the guided tours which even then were available to visitors. Thomas Platter took one of them on the day before he saw *Julius Caesar* at the Globe, writing that 'Before the entrance to the palace is the tilt-yard, in its centre a barrier about a horse's height on either side of which the participants joust'. After seeing this he and his party 'entered a chamber built over the water [the Thames], hung all round with emblems and mottoes'; he copied out a number of them, for example 'superat fortuna laborem. That is Good fortune vanquisheth effort, illustrated by a hand drawing a ring, with a diamond inset, from the water with a fishing line.'[38] By the time Shakespeare was a royal servant he could have seen hundreds of shields on occasions such as St Stephen's Night 1606 when the King's Men performed *King Lear* for the court.

He and Wilkins draw on the tradition in a scene in *Pericles* in which six knights joust before King Simonides and his daughter Thaisa in competition for her hand in marriage. The first five knights are richly armed, and accompanied by pageboys bearing their shields. The recently shipwrecked Pericles, however, wears only rusty armour reclaimed from the sea and, '*having neither page to deliver his shield nor shield to deliver*', presents an unexpected kind of device to the lady himself. The King asks:

> And what's the sixth and last, the which the knight himself
> With such a graceful courtesy delivereth?
> THAISA He seems to be a stranger, but his present is
> A withered branch that's only green at top.
> The motto, *In hac spe vivo* [in this hope I live].
> KING SIMONIDES From the dejected state wherein he is
> He hopes by you his fortunes yet may flourish.
>
> (Scene 6, 44–50)

Shakespeare may have taken ideas for this scene from his visits to Whitehall. Possibly he had himself already been commissioned to compose such devices.[39] That he eventually did so we know from an entry in the account books of Francis Manners, 6th Earl of Rutland (1578–1632), younger brother of the 5th Earl, Roger, who had spent so much time going to see plays with Southampton in 1599. On 31 March 1613 Francis's steward recorded a payment of forty-four shillings, 'To Mr Shakespeare in gold, about my lord's impresa', and of the same amount, also in gold, 'To Richard Burbage for painting and making it'.[40] The tournament had taken place a week before the payments were made; those taking part included the brother Earls of Pembroke and Montgomery, to whom the First Folio was to be dedicated. The payment for writing a few words may seem generous; it may appear to show Shakespeare in the guise of no more than an upmarket copywriter and the great actor Burbage, who played Pericles and whose death six years later the jousting Earl of Pembroke was to mourn, as a mere property-maker to the aristocracy. But the making of the impresa would have been an important occasion for Rutland, and the composition of an inscription to be presented to the King was a delicate matter calling for tact as well as skill. It has not survived, and we do not know in what language it was written. So, for one last time, Shakespeare worked together with the old friend with whom he had shared much for almost twenty years.

It is natural to ask why, in the closing stages of his career, after a period of a dozen or more years during which he produced a string of solo-authored masterpieces, Shakespeare turned to write plays jointly with Wilkins, Middleton and, finally, Fletcher. Did he need help because of some sort of recurring illness? This might be a plausible explanation if it looked as if the plays in question were started by him and then completed by someone else, but this is not so. There is every reason to suppose that he was fully involved in the planning and execution of all of them from start to finish. Was he acting as a kind of tutor to apprentice playwrights? There may have been an element of this, but Middleton, Fletcher, and even the less prolific Wilkins had written successful plays before their Shakespearian collaborations. Could it even be that Shakespeare's colleagues required him to work with a colleague who was more in touch with the demands of the public than the ageing, increasingly self-absorbed master? The plays of Shakespeare's late years, even the solo-authored *Coriolanus*, *The Winter's Tale*, *Cymbeline* and *The Tempest*, wonderful though they are, have never enjoyed the same degree of popular success as the masterpieces of his middle period – *Hamlet*, *Twelfth Night*, *Othello*, *King Lear*, *Macbeth*. Like Beethoven's late quartets and piano sonatas, Shakespeare's late plays exhibit a degree of introversion which, while being an indisputable part of their greatness, limits their appeal. They are works for connoisseurs, especially, as I have tried to show, in their verbal style, and Fletcher may have been brought in to alleviate their rigours.

8

The Succession: John Webster

In the film *Shakespeare in Love*, a scruffy-looking 13-year-old boy actor, named in the script simply as 'Urchin', aspires to the leading role of Ethel, the pirate's daughter, in a play that Shakespeare – 'Will' – is fighting against time to write. Will comes upon him outside the theatre, and the lad, who is playing with a cat, says: 'I was in a play. They cut my head off in *Titus Andronicus*. When I write plays, they will be like *Titus* ... I liked it when they cut heads off. And the daughter mutilated with knives.' Will asks him his name. 'John Webster. Here, kitty, kitty' – and he 'passes a white mouse to the cat and watches with sober interest'. 'Plenty of blood. That's the only writing.' At which 'Will backs away, unnerved'. 'Wait,' says the Urchin, 'you'll see the cat bites his head off.' Will: 'I've got to be back.'

That episode looks back to the beginnings of Shakespeare's career and forward to its ending. John Webster was born around 1578–80, which makes him a close contemporary of Middleton and Fletcher and some fifteen or so years younger than Shakespeare. No image of him survives. He studied briefly for the law, but started writing for the theatre in his early twenties. His career interacted with Shakespeare's during the first decade of the seventeenth century, but he did not find his individual voice until Shakespeare himself was fading from the scene. His great tragedy *The White Devil* was published in 1612, soon after it was written. It had failed on the stage. In his Address to the Reader Webster blames the weather ('it was acted in so dull a time of winter'), the playhouse (it was 'presented in so open and black a theatre'), and the audience (it lacked 'a full and understanding auditory'). But he is confident that it will succeed on the page. It is, he admits, 'no true dramatic poem' in that it does not observe the rules of neo-classical tragedy. But he has broken the rules deliberately, not through ignorance. And anyway the most correctly composed tragedy ever written would not have pleased the 'uncapable multitude' at the Red Bull.

Up to this point, Webster had always worked as a collaborator, with a remarkable range of other writers: Anthony Munday, Michael Drayton, Thomas Middleton, Henry Chettle, Thomas Heywood, Wentworth Smith (a member of the Henslowe stable in the early 1600s, none of whose plays is known to have survived), John Marston, George Chapman and Ben Jonson. Webster must have encountered Shakespeare in or before 1604 when he undertook the journeyman's task of adapting Marston's play *The Malcontent*, written originally for the Children of the Chapel Royal, for performance by the King's Men at the Globe. Shakespeare may have acted in it. After this enterprise Webster's playwriting activities tailed off, with a long gap between 1605 and 1612, years in which plague raged during the summer months and beyond. *The White Devil*, with which he broke his silence, was his first solo-authored play, and its composition had not come easily to him. He is sensitive about this: 'To those who report I was a long time in finishing this tragedy, I confess I do not write with a goose-quill winged with two feathers' (I suppose him to mean that his pen cannot fly across the paper twice as fast as other men's). And he defends himself with an anecdote: Euripides, when criticized by a minor writer for having 'composed three verses, whereas himself had written three hundred', admitted this was true, 'but here's the difference: thine shall only be read for three days, whereas mine shall continue three ages'. The judgement of posterity has vindicated Webster's smugness: *The White Devil*, along with its successor of only two years later, *The Duchess of Malfi*, performed by Shakespeare's company, the King's Men, is among the few English tragedies of the Jacobean – or indeed of any – period, apart from Shakespeare's, to have commanded the admiration of later ages.

Webster was a great borrower, his writings shot through with what M. C. Bradbrook called 'laminations or bondings of other men's images and short sayings into his text'.[1] Inevitably, Shakespeare was among the writers who stocked his mind and filled his notebooks. In a new Induction to *The Malcontent*, bringing the actors Burbage, Condell and William Sly on stage in their own persons, he virtually quotes from *Hamlet* as Condell says to a theatre patron: 'I beseech you, sir, be covered', which elicits the reply, 'No, in good faith, for mine ease' (Addition A, lines 33–5; so Hamlet: 'Put your bonnet to his right use . . .' Osric: 'Nay, good my lord, for mine ease, in good faith', 5.2.94–106). And at the end of the Induction is a brief parody of a line or two from the Epilogue to the as yet unpublished play *As You Like It*. 'Gentlemen,' says the Theatre Patron, improvising a Prologue, 'I could wish for the women's sakes you had all soft cushions. And gentlewomen, I could wish that for the men's sakes you had all more easy standings' (lines 133–5; *As You Like It*: 'I charge you, O women, for the love you bear to men, to like as much of this play as please you. And I charge you, O men, for the love you bear to women . . . That between you and the women the play may please', Epilogue, lines 11–14).

In *The White Devil*, too, we can hear echoes, both of Shakespeare plays that had appeared in print and of others that had not. Cornelia's words over the corpse of Marcello must recall Lear's over Cordelia: 'Fetch a looking-glass,' she says, 'see if his breath will not stain it; or pull out some feathers from my pillow, and lay them to his lips' (5.2.37–9). So Lear: 'Lend me a looking-glass. / If that her breath will mist or stain the stone, / Why, then she lives', and 'This feather stirs. She lives' (*Tragedy of King Lear*, 5.3.236–8, 240). In Cornelia's later scene of mourning, Webster's laminations include fragments of Ophelia's mad scene in *Hamlet* along with a memory of Lady Macbeth's as yet unpublished sleepwalking: 'There's rosemary for you, and rue for you', and 'Here's a white hand: / Can blood so soon be washed out?' (5.4.73, 77–8; *Hamlet*: 'There's rosemary, that's for remembrance', 4.5.175, and *Macbeth*: 'What, will these hands ne'er be clean?', 5.1.41, etc.). Flamineo's famously sudden access of compassion, 'I have a strange thing in me, to th'which / I cannot give a name, without it be / Compassion' (*The White Devil*, 5.4.109–11) recalls Edmond's recantation in *King Lear*: 'Some good I mean to do, / Despite of mine own nature' (5.3.218–19). And the white devil herself, Vittoria, about to die, is determined, like Cleopatra in a play that also was not yet published, that 'my servant / Shall never go before me' (*The White Devil*, 5.6.216–17; *Antony and Cleopatra*: 'If she first meet the curlèd Antony / He'll make demand of her . . .', 5.2.296–7).

The Duchess of Malfi, too, reverberates with Shakespearian echoes, though in this play they are more thoroughly absorbed and so more difficult to pin down. But it is easy to hear Lear in the storm through Ferdinand's hysterical wish to turn himself into a tempest so that he may toss his sister's

> palace 'bout her ears,
> Root up her goodly forest, blast her meads,
> And lay her general territory as waste
> As she hath done our honours.
>
> (2.5.18–21)

And Ferdinand later ruminates on reputation in lines that may recall Cassio's in *Othello*:

> 'Stay', quoth Reputation,
> 'Do not forsake me; for it is my nature
> If once I part from any man I meet
> I am never found again.'
>
> (3.2.131–4)

'Reputation, reputation, reputation – O, I ha' lost my reputation, I ha' lost the immortal part of myself . . .' (*Othello*, 2.3.255–6).

Shakespearian in their range and depth, in the brilliance of their verse and prose, and their vividness of characterization, *The White Devil* and *The Duchess of Malfi* are nevertheless the product of a unique imagination, brilliantly distilled by T. S. Eliot in his poem 'Whispers of Immortality':

> Webster was much possessed by death
> And saw the skull beneath the skin;
> And breastless creatures under ground
> Leaned backward with a lipless grin.
>
> Daffodil bulbs instead of balls
> Stared from the sockets of the eyes!
> He knew that thought clings round dead limbs
> Tightening its lusts and luxuries.

Tragedy had travelled a great distance over the quarter of a century since Marlowe wrote. Both his plays and Webster's have suffered because of Shakespeare's dominance in the eyes of posterity. Like Marlowe's, Webster's tragedies present their directors, their actors and their audiences with challenges quite different from Shakespeare's. Is there anything in Shakespeare quite so surreal as the episode in which the Duchess of Malfi is tormented by a 'wild consort of madmen', culminating in their dance *'with music answerable thereunto'*? Or that in which, just after Executioners strangle her waiting-woman Cariola, the Duchess is shown the bodies of her children strangled at the instigation of her brother, the Cardinal? Or that in which her other brother, Ferdinand, in the grip of lycanthropia – the diseased state of mind in which he believes himself to be a wolf – throws himself on his own shadow with the words 'I will throttle it'? Or the haunting 'echo scene' in which the Duchess's husband, Antonio, walking among ancient ruins, hears echoes 'very like [his] wife's voice'?:

> ANTONIO Echo, I will not talk with thee,
>   For thou art a dead thing.
> ECHO   Thou art a dead thing.
> ANTONIO My Duchess is asleep now,
>   And her little ones, I hope, sweetly. [In fact they are all dead.]
>   O heaven,
>   Shall I never see her more?
> ECHO   Never see her more.
>
> (5.3.38–42)

Webster's tragedies constantly shift their dramatic perspective. At times they adopt a formal style of presentation, as when, in the opening scene of *The Duchess of Malfi*, Antonio makes his friend Delio 'the partaker of the natures / Of some of your great courtiers', speaking a series of character sketches in the manner of the then-fashionable literary genre to which Webster himself was to contribute. At other times we are admitted to the inner recesses of characters' minds with devastating immediacy. The bizarre experiences to which Webster's tragedies subject their characters, their portrayal of extreme states of suffering, obsession, sexual tension and madness stretch their audiences' as well as their characters' imaginations to breaking-point and, sometimes, beyond. The people in these plays conform to no psychological norms. They are liable to leap suddenly from literariness to poignant informality, from intense subjectivity to choric commentary on their own as well as on others' fate. The white devil, Vittoria, stabbed to death, eloquently expresses her suffering with 'My soul, like to a ship in a black storm, / Is driven I know not whither'; moments later she dies on the sententious couplet 'O happy they that never saw the court, / Nor ever knew great man but by report' (*The White Devil*, 5.6. 247–8, 260–61). At his finest, Webster writes with a profundity that Shakespeare in his last years must have admired and might have envied. Bosola answering the Duchess's question 'Who am I?' is no less eloquent than Hamlet in his meditation on mortality:

Thou art a box of worm seed, at best, but a salvatory of green mummy. What's this flesh? A little curded milk, fantastical puff-paste; our bodies are weaker than those paper prisons boys use to keep flies in; more contemptible, since ours is to preserve earth-worms. Didst thou ever see a lark in a cage? Such is the soul in the body: this world is like her little turf of grass, and the heaven o'er our heads, like her looking-glass, only gives us a miserable knowledge of the small compass of our prison. (4.2.119–26)

And the Duchess faces death with no less splendour of spirit than Cleopatra:

> What would it pleasure me to have my throat cut
> With diamonds? or to be smothered
> With cassia? or to be shot to death with pearls?
> I know death hath ten thousand several doors
> For men to take their exits; and 'tis found
> They go on such strange geometrical hinges,
> You may open them both ways. Any way, for heaven' sake,
> So I were out of your whispering. Tell my brothers
> That I perceive death, now I am well awake,
> Best gift is they can give, or I can take.
>
> (4.2.208–17)

Antony and Cleopatra may well have helped Webster to shape the structure of *The Duchess of Malfi*. Both plays have double tragic climaxes, Shakespeare's in the widely separated deaths of Antony and Cleopatra, Webster's in those of the Duchess and Antonio.

Webster pays explicit tribute to Shakespeare in the address to the readers of *The White Devil*. Responding to his nameless critics, he claims that he has always reacted to the writings of his contemporaries with generosity, and he singles out for particular mention a number of those who have figured prominently in this book along with others who have not. He has admired 'that full and heightened style of Master Chapman, the laboured and understanding works of Master Jonson, the no less worthy composures [compositions] of the both worthily excellent Master Beaumont and Master Fletcher; and lastly (without wrong last to be named) the right happy and copious industry of Master Shakespeare, Master Dekker, and Master Heywood.' For whatever reason, he does not name Master Middleton, then in mid-career, even though they had worked together. But Middleton would write a generous commendatory poem on the first publication of what he calls that 'masterpiece of tragedy', *The Duchess of Malfi*, in 1623. Marston, whom Webster also leaves unnamed, had transmuted from playwright to clergyman in 1609.

In 1612 all of those whom Webster mentions were still active in the theatre. The writing careers of both Shakespeare and Beaumont came to an end in the following year. Fletcher would remain productive until the mid-1620s, as would Middleton. Dekker would go on until 1632, Jonson continued to write plays and other entertainments until a little later than that, and Thomas Heywood, the longest lived of all, was active until as late as 1641, the year he died. Webster himself was to follow his two great tragedies with *The Devil's Law-Case*, of 1617, and with additional collaborations – *Appius and Virginia* in 1622, *Keep the Widow Waking* in 1624, and *A Cure for a Cuckold* (with William Rowley), also in 1624. Nothing is known of him after this; even his death is unrecorded.

These men had formed the great generation of Jacobean dramatists. Some of them had worked directly with Shakespeare, all had come under his influence to some degree or another, and he had learnt from them. The two with least connections, and about whom I have consequently said least, are George Chapman and Thomas Heywood. Those whose careers blossomed after Shakespeare's death and extended beyond the reign of King James into that of King Charles I include, among other, lesser lights, Philip Massinger – who was to succeed Fletcher as chief dramatist for the King's Men – John Ford, William Davenant (1606–68), James Shirley (1596–1666) and Richard Brome (c. 1590–1652). As time passed and fashions changed, new influences exerted themselves, but Shakespeare's plays continued to be performed by the King's Men, to be reprinted both in quarto and folio – the second Folio appeared in 1632 – and to be read. And Davenant, reputed to have been Shakespeare's illegitimate son, became the first playwright to adapt his plays for the new theatrical conditions that prevailed after the restoration of the monarchy in 1660.

With the passing of the years Shakespeare has too often been isolated from his fellows. He is the greatest of them, but he would not have been what he is without them. As a playwright, he developed in technique and in the capacity to convey the depths of his human understanding throughout his career. But he remained essentially a romantic dramatist, setting virtually all his plays (except the English histories) in far-off places and in distant times, never, like Dekker, Jonson and Middleton, directly depicting the society around him, only rarely adopting the satirical stance that characterized the work of many playwrights of the Jacobean generation. To that extent he carried forward into the later period the traditions that he inherited from, and shared with, his Elizabethan contemporaries, Kyd and Marlowe in tragedy, Lyly and Greene in comedy. But as a working man of the theatre for a quarter of a century he never lost touch with the present; he was a thoroughgoing professional who worked hard to earn his living and to keep his family in some splendour in Stratford. The fact that half of his plays remained unpublished at his death suggests that he had more thought of the present than of posterity. He was deeply immersed in the world around him, and to see him as one among a great company is only to enhance our sense of what made him unique.

Documents

The pages that follow reproduce just a few of the key documents important to an understanding of the theatre of Shakespeare's time. Some of them have been partially quoted in earlier pages of this book.

DUTIES OF THE MASTER OF THE REVELS

[This is a digest of Queen Elizabeth I's patent of 24 December 1581 appointing Edmund Tilney (1535/6–1610) as Master of the Revels, an office that he held until he died. The patent is of interest partly in showing how many trades were involved in putting on shows for the court, as well as for the powers for licensing that it confers upon the Master of the Revels.]

He was 'authorized, licensed and commanded' to employ as many 'painters, embroiderers, tailors, cappers, haberdashers, joiners, carders, glaziers, armourers, basketmakers, skinners, saddlers, wagon makers, plasterers, feathermakers, as all other property makers' as are required 'for the speedy working and finishing of any [relevant] exploit, workmanship or piece of service'; to buy at reasonable prices 'any kind or kinds of stuff, ware or merchandise, wood or coal or other fuel, timber, wainscot, board, lathe, nails, brick, tile, lead, iron, wire and all other necessaries' for the works of the Office of the Revels, 'together with all carriages for the same both by land and by water as the case shall require'. He and his deputies have the right to arrest anyone who is unhelpful.

Most importantly, he has authority to license plays: 'we have and do by these presents authorize and command our said servant Edmund Tilney, Master of our said Revels, by himself or his sufficient deputy or deputies to warn, command, and appoint in all places within this our realm of England as well within franchises and liberties as without, all and every player or players with their play-makers either belonging to any nobleman or otherwise bearing the name or names of [or?] using the faculty of playmakers or players of comedies, tragedies, interludes or what other shows soever from time to time and at all times to appear before him with all such plays, tragedies, comedies or shows as they shall have in readiness or mean to set forth, and then to present and recite before our said servant or his sufficient deputy whom we ordain and appoint and authorize by these presents of all such shows, plays, players and playmakers, together with their playing places, to order and reform, authorize and put down, as shall be thought meet or unmeet unto himself or his deputy in that behalf . . .'

[The full document is transcribed in E. K. Chambers, *The Elizabethan Stage* (Oxford, Clarendon Press, 1923), vol. iv, pp. 285–7.]

AN INVENTORY OF THEATRICAL PROPERTIES

[This 'Inventory of the clowns' suits and hermits' suits, with divers other suits' belonging to the Lord Admiral's Men was made on 10 March 1598. It was preserved, along with other lists of costumes, playbooks, etc., at Dulwich College. The originals do not survive, but they were printed by Edmond Malone in his 1790 edition of Shakespeare and there is no reason to question their genuineness. The spelling, which I have attempted to modernize, is often eccentric, and a number of the words are unexplained or open to variant interpretation; some are names of actors or of characters in identifiable plays. The list gives a vivid idea of the contents of the wardrobes and property boxes in the tiring house of the Rose and is illuminating about staging methods.]

1 senator's gown, 1 hood, and 5 senators' caps
1 suit for Neptune; firedrakes' suits for Dobe [?]
4 janissaries' gowns, and 4 torchbearers' suits
3 pair of red strossers [tight hose] and 3 fares[?] gown of buckram
4 Heralds' [? 'Herwodes'] coats and 3 soldiers' coats, and 1 green gown for
    Marian
6 green coats for Robin Hood and 4 knaves' suits
2 pair of green hose, and Anderson's suit. 1 white shepen cloak
2 russet coats and 1 black frieze coat, and 3 priests' coats
2 white shepherds' coats, and 2 Danes' suits, and 1 pair of Dane's hose
The Moor's limbs, and Hercules' limbs, and Will Summers' suit
2 Orlate's [?] suits, hats and gorgets, and 7 antics' coats
Cathemer suit, 1 pair of cloth white stockings, 4 Turks' heads
4 friars' gowns and 4 hoods to them, and 1 fool's coat, cape, and bauble,
    and Branholt's bodice, and Merlin gown and cape

2 black say gowns, and 2 cotton gowns, and one red say gown

1 Maw gown of calico for the queen, 1 cardinal [? 'carnowll'] hat

1 red suit of cloth for Pig [John Pig, the boy actor], laid with white lace

5 pair of hose for the clown, and 5 jerkins for them

3 pair of canvas hose for asane [?], 2 pair of black strossers

1 yellow leather doublet for a clown, 1 Whitcome's doublet poke

Eve's bodice, 1 pedant trusser, and 3 dons' hats

1 pair of yellow cotton sleeves, 1 ghost's suit, and 1 ghost's bodice

18 copes and hats, Verone's son's hose

3 trumpets and a drum, and a treble viol, a bass viol, a bandore, a cittern, 1 ensign, 1 white hat

1 hat for Robin Hood, 1 hobbyhorse

5 shirts, and 1 surplice, 4 farthingales

6 head tires, 1 fan, 4 rebatos, 2 girkstrusses [?]

1 long sword

[From the same source comes the following list of properties for the Lord Admiral's Men, also made on 10 March 1598:]

1 rock, 1 cage, 1 tomb, 1 hell mouth

1 tomb of Guido, 1 tomb of Dido, 1 bedstead

8 lances, 1 pair of stairs for Phaeton

2 steeples and 1 chime of bells, and 1 beacon

1 heifer for the play of Phaeton, the limbs dead

1 globe, and 1 golden sceptre; 3 clubs

2 marchpanes, and the City of Rome

1 golden fleece, 2 rackets, 1 bay tree

1 wooden hatchet, 1 leather hatchet

1 wooden canopy; old Mahomet's head

1 lion skin, 1 bear's skin, and Phaeton's limbs, and Phaeton chariot, and Argus' head

Neptune fork and garland

1 croser's staff; Kent's wooden leg

Iris's [? 'Ierosses'] head and rainbow, 1 little altar

8 vizards; Tamburlaine bridle; 1 wooden mattock

Cupid's bow, and quiver; the cloth of the sun and moon

1 boar's head and Cerberus' 3 heads

1 caduceus; 2 moss banks, and 1 snake

2 fans of feathers; Bellendon's table [? 'Belendon stable']; 1 tree of golden apples; Tantalus' tree; 9 iron targets [shields]

1 copper target and 17 foils

4 wooden targets; 1 grieve armour

1 sign for Mother Redcap; 1 buckler

Mercury's wings; Tasso picture; 1 helmet with a dragon; 1 shield with 3 lions; 1 elm bowl

1 chain of dragons; 1 gilt spear

2 coffins; 1 bull's head; and 1 philtre [?'vylter']

3 timbrels, 1 dragon in *Faustus*

1 lion; 2 lion heads; 1 great horse with his legs; 1 sackbut

1 well and frame in *The Siege of London*

1 pair of rowghte [?] gloves

1 Pope's mitre

3 imperial crowns; 1 plain crown

1 ghost's crown; 1 crown with a sun

1 frame for the heading in *Black Joan*

1 black dog

1 cauldron for the Jew

[Transcribed and edited from *Henslowe Papers*, ed. Walter W. Greg (London, A. H. Bullen, 1907), pp. 116–18.]

EDWARD ALLEYN ON TOUR

[A letter written from Philip Henslowe, partly on behalf of his daughter Joan, in London to his son-in-law Edward Alleyn in the provinces on 14 August 1593, when plague was raging. The letter is subscribed: 'To my well-beloved husband Mr Edward Alleyn, one of my Lord Strange's players, this to be delivered with speed.' Henslowe uses no punctuation at all. I have edited the letter lightly to make it more intelligible while trying to retain something of its individuality.]

Well-beloved son Edward Alleyn, I and your mother and your sister Bess have all in general our hearty commendations unto you and very glad to hear of your good health which we pray God to continue long to His will and pleasure, for we heard that you were very sick at Bath and that one of your fellows were fain to play your part for you which was no little grief unto us to hear, but thanks be to God for amendment for we feared it much because we had no letter from you when the other wives had letters sent which made your mouse not to weep a little but took it very grievously thinking that you had conceived some unkindness of her because you were ever wont to write with the first and I pray ye do so still, for we would all be sorry but to hear as often from you as others do from their friends for we would write oftener to you than we do but we know not whither to send to you therefore I pray you forget not your mouse and us for you sent in one letter that we returned not answer whether we received them or no for we received one which you made at St James' tide wherein makes mention of your white waistcoat and your lute books and other things which we have received and now lastly a letter which Peter brought with your horse which I will be as careful as I can in it. Now son although long yet at the last I remember a hundred commendations from your mouse which is very glad to hear of your health and prayeth day and night to the Lord to continue the same and likewise prayeth unto the Lord to cease His hand from punishing us with His cross that she might have you at home with her hoping then that you should be eased of this heavy labour and toil and you said in your letter that she sent you not word how your garden and all your things doth prosper – very well thanks be to God for your beans are grown to high hedge and well codded and all other things doth very well but your tenants wax very poor for they can pay no rent nor will pay no rent while Michaelmas next and then we shall have it if we can get it, and likewise your joiner commends him unto you and says he will make you such good stuff and such good pennyworths as he hopeth shall well like you and content you which I hope he will do because he says he will prove himself an honest man, and for your good counsel which you gave us in your letter we all thank you which was for keeping of our house clean and watering of our doors and strewing our windows with wormwood and rue, which I hope all this we do and more, for we strew it with hearty prayers unto the Lord which unto us is more available than all things else in the world, for I praise the Lord God for that we are all in very good health, and I pray ye son commend me heartily to all the rest of your fellows in general for I grow poor for lack of them therefore have no gifts to send but as good and faithful a heart as they shall desire to have come amongst them, now son we thank you all for your tokens you sent us and as for news of the sickness I cannot send you no just note of it because there is commandment to the contrary, but as I think doth die within the City and without of all sicknesses to the number of seventeen or eighteen hundred in one week, and this praying to God for your health I end from London the 14 of August 1593

Your loving wife to	Your loving father and mother
command till death	To our powers P H A
Joan Alleyn	

[Transcribed and edited from Henslowe, ed. Greg, pp. 38–9.]

A WARRANT FROM A NOBLEMAN SEEKING PERMISSION FOR HIS COMPANY OF PLAYERS TO PERFORM ON TOUR

[The following warrant, signed and sealed by the Duke of Lennox, cousin and favourite of King James I, on 13 October 1604, is an example of the kind of document that travelling players would carry with them as a guarantee that they were under noble protection and in the attempt to overcome objections from local authorities. Subscribed 'To all Mayors, Justices of Peace, Sheriffs, Bailiffs, Constables, and all other His Highness' officers and loving subjects to whom it shall or may in any wise appertain', it is also addressed: 'To my loving friend Mr Dale Esquire and all other justices whatsoever.']

Sir, I am given to understand that you have forbidden the company of players that call themselves mine the exercise of their plays. I pray you to forbear any such course against them, and seeing they have my licence, to suffer them to continue the use of their plays, and until you receive other signification from me of them, to afford them your favour and assistance. And so I bid you heartily farewell; from Hampton Court the 13 of October 1604.

Your loving friend,

Lennox

[Transcribed and edited from Henslowe, ed. Greg, p. 62.]

AN ACT TO RESTRAIN ABUSES OF PLAYERS

[This Act dates from 27 May 1606. Prohibiting the use of oaths on stage, its effect is often visible in texts printed from theatre manuscripts; for instance, more than fifty oaths found in the quarto text of *Othello*, printed in 1622 (though the play had been written some twenty years earlier) are toned down in the more theatrical text printed in the First Folio, of 1623.]

For the preventing and avoiding of the great abuse of the holy name of God in stage plays, interludes, May games, shows, and such like: be it enacted by our sovereign Lord the King's Majesty and by the Lords Spiritual and Temporal, and commons in this present parliament assembled, and by the authority of the same: that if at any time or times after the end of this present session of parliament any person or persons do or shall in any stage play, interlude, show, May game or pageant jestingly or profanely speak or use the holy name of God or of Christ Jesus or of the Holy Ghost or of the Trinity, which are not to be spoken but with fear and reverence, [?such person or persons] shall forfeit for every such offence by him or them committed ten pounds, the one moiety thereof to the King's Majesty, his heirs and successors, the other moiety thereof to him or them that will sue for the same in any court of record at Westminster, wherein no essoin [excuse] protection or wager of law shall be allowed.

[Reprinted from Chambers, *Elizabethan Stage*, vol. iv, p. 339.]

SIMON FORMAN AT THE THEATRE

[A manuscript notebook by Simon Forman headed 'Book of Plays and Notes thereof' now in the Bodleian Library, Oxford, gives us the only accounts of visits to the theatre from Shakespeare's lifetime that provide any detail about performance. Partial, and containing curious discrepancies from the texts of the plays as they have come down to us, they are written from the point of view of an observer attempting in part to draw practical lessons from what he saw rather than from that of an objective witness, but even so they provide insights into both the expectations of playgoers and the nature of performance at the time. Forman saw three Shakespeare plays, none of which had appeared in print: *Macbeth* at the Globe on 20 April 1611, *The Winter's Tale*, also at the Globe, on 15 May 1611, and *Cymbeline*, probably also at the Globe on an unspecified date. He also saw a play about Richard II which was clearly not Shakespeare's. His accounts of the Shakespeare plays are of especial interest as they can be compared with the texts; *Macbeth* impressed him especially vividly as both story and performance. I offer the accounts in modernized spelling and punctuation.]

Cymbeline

Of Cymbeline, King of Britain. Remember also the story of Cymbeline King of England in Lucius' time, how Lucius came from Octavius Caesar for tribute, and being denied, after sent Lucius with a great army of soldiers who landed at Milford Haven, and after were vanquished by Cymbeline, and Lucius taken prisoner, and all by means of three outlaws, of the which two of them were the sons of Cymbeline, taken from him when they were but two years old by an old man whom Cymbeline banished, and he kept them as his own sons twenty years with him in a cave. And how one of them slew Cloten that was the Queen's son, going to Milford Haven to seek the love of Innogen the King's daughter whom he had banished also for loving his daughter. And how the Italian that came from her love conveyed himself into a chest and said it was a chest of plate sent from her love and others to be presented to the King; and in the deepest of the night, she being asleep, he opened the chest and came forth of it, and viewed her in her bed, and the marks of her body, and took away her bracelet, and after accused her of adultery to her love, etc. And in the end how he came with the Romans into England, and was taken prisoner and after revealed to Innogen, who had turned herself into man's apparel and fled to meet her love at Milford Haven, and chanced to fall on the cave in the woods where her two brothers were, and how by eating a sleeping dram they thought she had been dead, and laid her in the woods, and the body of Cloten by her in her love's apparel that he left behind him, and how she was found by Lucius, etc.

Macbeth

In *Macbeth* at the Globe 1611 the 20 of April, Saturday, there was to be observed first how Macbeth and Banquo, two noblemen of Scotland, riding through a wood, there stood before them three women fairies or nymphs, and saluted Macbeth saying three times unto him 'Hail Macbeth, King of Codon [Cawdor], for thou shalt be a king but shall beget no kings', etc. Then said Banquo 'What, all to Macbeth and nothing to me?' 'Yes' said the nymphs, 'Hail to thee, Banquo, thou shalt beget kings yet be no king.' And so they departed and came to the court of Scotland to Duncan King of Scots, and it was in the days of Edward the Confessor, and Duncan bade them both kindly welcome, and made Macbeth forthwith Prince of Northumberland, and sent him home to his own castle, and appointed Macbeth to provide for him, for he would sup with him the next day at night, and did so. And Macbeth contrived to kill Duncan, and through the persuasion of his wife did that night murder the King in his own castle, being his guest. And there were many prodigies seen that night and the day before. And when Macbeth had murdered the King the blood on his hands could not be washed off by any means, nor from his wife's hands, which handled the bloody daggers in hiding them, by which means they became both much amazed and affronted. The murder being known, Duncan's two sons fled, the one to England, the [other to] Wales to save themselves; they being fled they were supposed guilty of the murder of their father, which was nothing so. Then was Macbeth crowned king, and then he for fear of Banquo his old companion that he should beget kings but be no king himself he contrived the death of Banquo and caused him to be murdered on the way as he rode. The next night, being at supper with his noblemen whom he had bid to a feast to the which also Banquo should have come, he began to speak of 'noble Banquo', and to wish that he were there. And as he thus did, standing up to drink a carouse to him, the ghost of Banquo came and sat down in his chair behind him, and he turning about to sit down again saw the ghost of Banquo, which fronted him so that he fell into a great passion of fear and fury, uttering many words about his murder by which, when they heard that Banquo was murdered, they suspected Macbeth. Then Macduff fled to England to the King's son, and so they raised an army and came into Scotland, and at Dunstan [Dunsinane] Anyse overthrew Macbeth. In the meantime while Macduff was in England Macbeth slew Macduff's wife and children, and after in the battle Macduff slew Macbeth. Observe also how Macbeth's queen did rise in the night in her sleep, and walk and talked and confessed all, and the doctor noted her words.

The Winter's Tale

In *The Winter's Tale* at the Globe 1611, the 15 of May, Wednesday. Observe there how Leontes, the King of Sicilia, was overcome with jealousy of his wife with the King of Bohemia, his friend, that came to see him, and how he contrived his death, and would have had his cupbearer to have poisoned [him], who gave the King of Bohemia warning thereof and fled with him to Bohemia. Remember also how he sent to the oracle of Apollo, and the answer of Apollo – that she was guiltless and that the King was jealous, etc. And how, except the child was found again that was lost, the King should die without issue, for the child was carried into Bohemia and there laid in a forest and brought up by a shepherd, and the King of Bohemia his son married that wench, and how they fled into Sicilia to Leontes, and the shepherd, having showed the letter of the nobleman by whom Leontes sent a was [?away] that child, and the jewels found about her, she was known to be Leontes' daughter, and was then sixteen years old. Remember also the rogue that came in all tattered like Colt-pixie [a hobgoblin]; and how he feigned him sick and to have been robbed of all that he had, and how he cozened the poor man of all his money, and after came to the sheep-shear with a pedlar's pack and there cozened them again of all their money, and how he changed apparel with the King of Bohemia his son, and then how he turned courtier, etc. Beware of trusting feigned beggars or fawning fellows.

'A SONNET UPON THE PITIFUL BURNING OF THE GLOBE PLAYHOUSE IN LONDON'

Now sit thee down, Melpomene,
  Wrapped in a sea-coal robe,
And tell the doleful tragedy
  That late was played at Globe;
For no man that can sing and say
[But] was scared on St Peter's Day.
  O sorrow, pitiful sorrow, and yet all this is true.

All you that please to understand,
  Come listen to my story,
To see Death with his raking brand
  'Mongst such an auditory;
Regarding neither Cardinal's might,
Nor yet the rugged face of Henry the Eight.
  O sorrow, &c.

This fearful fire began above,
  A wonder strange and true,
And to the stage-house did remove,
  As round as tailor's clew;
And burnèd down both beam and snag,
And did not spare the silken flag.
  O sorrow, &c.

Out run the knights, out run the lords,
  And there was great ado;
Some lost their hats and some their swords;
  Then out run Burbage too;
The reprobates, though drunk on Monday,
Prayed for the Fool and Henry Condye.
  O sorrow, &c.

The periwigs and drum-heads fry
  Like to a butter firkin;
A woeful burning did betide
  To many a good buff jerkin.
Then with swoll'n eyes, like drunken Flemings,
Distressèd stood old stuttering Heminges.
  O sorrow, &c.

No shower his rain did there down force
   In all that sunshine weather,
To save that great renownèd house;
   Nor thou, O ale-house, neither.
Had it begun below, sans doubt,
Their wives for fear had pissed it out.
   O sorrow, &c.

Be warnèd, you stage strutters all,
   Lest you again be catched,
And such a burning do befall,
   As to them whose house was thatched;
Forbear your whoring, breeding biles,
And lay up that expense for tiles.
   O sorrow, &c.

Go draw you a petition,
   And do you not abhor it,
And get, with low submission,
   A licence to beg for it
In churches, sans churchwardens' checks,
In Surrey and in Middlesex.
   O sorrow, pitiful sorrow, and yet all this is true.

[Edited from Peter Beal, 'The Burning of the Globe', *TLS*, 20 June 1986, pp. 689–90.]

'THE CHARACTER OF A VIRTUOUS PLAYER'

He knows the right use of the world, wherein he comes to play a part and so away. His life is not idle for it is all action, and no man need be more wary in his doings, for the eyes of all men are upon him. His profession has in it a kind of contradiction, for none is more disliked, and yet none more applauded: and he has this misfortune of some scholar, too much wit makes him a fool. He is like our painting gentlewomen, seldom in his own face, seldomer in his clothes, and he pleases the better he counterfeits, except only when he is disguised with straw for gold lace. He does not only personate on the stage, but sometime in the street, for he is masked still in the habit of a gentleman. His parts find him oaths and good words, which he keeps for his use and discourse, and makes show with them of a fashionable companion. He is tragical on the stage, but rampant in the tiring house, and swears oaths there which he never conned. The waiting-women spectators are over ears in love with him, and ladies send for him to act in their chambers. Your Inns of Court men were undone but for him, he is their chief guest and employment, and the sole business that makes them afternoon's men. The poet only is his tyrant, and he is bound to make his friend's friend drunk at his charges. Shrove Tuesday he fears as much as the bawds, and Lent is more damage to him than [to] the butcher. He was never so much discredited as in one act, and that was of Parliament, which gives ostlers privilege before him, for which he abhors it more than a corrupt judge. But to give him his due, one well furnished actor has enough in him for five common gentlemen, and, if he have a good body, for six; and for resolution, he shall challenge any Cato, for it has been his practice to die bravely.

[From John Earle, *Microcosmography; or a Piece of the World Discovered in Essays and Characters* (1628); reprinted in Glynne Wickham, Herbert Berry and William Ingram (eds.), *English Professional Theatre, 1530–1660* (Cambridge, Cambridge University Press, 2000), pp. 186–7.]

Notes

	(Cambridge, Cambridge University Press, 2002)
Henslowe, ed. Greg	*Henslowe Papers*, ed. Walter W. Greg (London, A. H. Bullen, 1907)
Jonson, ed. Donaldson	*Ben Jonson*, ed. Ian Donaldson, The Oxford Authors (Oxford, Oxford University Press, 1985)
Jonson, ed. Herford and Simpson	*Ben Jonson*, ed. C. H. Herford and Percy and Evelyn Simpson, 11 vols. (Oxford, Clarendon Press, 1925–52)
Marlowe, *Poems*	*Christopher Marlowe: The Complete Poems and Translations*, ed. Stephen Orgel (Harmondsworth, Penguin Books, 1971)
Middleton, ed. Bullen	*The Works of Thomas Middleton*, ed. A. H. Bullen, 8 vols. (London, John C. Nimmo, 1885–6)
Nashe, ed. McKerrow	*The Works of Thomas Nashe*, ed. R. B. McKerrow, 5 vols. (Oxford, Clarendon Press, 1904–10, revised edition 1958)
Nashe, ed. Wells	*Thomas Nashe: Selected Works*, ed. Stanley Wells (London, Edward Arnold, 1964)
Platter, trans. Schanzer	E. Schanzer, 'Thomas Platter's Observations of the Elizabethan Stage', *Notes and Queries*, NS, 3/11 (Nov. 1956), pp. 465–7
Platter, *Travels*	*Thomas Platter's Travels in England 1599*, trans. Clare Williams (London, Jonathan Cape, 1937) (for excerpts not translated by Schanzer)
Shakespeare, *Complete Works*	William Shakespeare, *The Complete Works*, general editors Stanley Wells and Gary Taylor, second edn. (Oxford, Oxford University Press, 2005)
Textual Companion	*William Shakespeare: A Textual Companion*, by Stanley Wells, Gary Taylor, John Jowett and William Montgomery (Oxford, Clarendon Press, 1987)

Wickham   Glynne Wickham, Herbert Berry and
                           William Ingram (eds.), *English
                           Professional Theatre, 1530–1660*
                           (Cambridge, Cambridge University
                           Press, 2000)

CHAPTER I THE THEATRICAL SCENE

1. Wickham, p. 146.

2. C. M. Ingleby *et al.* (eds.), *The Shakspere* [sic] *Allusion-Book*, 2 vols., revised edition (London, Oxford University Press, 1932), vol. i, p. 56.

3. Wickham, p. 51.

4. Ibid., p. 208.

5. The Oxford *Complete Works* prints two versions of *King Lear*: *The History of King Lear*, edited from the first quarto, of 1608, and *The Tragedy of King Lear*, edited from the First Folio. Unless otherwise stated, my references are to the latter.

6. John Taylor, *All the Workes of John Taylor the Water Poet* (London, James Bowles, 1630), sig. Ddd3v.

7. Plays were certainly performed throughout the winter months of some years at the Rose, as Henslowe's accounts show. The frost fair forms a vivid scene in Virginia Woolf's novel *Orlando* (1928).

8. Though highly probable, it is not absolutely certain that Platter visited the Globe, or that the play he saw about Julius Caesar was Shakespeare's.

9. Platter, trans. Schanzer, p. 466.

10. Gurr, *Playgoing*, p. 21.

11. *The First Quarto of Hamlet*, ed. Kathleen O. Irace (Cambridge, Cambridge University Press, 1998), Scene 9, line 6.

12. *The Poems of Sir John Davies*, ed. Robert Kreuger and Ruby Nemser (Oxford, Oxford University Press, 1975), p. 136. Gurr, *Stage*, p. 217.

13. Chambers, *Elizabethan Stage*, vol. iv, p. 211.

14. Ibid.

15. Sheldon Zitner, 'Gosson, Ovid and the Elizabethan Audience', *Shakespeare Quarterly*, 9 (1958), pp. 206–8.

16. Gurr, *Playgoing*, p. 250.

17. Ibid., p. 258.

18. Ibid., p. 265.

19. Platter, *Travels*, pp. 174–5.

20. Inigo Jones's plans for the building survive, and the exterior has been reconstructed alongside the Globe, but sadly it is not yet fitted out for performances.

21. Gurr, *Stage*, p. 14.

22. Philip Gawdy, cited in Gurr, *Playgoing*, p. 260.

23. Gurr, *Playgoing*, p. 236.

24. Ibid., p. 246.

25. Ibid., pp. 230, 238.

26. Ibid., p. 224.

27. 'Upon Master William Shakespeare, the Deceased Author, and his Poems', in Shakespeare, *Complete Works*, p. lxxiv.

28. Wickham, pp. 507–8.

29. A replica of the Blackfriars has been constructed in Staunton, Virginia, and is regularly used for performances. It makes a comfortably intimate playing space.

30. Gurr, *Playgoing*, p. 259.

31. Ibid., p. 226.

32. Platter, trans. Schanzer, p. 466.

33. P. L. Hughes and J. F. Larkin (eds.), *Tudor Royal Proclamations*, vol. ii, *The Later Tudors (1553–1587)* (New Haven and London, Yale University Press, 1969), p. 383.

34. Bentley, *Player*, p. 102.

35. Henslowe, ed. Foakes, p. 269.

36. Bentley, *Player*, p. 49.

37. Henslowe, ed. Greg, p. 67.

38. Peter Holland, 'Reading to the Company', in Hanna Scolnicov and Peter Holland (eds.), *Reading Plays: Interpretation and Reception* (Cambridge, Cambridge University Press, 1991), pp. 8–29.

39. Henslowe, ed. Foakes, p. 88.

40. 'Nearly half of the plays written for the public theatres during the early modern period were the product of joint authorship.' Eric Rasmussen, 'Collaboration', in Michael Dobson and Stanley Wells (eds.), *The Oxford Companion to Shakespeare* (Oxford, Oxford University Press, 2001).

CHAPTER 2 WILLIAM SHAKESPEARE AND THE ACTORS

1. Shakespeare, *Complete Works*, p. xliii.

2. By Nicholas Rowe (Ghost) and William Oldys (Adam).

3. In a review of Johnston Forbes-Robertson's Hamlet, 2 October 1897; reprinted in Edwin Wilson (ed.), *Shaw on Shakespeare* (London, Cassell, 1962), p. 85.

4. See my *Shakespeare: For All Time* (London, Macmillan, 2002), p. 113, and the illustration of a page from the quarto on p. 114.

5. C. J. Sisson, *Lost Plays of Shakespeare's Age* (Cambridge, Cambridge

University Press, 1936), p. 126. This book has a valuable section (pp. 125–56) on the jig, and prints examples from manuscripts discovered by Sisson. James Shapiro writes judiciously on the topic in *1599: A Year in the Life of William Shakespeare* (London, Faber and Faber, 2005), pp. 46–8.

6. Nashe, ed. Wells, pp. 47–8.

7. His date of birth is unknown; he is first heard of as an actor in 1585.

8. Thomas Nashe, *An Almond for a Parrot*, in Nashe, ed. McKerrow, vol. iii, p. 341.

9. David Wiles, *Shakespeare's Clown: Actor and Text in the Elizabethan Playhouse* (Cambridge, Cambridge University Press, 1987), offers extensive discussion of the stage roles of Kemp and of other clowns of the period.

10. Quotations are modernized from the reprint ed. Susan Yaxley (Stibbard, Norfolk, Larks Press, 1985).

11. John Davies, *Complete Works*, ed. A. B. Grosart, 3 vols. (privately circulated, University of Edinburgh Press, 1878), vol. ii, p. 60.

12. Henslowe, ed. Foakes, p. 276.

13. Ibid., pp. 277–8.

14. Nashe, ed. McKerrow, p. 296.

15. Nashe, ed. Wells, p. 66.

16. Jonson, ed. Donaldson, p. 252.

17. Alleyn's acting is discussed by William A. Armstrong in 'Shakespeare and the Acting of Edward Alleyn', *Shakespeare Survey*, 7 (1954), pp. 82–9. S. P. Cerasano's *Oxford DNB* entry is invaluable, as also is her article 'Tamburlaine and Edward Alleyn's Ring', *Shakespeare Survey*, 47 (1994), pp. 17–19.

18. Chambers, *Elizabethan Stage*, vol. ii, p. 388.

19. Wickham, pp. 361–2.

20. Ibid., p. 182.

21. The comparison is drawn by R. A. Foakes, in Jonathan Bate and Russell Jackson (eds.), *Shakespeare: An Illustrated Stage History* (Oxford, Oxford University Press, 1996), p. 14.

22. Wickham, p. 181.

23. Quoted by Mary Edmond in her *Oxford DNB* entry for Burbage.

24. Wickham, p. 173.

25. *The Diary of John Manningham of the Middle Temple, 1602–3*, ed. Robert Parker Sorlien (Hanover, NH, University Press of New England, 1976), pp. 208–9.

26. Wickham, p. 17.

27. Duncan Salkeld, 'Literary Traces in Bridewell and Bethlem, 1602–24', *RES*, NS, 56/225 (2005), pp. 379–85, quotation from p. 382.

28. 'A representative life: Augustine Phillips', in Wickham, pp. 191–203, gathers together the documentary evidence about his life.

29. They are discussed in detail and reproduced in David Bradley, *From Text to Performance in the Elizabethan Theatre: Preparing the Play for the Stage* (Cambridge, Cambridge University Press, 1992).

30. Wilhelm Schrickx, 'English Actors' Names in German Archives and Elizabethan Theatre History', *Deutsche Shakespeare-Gesellschaft West Jahrbuch* (1982), p. 155.

31. Andrew Gurr writes on Sinklo's roles in *The Shakespearian Playing Companies* (Oxford, Clarendon Press, 1996), p. 280.

32. Wickham, pp. 262–3.

33. Ibid., p. 263.

34. Ibid., pp. 264–7.

35. Ibid.

36. Jonson, ed. Donaldson, p. 270.

37. The first known training school for young players dates from around 1630: Bentley, *Player*, pp. 137–8.

38. 'As stage-players had no formal recognition as a guild, this sort of training conferred no rights of freedom upon its graduates, nor was it hedged round with the constraints of age and marital status imposed by the City on more formal kinds of apprenticeship'; Wickham, p. 155.

39. Bentley, *Player*, p. 145.

40. Henslowe, ed. Foakes, pp. 282–3.

CHAPTER 3 CHRISTOPHER MARLOWE AND SHAKESPEARE'S OTHER EARLY CONTEMPORARIES

1. This and all the following details are from D. Kathman, *Oxford DNB* entry for Meres.

2. D. Cameron Allen, *Francis Meres' Treatise 'Poetrie'* (Urbana, University of Illinois Press, 1933), p. 84.

3. Dekker, ed. Pendry, p. 168.

4. Quoted G. K. Hunter, *John Lyly: The Humanist as Courtier* (London, Routledge and Kegan Paul, 1962), p. 49.

5. Quoted in *1 Henry IV*, ed. David Bevington (Oxford, Oxford University Press, 1987), note to 2.4.387.

6. He is also the only one not known to have written in collaboration, if we believe that Nashe helped Marlowe with *Dido, Queen of Carthage*.

7. Hunter, *John Lyly*, p. 86.

8. See John Jowett, 'Johannes Factotum: Henry Chettle and *Greene's Groatsworth of Wit*', *Publications of the Bibliographical Society of America*, 87 (1993), pp. 453–86. The book may have been wholly or partly written by Henry Chettle.

9. From *Strange News*, 1593; reprinted in Nashe, ed. Wells, pp. 279–80.

10. Reprinted in Emrys Jones (ed.), *The New Oxford Book of Sixteenth-Century Verse* (Oxford, Oxford University Press, 1991), p. 421.

11. The exact canon of Greene's plays, by which he is best remembered, is uncertain. His early work, especially *Alphonsus, King of Aragon* (*c.* 1587), is heavily influenced by Marlowe, and especially by *Tamburlaine. Alphonsus* includes as a grand climax the nicely pragmatic stage direction: '*Exit Venus; or if you can conveniently, let a chair come down from the top of the stage and draw her up.*' Greene collaborated with Thomas Lodge on a moralistic biblical drama, *A Looking Glass for London and England* (1589?), which has robust comic interludes and calls for elaborate stage effects: '*Upon this prayer she departeth, and a flame of fire appeareth from beneath, and Radagon is swallowed*'; '*Jonas the prophet cast out of the whale's belly upon the stage, and a hand from out a cloud threateneth a burning sword.*'

12. *Plays and Poems*, ed. J. Churton Collins, 2 vols. (Oxford, Clarendon Press, 1905), vol. i, p. 47.

13. Preface to Greene's *Menaphon*, in Nashe, ed. McKerrow, vol. iii, p. 323.

14. The case is passionately summarized, supported and re-argued by Brian Vickers in his *Shakespeare, Co-author* (Oxford, Oxford University Press, 2002), pp. 148–243.

15. Nashe, ed. Wells, p. 130.

16. Nashe, ed. McKerrow, vol. iii, pp. 408–9.

17. Gary Taylor, 'Shakespeare and Others: The Authorship of *1 Henry VI*', *Medieval and Renaissance Drama in England*, 7 (1995), 145–205.

18. Nashe, ed. Wells, pp. 64–5.

19. Dover Wilson lists these and other parallels, some more suggestive of direct influence than others, in an appendix, 'Parallels from Nashe', in his New Shakespeare edition of *Henry the Fourth Part One* (Cambridge, 1946), pp. 191–6.

20. It had been entered in the Stationers' Register in 1593, and may have been printed then; only one copy of the first 1598 edition survives.

21. Marlowe, *Poems*, p. 119.

22. Park Honan, *Christopher Marlowe: Poet and Spy* (Oxford, Oxford University Press, 2005), p. 154.

23. Quoted in this context by Charles Nicholl in his brilliant study *The*

Reckoning (London, Jonathan Cape, 1992; revised edition, London, Vintage Books, 2002, p. 121) to which all students of Marlowe owe a great debt.

24. Nashe, ed. McKerrow, vol. iii, pp. 126–7.

25. Charles Nicholl, *Oxford DNB*; also entry for William Corkine which does not refer to the father.

26. T. S. Eliot, *Elizabethan Essays* (London, Faber and Faber, 1934), p. 28.

27. Its date is uncertain; some scholars put it before *Edward II*.

28. Paul Hammond, *Figuring Sex between Men from Shakespeare to Rochester* (Oxford, Clarendon Press, 2002), pp. 72–84.

29. There is a useful discussion in Alan Nelson, *Monstrous Adversary: The Life of Edward de Vere, 17th Earl of Oxford* (Liverpool, Liverpool University Press, 2003), pp. 209–13.

30. Ibid., p. 210.

31. The Baines and Kyd documents, along with the coroner's report, are reproduced in Honan, *Marlowe*, pp. 374–81.

32. Ibid., p. 337.

33. Ibid., pp. 278–80.

34. Ibid., p. 352. Honan reprints the coroner's report and reproduces a mock-up photograph of the damage done to Marlowe's skull.

35. Leslie Hotson, *The Death of Christopher Marlowe* (London, Nonsuch Press, 1925).

36. Nicholl, *The Reckoning*, pp. 204–5. Honan, however, is inclined to believe that the anecdote relates to a John Fineaux who is unlikely to have known Marlowe personally (*Marlowe*, pp. 249–50).

37. These tributes are all cited from C. F. Tucker Brooke, *The Life of Marlowe* (London, Methuen, 1930), pp. 79–80.

38. E. K. Chambers, *William Shakespeare: A Study of Facts and Problems*, 2 vols. (Oxford, Clarendon Press, 1930), vol. ii, p. 252.

CHAPTER 4 THOMAS DEKKER AND LONDON

1. Dekker's *Plague Pamphlets*, ed. F. P. Wilson (Oxford, Clarendon Press, 1925), p. 146.

2. Henslowe, whose spelling is very flexible, actually wrote 'Dickers', but here as elsewhere I normalize the form of names.

3. James Agate, *Brief Chronicles* (London, Jonathan Cape, 1943), p. 71.

4. The total cost amounted to close on £1,000; a modern scholar's analysis of how the money was spent gives a good idea of the splendour of the occasion. 'The expenses covered charges for the mayor's galley foist and three other galleys to accompany him by water to Westminster for the swearing-in

ceremony and back again to the City; fees for gunfire; payments for thirty-two trumpeters, seven drums, three ensigns and four fifes; for sixteen fencers with handswords; for six greenmen and the fireworks they would scatter to disperse the crowds and so make way for the procession; to the City waits for music; to an unspecified number of porters who carried parts of the shows; to guards for watching over the pageants during the night before they were brought into the streets, and for miscellaneous items of food and drink' (Cyrus Hoy, Introductions, Notes and Commentaries to texts in *The Dramatic Works of Thomas Dekker*, ed. Fredson Bowers, 4 vols. (Cambridge, Cambridge University Press, 1980), vol. ii, p. 133).

5. The play came into its own in 2005 with a powerful production by the Royal Shakespeare Company in the Swan Theatre, Stratford-upon-Avon. Before that it had received occasional performances in reconstructed form, most notably in a Nottingham production of 1964 in which Ian McKellen played More.

6. The Oxford edition of the *Complete Works* of 1986 printed only the Shakespearian passages, but the whole play is given in the second edition of 2005.

7. It is tempting to suggest that Shakespeare may have had special reason to sympathize with immigrants since he lived for some time with a Huguenot family, the Mountjoys, apparently in the early years of the seventeenth century.

8. For information on the plague I am much indebted to F. P. Wilson's classic study, *The Plague in Shakespeare's London* (Oxford, Clarendon Press, 1927, reprinted 1999).

9. The connection is made by Wilson, *The Plague*, p. 98.

10. Dekker, ed. Pendry, pp. 32–7.

11. Ibid., p. 39.

12. Ibid., pp. 43–4.

13. *Plague Pamphlets*, ed. Wilson, p. 94.

14. Ibid., pp. 102–3.

15. *Dramatic Works of Thomas Dekker*, ed. Bowers, vol. ii, p. 258.

16. *The Roaring Girl*, ed. Paul Mulholland (Manchester, Manchester University Press, 1987), appendix E, p. 262.

17. Dekker, ed. Pendry, pp. 98–102.

18. Ibid., p. 274.

19. They are recounted in *Lost Plays of Shakespeare's Age*, by C. J. Sisson (Cambridge, Cambridge University Press, 1936), to which I am deeply indebted for this account. The book has been oddly neglected, especially by

students of the place of women in the period. The account of the events on which the play is based is on pp. 80–124.

20. *Thomas Dekker*, ed. Bowers, vol. iii, p. 265.

CHAPTER 5 BEN JONSON

1. I use the edition in Jonson, ed. Donaldson, pp. 595–661.

2. Ibid., pp. 236–7.

3. David Riggs, *Ben Jonson: A Life* (Cambridge, Mass., Harvard University Press, 1989), p. 30.

4. Wickham, p. 102.

5. Ibid., p. 100.

6. Henslowe, ed. Foakes, p. 286.

7. Jonson, ed. Donaldson, p. 602.

8. It has been described as 'the first English comedy to have a realistic modern setting'; Martin Wiggins, *Shakespeare and the Drama of His Time* (Oxford, Oxford University Press, 2000), p. 65.

9. Quoted in E. K. Chambers, *William Shakespeare: A Study of Facts and Problems*, 2 vols. (Oxford, Clarendon Press, 1930), vol. ii, p. 267.

10. See James Shapiro, *Rival Playwrights: Marlowe, Jonson, Shakespeare* (New York, Columbia University Press, 1991), p. 142, for a measured discussion of the links between Shakespeare and *Every Man Out of His Humour*.

11. Anne Barton, *Ben Jonson, Dramatist* (Cambridge, Cambridge University Press, 1984), p. 94.

12. Jonson, ed. Donaldson, p. 603.

13. 'Introduction' to *Sejanus, His Fall*, in *Ben Jonson: The Devil is an Ass and Other Plays*, ed. M. J. Kidnie (Oxford, Oxford University Press, 2000), p. xvi.

14. Jonson, ed. Donaldson, p. 601.

15. H. Chettle, *England's Mourning Garment*, 1603, sigs. D2v–D3r.

16. 'Ode. To Himself', appended to *The New Inn* (Jonson, ed. Donaldson, p. 502).

17. Jonson, ed. Donaldson, p. 603.

18. Donald Wolfit, *First Interval* (London, Odhams Press, 1954), p. 180.

19. Samuel Pepys, *The Shorter Pepys*, ed. Robert Latham (Harmondsworth, Penguin Books, 1985), p. 109. In 1664, however, he enjoyed it less, finding it 'not so well done or so good [a] play as I formerly thought it to be, or else I am nowadays out of humour'; p. 390.

20. *The Diary of Samuel Pepys*, ed. Robert Latham and William Matthews

11 vols. (London, Bell and Hyman, 1970–83), vol. viii, p. 169 (not included in *The Shorter Pepys*).

21. *The Shorter Pepys*, p. 109.

22. Jonson, ed. Donaldson, p. 601.

23. 'Guthrie Believes in Keeping Ben Jonson Topical', an interview in *The Times*, 19 November 1962.

24. Quoted from James Boaden, *Private Correspondence of David Garrick*, in Jonson, ed. Herford and Simpson, vol. ix, pp. 232–3.

25. Could Jonson be remembering Cleopatra's 'I am fire and air' (*Antony and Cleopatra*, 5.2.284)?

26. Jonson, ed. Donaldson, p. 368.

27. Ibid., p. 597.

28. Shakespeare, *Complete Works*, pp. lxxi–lxxii.

29. Edmund Spenser, however, had received a pension from Queen Elizabeth in 1591 after his compliments to her in the first three books of *The Faerie Queene* (1590).

30. Jonson, ed. Donaldson, p. 209.

31. Ibid., p. 229.

32. Ibid., p. 463.

CHAPTER 6 THOMAS MIDDLETON AND SHAKESPEARE

1. There are accounts of Middleton's life in Richard Hindry Barker, *Thomas Middleton* (New York, Columbia University Press, 1958), and a more up-to-date but less detailed one by Gary Taylor in *Oxford DNB*.

2. See *http://statelibrary.dcr.state.nc.us/nc/ncsites/english1.htm* for information about this expedition.

3. Middleton, ed. Bullen, vol. viii, p. 297.

4. There is an excellent edition by Joseph Quincy Adams (New York and London, Scribner's, 1937).

5. This little book was completely unknown until 1920, when it turned up in the lumber room of an English country gentleman, handsomely bound in vellum along with four other books of verse, three of them by or attributed to Shakespeare. One of the books is a defective copy of *The Passionate Pilgrim*, put together from leaves of the first edition (1599) and others from what appears to be the second edition. Another is the previously unknown third edition (1599) of Shakespeare's *Venus and Adonis*; and there is also a copy of the third edition (1600) of Shakespeare's other narrative poem, *The Rape of Lucrece*. A wealthy admirer of Shakespeare had assembled the

collection and had it specially bound for his private library in or soon after 1600. He is known only by his initials, 'G.O.', which are emblazoned on the cover. Soon after the volume was discovered, Henry Clay Folger, the American collector, snapped it up, and it is now in the Folger Shakespeare Library, Washington.

6. Middleton, ed. Bullen, vol. viii, p. 77.

7. Leanda de Lisle, *After Elizabeth* (London, HarperCollins, 2005), p. 257.

8. Curiously, the first two lines of this speech are lifted directly from one of Middleton's favourite books, Nashe's *Pierce Penniless*.

9. 9 October 1966.

10. There are no references to Shakespeare as an actor after 1603, but then there are very few of any date, so it is not impossible that he went on acting till the end of his career.

11. John Jowett, 'Introduction', *Timon of Athens*, The Oxford Shakespeare (Oxford, Oxford University Press, 2004), p. 1; there is a tabulation of Jowett's assessment of Middleton's contributions on p. 2.

12. The case is argued by Anne Lancashire in '*The Witch*: Stage Flop or Political Mistake?', in Kenneth Friedenreich (ed.), '*Accompaninge the players*': *Essays Celebrating Thomas Middleton, 1580–1980* (New York, AMS Press, 1983), pp. 161–81.

13. For purposes of comparison I have deliberately chosen plays that exist in only one early text.

14. The case sketched below is argued at length by John Jowett and Gary Taylor in their book *Shakespeare Reshaped, 1606–1623* (Oxford, Oxford University Press, 1993). Jowett puts the case more succinctly in his excellent article, 'The Audacity of *Measure for Measure* in 1621', *Ben Jonson Journal*, 8 (2001), pp. 229–48.

15. Gary Taylor, 'Shakespeare's Mediterranean *Measure for Measure*', in Tom Clayton, Susan Brock and Vicente Forés (eds.), *Shakespeare and the Mediterranean* (Newark, University of Delaware Press, 2004), pp. 243–69.

16. The relevant documents are most conveniently reprinted in appendix 1 to the Revels edition, ed. T. Howard-Hill (Manchester, Manchester University Press, 1993).

17. Wickham, p. 615.

18. To raise £100 from 3,000 spectators at a single performance would have required gross inflation of the normal entry charges.

CHAPTER 7 THE MOVE TO TRAGICOMEDY: JOHN FLETCHER AND OTHERS

1. This is the only recorded use of this word, which means resemblance.

2. Aubrey, *Brief Lives*, p. 21.

3. Ibid.

4. This quotes from *1 Henry IV*, 1.3.199–203, where, however, 'sea' reads 'deep', 'never fathom-line touched any ground' reads 'fathom-line could never touch the ground', and 'from the lake of hell' reads 'by the locks'.

5. It was broadcast by the BBC in 1988, with Roy Kinnear in the role of the hungry courtier.

6. Compare *The Merchant of Venice*, '... warmed and cooled by the same winter and summer as a Christian is? If you prick us, do we not bleed?' (3.1.58–60), and *The History of King Lear*, 'Through the sharp hawthorn blows the cold wind ... Tom's a-cold!' (Scene 11, lines 40–41, 51–2).

7. It is undated.

8. The definitive study is *Defining Shakespeare: Pericles as Test Case*, by MacDonald P. Jackson (Oxford, Oxford University Press, 2003).

9. Roger Prior, 'The Life of George Wilkins', *Shakespeare Survey*, 25 (1972), pp. 137–52; quotations from pp. 144 and 147.

10. Jackson, *Defining Shakespeare*, p. 216.

11. The play also lifts passages from an earlier version of the tale, *The Pattern of Painful Adventures*, by Laurence Twine, published originally in the mid-1570s and reprinted in 1607, which the dramatists had used as source material.

12. 'Part of *Cymbeline*'s pleasure will come from the way it mines Fletcher's seam, drawing the tragic emotions of pity and fear into the tragicomic modes of admiration and wonder'; Martin Butler, 'Introduction' to *Cymbeline* (Cambridge, Cambridge University Press, 2005), p. 19.

13. *Shaw on Shakespeare*, ed. Edwin Wilson (London, Cassell, 1962), p. 180.

14. Gordon McMullan, 'Introduction' to *The Royal Shakespeare Company Production of 'The Tamer Tamed'* (London, Nick Hern Books, 2003), p. xiv. This is a somewhat rewritten acting version. My quotations are modernized from the edition by Fredson Bowers.

15. The affair is discussed by Meg Powers Livingston in 'Fletcher's *The Woman's Prize* in 1633' (April 1999), paper presented at the NEMLA Convention, Pittsburgh, Pa., available at *http://www.personal.psu.edu/faculty/m/p/mpl10/*

16. *Samuel Johnson on Shakespeare*, ed. Henry Woudhuysen (Harmondsworth, Penguin Books, 1989), p. 235.

17. The case for *Philaster* being the earlier play is summarized by Martin Butler in his New Cambridge edition of *Cymbeline* (2005), p. 4. Butler valuably points to Shakespeare's indebtedness to much earlier dramatic romances, pp. 13–14.

18. His contribution to *Sir Thomas More* does not constitute collaboration in the normal sense of the word.

19. And *Timon of Athens* only got in by the skin of its teeth: see p. 185. It appears to have been added at the last minute because of difficulties relating to the copyright of *Troilus and Cressida*.

20. Brean S. Hammond, 'Theobald's *Double Falsehood*: An "Agreeable Cheat"?', *Notes and Queries*, 229 (1984), pp. 2–3.

21. In recent years Gary Taylor imaginatively reconstructed the original play in a pastiche style (http://www.shaksper.net/archives/1993/0425.html), and Stephen Greenblatt, in collaboration with Charles Mee, has written a play based – very freely, it would seem – on the same material (http://www.wiko-berlin.de/kolleg/fellows/fruefell/flo405/0304greenblatt?hp1=2). There have also been claims that *Cardenio* is an alternative title for the lurid play known until recently as *The Second Maiden's Tragedy* (see p. 188) but which is to be included in the forthcoming edition of the *Complete Works* of Thomas Middleton as *The Lady's Tragedy*. The claim, based largely on the evidence of handwriting, has received little credence.

22. The accounts are printed in facsimile in *Textual Companion*, pp. 29–30.

23. There is an excellent account of balladeering in Bruce R. Smith, *The Acoustic World of Early Modern England* (Chicago and London, Chicago University Press, 1999), pp. 168–205.

24. Brian Vickers, *Shakespeare, Co-author* (Oxford, Oxford University Press, 2002), p. 333. My discussion of this play draws heavily on Vickers's exhaustive study. He mistakenly dates Charles Knight's remarks 'some fifty years later' than Roderick's.

25. *Gentleman's Magazine*, 178, NS 34 (1850), pp. 115–23.

26. Cited Vickers, *Shakespeare, Co-author*, p. 337.

27. Vickers summarizes the linguistic characteristics, ibid., p. 395.

28. From his *Specimens of English Dramatic Poets Contemporary with Shakespeare* (London, Longman, Hurst, Rees and Orme, 1808), quoted in Jonathan Bate, *The Romantics on Shakespeare* (Harmondsworth, Penguin Books, 1992), p. 556.

29. Edited by Philip Edwards in *A Book of Masques in Honour of Allardyce Nicoll* (Cambridge, Cambridge University Press, 1967), p. 139.

30. Emended from the quarto's 'happele, her careless, were'.

31. Emended from the quarto's 'on'.

32. Emended from the quarto's 'misicall'.

33. Shakespeare, *Complete Works*, p. lxx. The lines, which circulated widely in manuscript, were first printed in the 1633 collection of John Donne's *Poems*. Donne has been proposed as their author (Brandon S. Centerwall, 'Who Wrote William Basse's "Elegy on Shakespeare"?: Rediscovering a Poem Lost from the Donne Canon', forthcoming in *Shakespeare Survey*, 59 (2006)).

34. Paul Edmondson intriguingly asks whether this tailor might also have supplied Aubrey with his information about Shakespeare. May he also be the man who designed the doublet shown in the Droeshout engraving of Shakespeare?!

35. Aubrey, *Brief Lives*, p. 22.

36. There are detailed accounts by Alan Young, 'The English Tournament Imprese', in Peter M. Daly (ed.), *The English Emblem and the Continental Tradition* (New York, AMS Press, 1988), pp. 61–81, and in his book, *The English Tournament Imprese* (New York, AMS Press, 1988).

37. James Shapiro describes the Palace and suggests that Shakespeare may have been the anonymous author of a number of the imprese on display; *1599: A Year in the Life of William Shakespeare* (London, Faber and Faber, 2005), pp. 28–37.

38. Platter, *Travels*, pp. 163–4.

39. Shapiro, *1599*, p. 34.

40. The document is reproduced in S. Schoenbaum, *William Shakespeare: A Documentary Life* (Oxford, Clarendon Press, 1975), p. 220.

CHAPTER 8 THE SUCCESSION: JOHN WEBSTER

1. M. C. Bradbrook, *John Webster: Citizen and Dramatist* (London, Weidenfeld and Nicolson, 1980), p. 137.

Index

Works by Shakespeare and anonymous writings are indexed under their titles. Other works are indexed under their authors' names (at the end of the entry). Collaborators are normally listed in alphabetical order of their surnames.

Pages containing relevant illustrations are indexed in italic.

Printed in the United States
by Baker & Taylor Publisher Services